Bilingual VISUAL dictionary

...paired

D1428145

522 067 30 9

Bilingual

VISUAL

dictionary

Penguin Random House

Senior Editor Angeles Gavira
Senior Art Editor Ina Stradins
DTP Designers Sunil Sharma, Balwant Singh,
Harish Aggarwal, John Goldsmid, Ashwani Tyagi
DTP Coordinator Pankaj Sharma
Production Controller Liz Cherry
Picture Researcher Anna Grapes
Managing Editor Liz Wheeler
Managing Art Editor Phil Ormerod
Category Publisher Jonathan Metcalf

Designed for Dorling Kindersley by WaltonCreative.com
Art Editor Colin Walton, assisted by Tracy Musson
Designers Peter Radcliffe, Earl Neish, Ann Cannings
Picture Research Marissa Keating

Language content for Dorling Kindersley by
g-and-w PUBLISHING
Managed by Jane Wightwick, assisted by Ana Bremón
Translation and editing by Christine Arthur
Additional input by Dr. Arturo Pretel, Martin Prill,
Frédéric Monteil, Meinrad Prill, Mari Bremón,
Oscar Bremón, Anunchi Bremón, Leila Gaafar

First published in Great Britain in 2005
This revised edition published in 2015 by
Dorling Kindersley Limited,
80 Strand, London WC2R 0RL

Copyright © 2005, 2015 Dorling Kindersley Limited

A Penguin Random House Company

Content first published as
5 Language Visual Dictionary in 2003

2 4 6 8 10 9 7 5 3 1
001 – BD221 – June/15

All rights reserved. No part of this publication may
be reproduced, stored in a retrieval system, or
transmitted in any form or by any means, electronic,
mechanical, photocopying, recording or otherwise,
without the prior written permission
of the copyright owner.

A CIP catalogue record for this
book is available from the British Library.
ISBN: 978-0-2411-9918-3

Printed in China

A WORLD OF IDEAS:
SEE ALL THERE IS TO KNOW

www.dk.com

Inhalt
contents

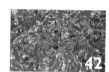

42
die Gesundheit
health

146
auswärts essen
eating out

252
die Freizeit
leisure

über das Wörterbuch
about the dictionary

die Benutzung des Buchs
how to use this book

die Menschen
people

die äußere Erscheinung
appearance

das Haus
home

die Dienstleistungen
services

der Einkauf
shopping

die Nahrungsmittel
food

das Lernen
study

die Arbeit
work

der Verkehr
transport

der Sport
sports

die Umwelt
environment

die Information
reference

Register
index

Dank
acknowledgments

die Menshen •
people

der Körper | body 12

das Gesicht | face 14

die Hand | hand 15

der Fuß | foot 15

die Muskeln | muscles 16

das Skelett | skeleton 17

die inneren Organe 18
internal organs

die Fortpflanzungsorgane 20
reproductive organs

die Familie | family 22

die Beziehungen | relationships 24

die Gefühle | emotions 25

die Ereignisse des Lebens 25
life events

die äußere Erscheinung • appearance

die Kinderkleidung 30
children's clothing

die Herrenkleidung 32
men's clothing

die Damenkleidung 34
women's clothing

die Accessoires | accessories 36

das Haar | hair 38

die Schönheit | beauty 40

die Gesundheit •
health

die Krankheit | illness 44

der Arzt | doctor 45

die Verletzung | injury 46

die erste Hilfe | first aid 47

das Krankenhaus | hospital 48

der Zahnarzt | dentist 50

der Augenoptiker | optician 51

die Schwangerschaft 52
pregnancy

die Geburt | childbirth 53

die Alternativtherapien 54
alternative therapy

das Haus • home

das Haus | house 58

die Hausanschlüsse 60
internal systems

das Wohnzimmer | living room 62

das Esszimmer | dining room 64

die Küche | kitchen 66

die Küchengeräte 68
kitchenware

das Schlafzimmer | bedroom 70

das Badezimmer 72
bathroom

das Kinderzimmer 74
nursery

der Allzweckraum | utility room 76

die Heimwerkstatt | workshop 78

der Werkzeugkasten 80
toolbox

das Tapezieren | decorating 82

der Garten | garden 84

die Gartenpflanzen 86
garden plants

die Gartengeräte | garden tools 88

die Gartenarbeit | gardening 90

die Dienstleistungen • services

die Notdienste 94
emergency services

die Bank | bank 96

die Kommunikation 98
communications

das Hotel | hotel 100

der Einkauf •
shopping

das Einkaufszentrum 104
shopping centre

das Kaufhaus 105
department store

der Supermarkt 106
supermarket

die Apotheke | chemist 108

das Blumengeschäft | florist 110

der Zeitungshändler 112
newsagent

der Konditor | confectioner 113

andere Geschäfte 114
other shops

die Nahrungsmittel • food

das Fleisch | meat 118

der Fisch | fish 120

das Gemüse | vegetables 122

das Obst | fruit 126

die Getreidearten und die Hülsenfrüchte 130
grains and pulses

die Kräuter und Gewürze 132
herbs and spices

die Nahrungsmittel in Flaschen | bottled foods 134

die Milchprodukte 136
dairy produce

das Brot und das Mehl 138
breads and flours

Kuchen und Nachspeisen 140
cakes and desserts

die Feinkost | delicatessen 142

die Getränke | drinks 144

deutsch • english

auswärts essen •
eating out

das Café | café	148
die Bar | bar	150
das Restaurant | restaurant	152
der Schnellimbiss fast food	154
das Frühstück | breakfast	156
die Hauptmahlzeit dinner	158

das Lernen • study

die Schule | school	162
die Mathematik | maths	164
die Wissenschaft | science	166
die Hochschule | college	168

die Arbeit • work

das Büro | office	172
der Computer | computer	176
die Medien | media	178
das Recht | law	180
der Bauernhof | farm	182
der Bau | construction	186
die Berufe | professions	188

der Verkehr •
transport

die Straßen | roads	194
der Bus | bus	196
das Auto | car	198
das Motorrad | motorbike	204
das Fahrrad | bicycle	206
der Zug | train	208
das Flugzeug | aircraft	210
der Flughafen | airport	212
das Schiff | ship	214
der Hafen | port	216

der Sport • sport

der Football American football	220
das Rugby | rugby	221
der Fußball | soccer	222
das Hockey | hockey	224
das Kricket | cricket	225
der Basketball | basketball	226
der Baseball | baseball	228
das Tennis | tennis	230
das Golf | golf	232
die Leichtathletik | athletics	234
der Kampfsport combat sports	236
der Schwimmsport | swimming	238
der Segelsport | sailing	240
der Reitsport | horse riding	242
der Angelsport | fishing	244
der Skisport | skiing	246
die anderen Sportarten other sports	248
die Fitness | fitness	250

die Freizeit • leisure

das Theater | theatre	254
das Orchester | orchestra	256
das Konzert | concert	258
die Besichtigungstour sightseeing	260
die Aktivitäten im Freien outdoor activities	262
der Strand | beach	264
das Camping | camping	266
die Privatunterhaltung home entertainment	268
die Fotografie | photography	270
die Spiele | games	272
das Kunsthandwerk arts and crafts	274

die Umwelt •
environment

der Weltraum | space	280
die Erde | Earth	282
die Landschaft | landscape	284
das Wetter | weather	286
das Gestein | rocks	288
die Mineralien | minerals	289
die Tiere | animals	290
die Pflanzen | plants	296
die Stadt | town	298
die Architektur architecture	300

die Information •
reference

die Uhrzeit | time	304
der Kalender | calendar	306
die Zahlen | numbers	308
die Maße und Gewichte weights and measures	310
die Weltkarte world map	312
Partikeln und Antonyme particles and antonyms	320
praktische Redewendungen useful phrases	322

über das Wörterbuch

Bilder helfen erwiesenermaßen, Informationen zu verstehen und zu behalten. Dieses zweisprachige Wörterbuch enthält eine Fülle von Illustrationen und präsentiert gleichzeitig ein umfangreiches aktuelles Vokabular in zwei europäischen Sprachen.

Das Wörterbuch ist thematisch gegliedert und behandelt eingehend die meisten Bereiche des heutigen Alltags, vom Restaurant und Fitnesscenter, Heim und Arbeitsplatz bis zum Tierreich und Weltraum. Es enthält außerdem Wörter und Redewendungen, die für die Unterhaltung nützlich sind und das Vokabular erweitern.

Dies ist ein wichtiges Nachschlagewerk für jeden, der sich für Sprachen interessiert – es ist praktisch, anregend und leicht zu benutzen.

Einige Anmerkungen
Die zwei Sprachen werden immer in der gleichen Reihenfolge aufgeführt – Deutsch und Englisch.

Substantive werden mit den bestimmten Artikeln, die das Geschlecht (Maskulinum, Femininum oder Neutrum) und den Numerus (Singular oder Plural) ausdrücken, angegeben, zum Beispiel:

der Samen **die Mandeln**
seed almonds

Die Verben sind durch ein (v) nach dem englischen Wort gekennzeichnet:

ernten • harvest (v)

Am Ende des Buchs befinden sich Register für jede Sprache. Sie können dort ein Wort in einer der zwei Sprachen und die jeweilige Seitenzahl nachsehen.
Die Geschlechtsangabe erfolgt mit folgenden Abkürzungen:

m = Maskulinum
f = Femininum
n = Neutrum

about the dictionary

The use of pictures is proven to aid understanding and the retention of information. Working on this principle, this highly-illustrated bilingual dictionary presents a large range of useful current vocabulary in two European languages.

The dictionary is divided thematically and covers most aspects of the everyday world in detail, from the restaurant to the gym, the home to the workplace, outer space to the animal kingdom. You will also find additional words and phrases for conversational use and for extending your vocabulary.

This is an essential reference tool for anyone interested in languages – practical, stimulating, and easy-to-use.

A few things to note
The two languages are always presented in the same order – German and English.

In German, nouns are given with their definite articles reflecting the gender (masculine, feminine or neuter) and number (singular or plural), for example:

der Samen **die Mandeln**
seed almonds

Verbs are indicated by a (v) after the English, for example:

ernten • harvest (v)

Each language also has its own index at the back of the book. Here you can look up a word in either of the two languages and be referred to the page number(s) where it appears. The gender is shown using the following abbreviations:

m = masculine
f = feminine
n = neuter

die Benutzung des Buchs

how to use this book

Ganz gleich, ob Sie eine Sprache aus Geschäftsgründen, zum Vergnügen oder als Vorbereitung für einen Auslandsurlaub lernen, oder Ihr Vokabular in einer Ihnen bereits vertrauten Sprache erweitern möchten, dieses Wörterbuch ist ein wertvolles Lernmittel, das Sie auf vielfältige Art und Weise benutzen können.

Wenn Sie eine neue Sprache lernen, achten Sie auf Wörter, die in verschiedenen Sprachen ähnlich sind sowie auf falsche Freunde (Wörter, die ähnlich aussehen aber wesentlich andere Bedeutungen haben). Sie können ebenfalls feststellen, wie die Sprachen einander beeinflusst haben. Englisch hat zum Beispiel viele Ausdrücke für Nahrungsmittel aus anderen europäischen Sprachen übernommen und andererseits viele Begriffe aus der Technik und Popkultur ausgeführt.

Praktische Übungen

• Versuchen Sie sich zu Hause, am Arbeits- oder Studienplatz den Inhalt der Seiten einzuprägen, die Ihre Umgebung behandeln. Schließen Sie dann das Buch und prüfen Sie, wie viele Gegenstände Sie in den anderen Sprachen sagen können.
• Schreiben Sie eine Geschichte, einen Brief oder Dialog und benutzen Sie dabei möglichst viele Ausdrücke von einer bestimmten Seite des Wörterbuchs. Dies ist eine gute Methode, sich das Vokabular und die Schreibweise einzuprägen. Sie können mit kurzen Sätzen von zwei bis drei Worten anfangen und dann nach und nach längere Texte schreiben.
• Wenn Sie ein visuelles Gedächtnis haben, können Sie Gegenstände aus dem Buch abzeichnen oder abpausen. Schließen Sie dann das Buch und schreiben Sie die passenden Wörter unter die Bilder.
• Wenn Sie mehr Sicherheit haben, können Sie Wörter aus einem der Fremdsprachenregister aussuchen und deren Bedeutung aufschreiben, bevor Sie auf der entsprechenden Seite nachsehen.

Whether you are learning a new language for business, pleasure, or in preparation for a holiday abroad, or are hoping to extend your vocabulary in an already familiar language, this dictionary is a valuable learning tool which you can use in a number of different ways.

When learning a new language, look out for cognates (words that are alike in different languages) and false friends (words that look alike but carry significantly different meanings). You can also see where the languages have influenced each other. For example, English has imported many terms for food from other European languages but, in turn, exported terms used in technology and popular culture.

Practical learning activities

• As you move about your home, workplace, or college, try looking at the pages which cover that setting. You could then close the book, look around you and see how many of the objects and features you can name.
• Challenge yourself to write a story, letter, or dialogue using as many of the terms on a particular page as possible. This will help you retain the vocabulary and remember the spelling. If you want to build up to writing a longer text, start with sentences incorporating 2–3 words.
• If you have a very visual memory, try drawing or tracing items from the book onto a piece of paper, then close the book and fill in the words below the picture.
• Once you are more confident, pick out words in a foreign-language index and see if you know what they mean before turning to the relevant page to check if you were right.

die Menschen
people

der Körper • body

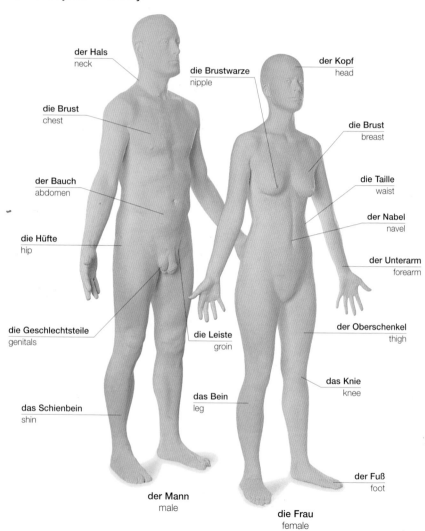

der Hals
neck

die Brustwarze
nipple

der Kopf
head

die Brust
chest

die Brust
breast

die Taille
waist

der Bauch
abdomen

der Nabel
navel

die Hüfte
hip

der Unterarm
forearm

die Geschlechtsteile
genitals

die Leiste
groin

der Oberschenkel
thigh

das Knie
knee

das Schienbein
shin

das Bein
leg

der Fuß
foot

der Mann
male

die Frau
female

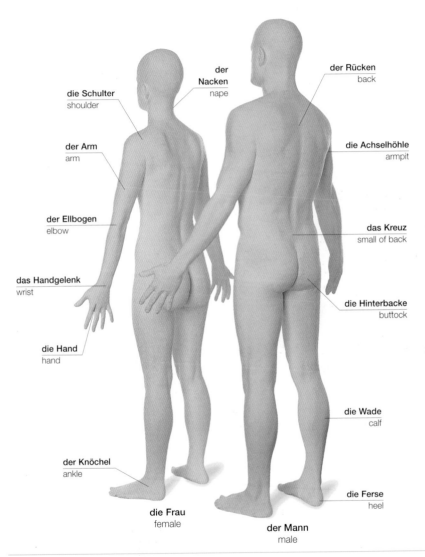

die Schulter
shoulder

der Nacken
nape

der Rücken
back

der Arm
arm

die Achselhöhle
armpit

der Ellbogen
elbow

das Kreuz
small of back

das Handgelenk
wrist

die Hinterbacke
buttock

die Hand
hand

die Wade
calf

der Knöchel
ankle

die Ferse
heel

die Frau
female

der Mann
male

das Gesicht • face

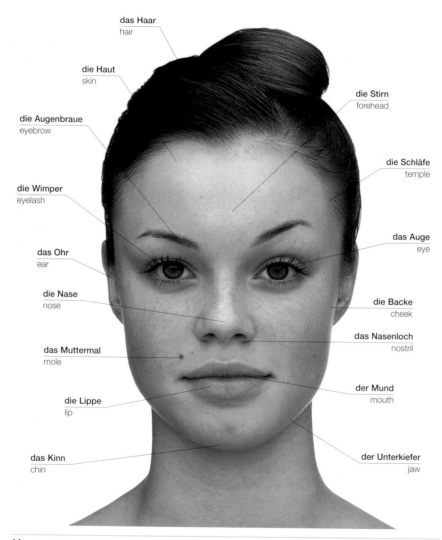

das Haar
hair

die Haut
skin

die Stirn
forehead

die Augenbraue
eyebrow

die Schläfe
temple

die Wimper
eyelash

das Auge
eye

das Ohr
ear

die Nase
nose

die Backe
cheek

das Nasenloch
nostril

das Muttermal
mole

der Mund
mouth

die Lippe
lip

das Kinn
chin

der Unterkiefer
jaw

die Falte
wrinkle

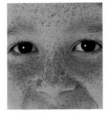

die Sommersprosse
freckle

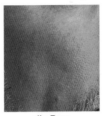

die Pore
pore

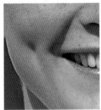

das Grübchen
dimple

die Hand • hand

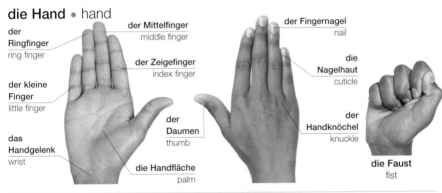

der
Ringfinger
ring finger

der Mittelfinger
middle finger

der Zeigefinger
index finger

der Fingernagel
nail

der kleine
Finger
little finger

die
Nagelhaut
cuticle

das
Handgelenk
wrist

der
Daumen
thumb

der
Handknöchel
knuckle

die Handfläche
palm

die Faust
fist

der Fuß • foot

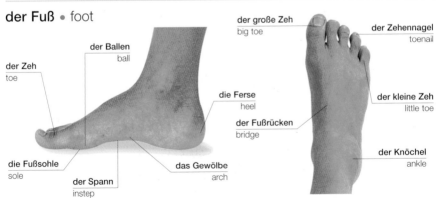

der
Ballen
ball

der große Zeh
big toe

der Zehennagel
toenail

der Zeh
toe

die Ferse
heel

der kleine Zeh
little toe

der Fußrücken
bridge

die Fußsohle
sole

das Gewölbe
arch

der Knöchel
ankle

der Spann
instep

die Muskeln • muscles

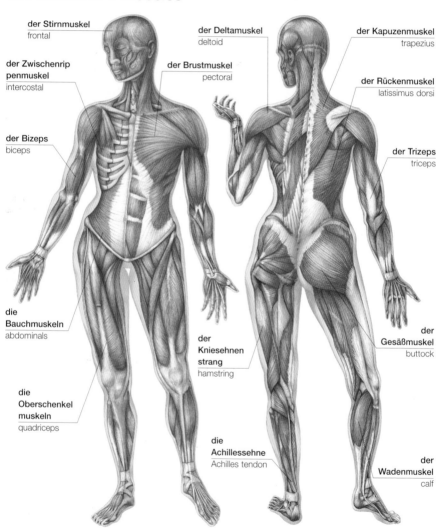

der Stirnmuskel
frontal

der Deltamuskel
deltoid

der Kapuzenmuskel
trapezius

der Zwischenrip
penmuskel
intercostal

der Brustmuskel
pectoral

der Rückenmuskel
latissimus dorsi

der Bizeps
biceps

der Trizeps
triceps

die
Bauchmuskeln
abdominals

der
Kniesehnen
strang
hamstring

der
Gesäßmuskel
buttock

die
Oberschenkel
muskeln
quadriceps

die
Achillessehne
Achilles tendon

der
Wadenmuskel
calf

deutsch • english

das Skelett • skeleton

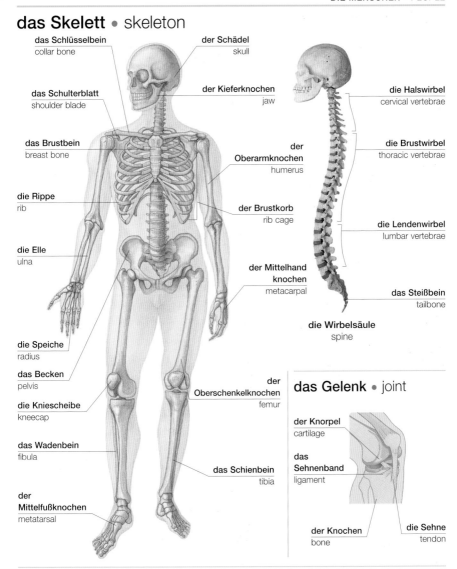

das Schlüsselbein
collar bone

der Schädel
skull

das Schulterblatt
shoulder blade

der Kieferknochen
jaw

die Halswirbel
cervical vertebrae

das Brustbein
breast bone

der
Oberarmknochen
humerus

die Brustwirbel
thoracic vertebrae

die Rippe
rib

der Brustkorb
rib cage

die Elle
ulna

die Lendenwirbel
lumbar vertebrae

der Mittelhand
knochen
metacarpal

das Steißbein
tailbone

die Speiche
radius

die Wirbelsäule
spine

das Becken
pelvis

der
Oberschenkelknochen
femur

das Gelenk • joint

die Kniescheibe
kneecap

der Knorpel
cartilage

das Wadenbein
fibula

das
Sehnenband
ligament

das Schienbein
tibia

der
Mittelfußknochen
metatarsal

der Knochen
bone

die Sehne
tendon

die inneren Organe • internal organs

die Schilddrüse
thyroid gland

die Leber
liver

die Luftröhre
windpipe

der
Zwölffingerdarm
duodenum

die Lunge
lung

die Niere
kidney

das Herz
heart

der Magen
stomach

die
Bauchspeichel-
drüse
pancreas

der Dünndarm
small intestine

die Milz
spleen

der
Dickdarm
large intestine

der Blinddarm
appendix

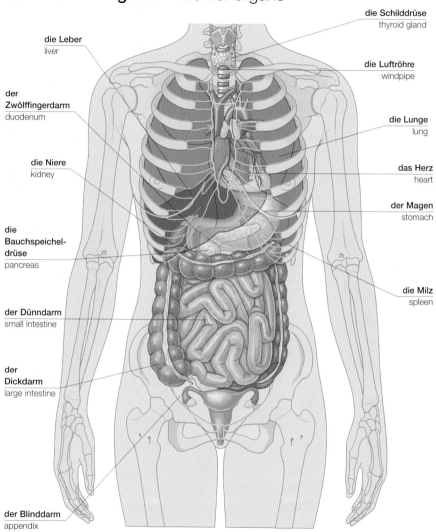

der Kopf • head

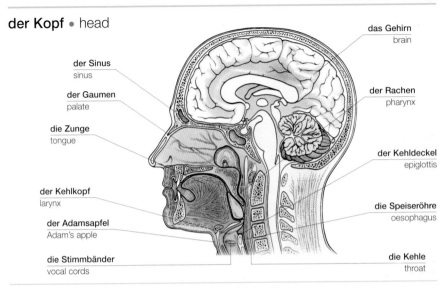

der Sinus
sinus

das Gehirn
brain

der Gaumen
palate

der Rachen
pharynx

die Zunge
tongue

der Kehldeckel
epiglottis

der Kehlkopf
larynx

der Adamsapfel
Adam's apple

die Speiseröhre
oesophagus

die Stimmbänder
vocal cords

die Kehle
throat

die Körpersysteme • body systems

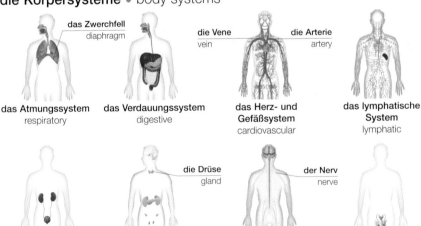

das Zwerchfell
diaphragm

die Vene
vein

die Arterie
artery

das Atmungssystem
respiratory

das Verdauungssystem
digestive

das Herz- und
Gefäßsystem
cardiovascular

das lymphatische
System
lymphatic

die Drüse
gland

der Nerv
nerve

das Harnsystem
urinary

das endokrine System
endocrine

das Nervensystem
nervous

das Fortpflanzungssystem
reproductive

---

die Fortpflanzungsorgane • reproductive organs

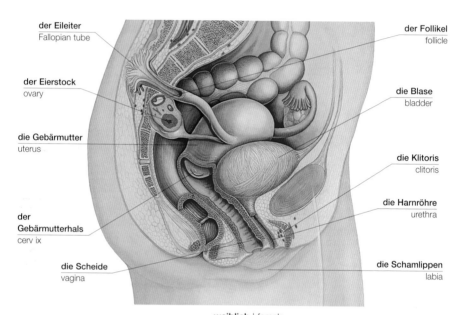

der Eileiter
Fallopian tube

der Eierstock
ovary

die Gebärmutter
uterus

der
Gebärmutterhals
cerv ix

die Scheide
vagina

der Follikel
follicle

die Blase
bladder

die Klitoris
clitoris

die Harnröhre
urethra

die Schamlippen
labia

weiblich | female

die Fortpflanzung •
reproduction

das Spermium
sperm

das Ei
egg

die Befruchtung | fertilization

Vokabular • vocabulary

steril infertile	**impotent** impotent	**die Menstruation** menstruation
fruchtbar fertile	**empfangen** conceive	**der Geschlechtsverkehr** intercourse
das Hormon hormone	**der Eisprung** ovulation	**die Geschlechtskrankheit** sexually transmitted disease

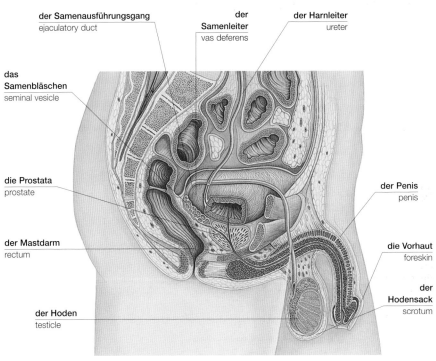

der Samenausführungsgang
ejaculatory duct

der
Samenleiter
vas deferens

der Harnleiter
ureter

das
Samenbläschen
seminal vesicle

die Prostata
prostate

der Penis
penis

der Mastdarm
rectum

die Vorhaut
foreskin

der
Hodensack
scrotum

der Hoden
testicle

männlich | male

die Empfängnisverhütung • contraception

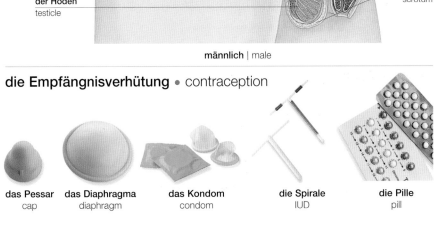

das Pessar
cap

das Diaphragma
diaphragm

das Kondom
condom

die Spirale
IUD

die Pille
pill

die Familie • family

die Großmutter
grandmother

der Großvater
grandfather

der Onkel
uncle

die Tante
aunt

der Vater
father

die Mutter
mother

der Cousin
cousin

der Bruder
brother

die Schwester
sister

die Ehefrau
wife

die Schwiegertochter
daughter-in-law

der Sohn
son

die Tochter
daughter

der Schwiegersohn
son-in-law

der Enkel
grandson

die Enkelin
granddaughter

der Ehemann
husband

Vokabular • vocabulary

die **Großeltern** grandparents	die **Verwandten** relatives	die **Enkelkinder** grandchildren	die **Stiefmutter** stepmother	die **Stieftochter** stepdaughter	die **Generation** generation
die **Eltern** parents	die **Kinder** children	der **Stiefvater** stepfather	der **Stiefsohn** stepson	der **Partner/die Partnerin** partner	die **Zwillinge** twins

die **Schwiegermutter**
mother-in-law

der **Schwiegervater**
father-in-law

der **Schwager**
brother-in-law

die **Schwägerin**
sister-in-law

die **Nichte**
niece

der **Neffe**
nephew

die Stadien • stages

das **Baby**
baby

das **Kind**
child

der **Junge**
boy

das **Mädchen**
girl

die **Jugendliche**
teenager

der **Erwachsene**
adult

der **Mann**
man

die **Frau**
woman

die Anreden • titles

Frau
Mrs

Herr
Mr

Fräulein
Miss

die Beziehungen • relationships

die
Assistentin
assistant

der **Chef**
manager

die
Geschäftspartnerin
business partner

der
Arbeitnehmer
employee

die
Arbeitgeberin
employer

der
Kollege
colleague

das Büro | office

der **Nachbar**
neighbour

der **Freund**
friend

der **Bekannte**
acquaintance

der **Brieffreund**
penfriend

der **Freund**
boyfriend

die **Freundin**
girlfriend

das Paar | couple

der **Verlobte**
fiancé

die **Verlobte**
fiancée

die Verlobten | engaged couple

die Gefühle • emotions

das Lächeln
smile

glücklich
happy

traurig
sad

aufgeregt
excited

gelangweilt
bored

überrascht
surprised

erschrocken
scared

das
Stirnrunzeln
frown

verärgert
angry

verwirrt
confused

besorgt
worried

nervös
nervous

stolz
proud

selbstsicher
confident

verlegen
embarrassed

schüchtern
shy

Vokabular • vocabulary

bestürzt upset	**schreien** shout (v)	**lachen** laugh (v)	**seufzen** sigh (v)
schockiert shocked	**gähnen** yawn (v)	**weinen** cry (v)	**in Ohnmacht fallen** faint (v)

die Ereignisse des Lebens • life events

geboren werden
be born (v)

zur Schule kommen
start school (v)

sich befreunden
make friends (v)

graduieren
graduate (v)

eine Stelle bekommen
get a job (v)

sich verlieben
fall in love (v)

heiraten
get married (v)

ein Baby bekommen
have a baby (v)

die Hochzeit | wedding

die Scheidung
divorce

das Begräbnis
funeral

vokabular • vocabulary

die Taufe christening	**emigrieren** emigrate (v)
die Bar Mizwa bar mitzvah	**sterben** die (v)
der Hochzeitstag anniversary	**die Hochzeitsfeier** wedding reception
in den Ruhestand treten retire (v)	**die Hochzeitsreise** honeymoon
sein Testament machen make a will (v)	**die Geburtsurkunde** birth certificate

die Feste • celebrations

die Geburtstagsfeier
birthday party

die Karte
card

der Geburtstag
birthday

das Geschenk
present

das Weihnachten
Christmas

die Feste •
festivals

das Passah
Passover

das Neujahr
New Year

der Karneval
carnival

der Umzug
procession

der Ramadan
Ramadan

das Band
ribbon

der Thanksgiving Day
Thanksgiving

das Ostern
Easter

das Halloween
Halloween

das Diwali
Diwali

die äußere Erscheinung
appearance

die Kinderkleidung • children's clothing

das Baby • baby

der Schneeanzug
snowsuit

das
Hemdchen
vest

der Schlafanzug
sleepsuit

der Spielanzug
romper suit

das Lätzchen
bib

der
Druckknopf
popper

der
Strampelanzug
babygro

die
Babyhandschuhe
mittens

die
Babyschuhe
booties

die
Stoffwindel
terry nappy

die
Wegwerfwindel
disposable nappy

das
Gummihöschen
plastic pants

das Kleinkind • toddler

die Latzhose
dungarees

das T-Shirt
t-shirt

der Sonnenhut
sunhat

die Schürze
apron

die Shorts
shorts

der Rock
skirt

das Kind • child

das Kleid
dress

die Kapuze
hood

die Jeans
jeans

die Sandalen
sandals

der Sommer
summer

der Regenmantel
raincoat

der Rucksack
backpack

der Knebelknopf
toggle

der Herbst
autumn

der Dufflecoat
duffel coat

der Schal
scarf

der Anorak
anorak

die Gummistiefel
wellington boots

der Winter
winter

der Morgenrock
dressing gown

das Logo
logo

die Sportschuhe
trainers

das Nachthemd
nightie

die Hausschuhe
slippers

die Nachtwäsche
nightwear

der Fußballdress
football strip

der Trainingsanzug
tracksuit

die Leggings
leggings

Vokabular • vocabulary

die Naturfaser natural fibre	**Ist es waschmaschinenfest?** Is it machine washable?
synthetisch synthetic	**Passt das einem Zweijährigen?** Will this fit a two-year-old?

die Herrenkleidung • men's clothing

der Kragen
collar

die Krawatte
tie

der Gürtel
belt

das Revers
lapel

das Knopfloch
buttonhole

die Manschette
cuff

die Jacke
jacket

die Hose
trousers

der Knopf
button

die
Tasche
pocket

die Leder
schuhe
leather
shoes

der Straßenanzug
business suit

der Regenmantel
raincoat

das Futter
lining

Vokabular • vocabulary

die Strickjacke cardigan	die Unterwäsche underwear	der Trainingsanzug tracksuit
der Bademantel dressing gown	der Mantel coat	lang long / kurz short

Haben Sie das eine Nummer größer/kleiner?
Do you have this in a larger/smaller size?

Kann ich das anprobieren?
May I try this on?

der Blazer
blazer

das Sportjackett
sports jacket

die Weste
waistcoat

der V-Ausschnitt
v-neck

der runde Ausschnitt
round neck

das T-Shirt
t-shirt

der Anorak
anorak

das Sweatshirt
sweatshirt

das Hemd
shirt

die Jeans
jeans

der Pullover
sweater

der Schlafanzug
pyjamas

das Unterhemd
vest

die Freizeitkleidung
casual wear

die Shorts
shorts

der Slip
briefs

die Boxershorts
boxer shorts

die Socken
socks

die Damenkleidung • women's clothing

die Jacke
jacket

die Naht
seam

der Ärmel
sleeve

knöchellang
ankle length

der Rock
skirt

der Saum
hem

knielang
knee-length

die Schuhe
shoes

formell
formal

trägerlos
strapless

ärmellos
sleeveless

das Abendkleid
evening dress

das Kleid
dress

die Bluse
blouse

die Hose
trousers

leger
casual

die Unterwäsche • lingerie

die Hochzeit • wedding

der Träger
strap

der Morgenmantel
dressing gown

der Unterrock
slip

das Mieder
camisole

der Schleier
veil

die
Spitze
lace

das Bukett
bouquet

die
Schleppe
train

das Hochzeitskleid
wedding dress

der
Strumpfhalter
suspender

das Bustier
basque

der Strumpf
stocking

die Strumpfhose
tights

der Büstenhalter
bra

der Slip
knickers

das Nachthemd
nightdress

Vokabular • vocabulary

das Korsett corset	**gut geschnitten** tailored
rückenfrei halter neck	**das Strumpfband** garter
der Rockbund waistband	**der Sport-BH** sports bra
das Schulter polster shoulder pad	**mit Formbügeln** underwired

die Accessoires • accessories

die
Gürtelschnalle
buckle

der Griff
handle

die Mütze
cap

der Hut
hat

das Halstuch
scarf

der Gürtel
belt

die Spitze
tip

das Taschentuch
handkerchief

die Fliege
bow tie

**die
Krawattennadel**
tie-pin

die Handschuhe
gloves

der Regenschirm
umbrella

der Schmuck • jewellery

die Perlenkette
string of pearls

der Anhänger
pendant

die Brosche
brooch

der Manschettenknopf
cufflink

das Glied
link

der Verschluß
clasp

der Ohrring
earring

der Ring
ring

der Edelstein
stone

die Halskette
necklace

das Armband
bracelet

die Kette
chain

die Uhr
watch

der Schmuckkasten | jewellery box

die Taschen • bags

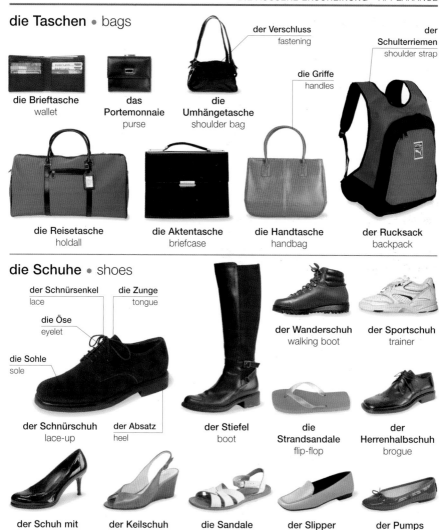

die Brieftasche
wallet

das Portemonnaie
purse

die Umhängetasche
shoulder bag

der Verschluss
fastening

die Griffe
handles

der Schulterriemen
shoulder strap

die Reisetasche
holdall

die Aktentasche
briefcase

die Handtasche
handbag

der Rucksack
backpack

die Schuhe • shoes

der Schnürsenkel
lace

die Zunge
tongue

die Öse
eyelet

die Sohle
sole

der Schnürschuh
lace-up

der Absatz
heel

der Stiefel
boot

der Wanderschuh
walking boot

der Sportschuh
trainer

die Strandsandale
flip-flop

der Herrenhalbschuh
brogue

der Schuh mit hohem Absatz
high heel shoe

der Keilschuh
wedge

die Sandale
sandal

der Slipper
slip-on

der Pumps
pump

das Haar • hair

der Kamm
comb

kämmen
comb (v)

die Haarbürste
brush

bürsten | brush (v)

ausspülen
rinse (v)

die Friseurin
hairdresser

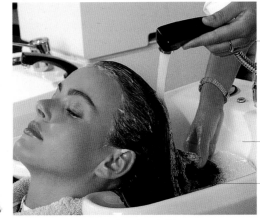

das Waschbecken
sink

die Kundin
client

waschen | wash (v)

der Frisierumhang
robe

schneiden
cut (v)

föhnen
blow dry (v)

legen
set (v)

die Frisierartikel • accessories

der Föhn
hairdryer

das Shampoo
shampoo

die Haarspülung
conditioner

das Haargel
gel

das Haarspray
hairspray

der Lockenstab
curling tongs

die Schere
scissors

der Haarreif
hairband

der Haarglätter
hair straighteners

die Haarklammer
hairpin

die Frisuren • styles

der Pferdeschwanz
ponytail

der Zopf
plait

die Hochfrisur
french pleat

der Haarknoten
bun

die Schwänzchen
pigtails

der Bubikopf
bob

der Kurzhaarschnitt
crop

kraus
curly

die Dauerwelle
perm

glatt
straight

die Wurzeln
roots

die Strähnen
highlights

kahl
bald

die Perücke
wig

Vokabular • vocabulary

das Haarband hairtie	**fettig** greasy
nachschneiden trim (v)	**trocken** dry
der Herrenfriseur barber	**normal** normal
die Schuppen dandruff	**die Kopfhaut** scalp
der Haarspliss split ends	**glätten** straighten (v)

die Haarfarben • colours

blond
blonde

brünett
brunette

rotbraun
auburn

rot
ginger

schwarz
black

grau
grey

weiß
white

gefärbt
dyed

die Schönheit • beauty

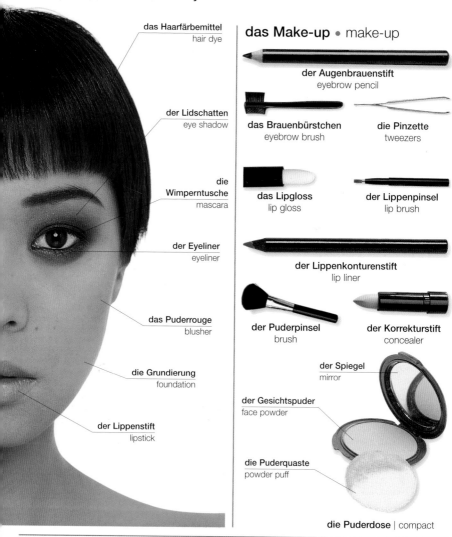

das Haarfärbemittel
hair dye

der Lidschatten
eye shadow

die Wimperntusche
mascara

der Eyeliner
eyeliner

das Puderrouge
blusher

die Grundierung
foundation

der Lippenstift
lipstick

das Make-up • make-up

der Augenbrauenstift
eyebrow pencil

das Brauenbürstchen
eyebrow brush

die Pinzette
tweezers

das Lipgloss
lip gloss

der Lippenpinsel
lip brush

der Lippenkonturenstift
lip liner

der Puderpinsel
brush

der Korrekturstift
concealer

der Spiegel
mirror

der Gesichtspuder
face powder

die Puderquaste
powder puff

die Puderdose | compact

die Schönheitsbehandlungen •
beauty treatments

die Gesichtsmaske
face pack

die Sonnenbank
sunbed

die Gesichtsbehandlung
facial

die Haut schälen
exfoliate (v)

die Enthaarung
wax

die Pediküre
pedicure

die Toilettenartikel • toiletries

der Reiniger
cleanser

das Gesichts-wasser
toner

die Feuchtig-keitscreme
moisturizer

die Selbst-bräunungscreme
self-tanning cream

das Parfum
perfume

das Eau de Toilette
eau de toilette

die Maniküre • manicure

der Nagellackentferner
nail varnish remover

die Nagelfeile
nail file

der Nagellack
nail varnish

die Nagelschere
nail scissors

der Nagelknipser
nail clippers

Vokabular • vocabulary

die Sonnenbräune tan	**empfindlich** sensitive	**hell** fair
die Tätowierung tattoo	**der Farbton** shade	**dunkel** dark
die Wattebällchen cotton balls	**Antifalten-** anti-wrinkle	**trocken** dry
hypoallergen hypoallergenic	**der Teint** complexion	**fettig** oily

die Gesundheit
health

die Krankheit • illness

das Fieber | fever

die
Kopfschmerzen
headache

das
Nasenbluten
nosebleed

der
Husten
cough

das Niesen
sneeze

die Erkältung
cold

die Grippe
flu

der **Inhalations
apparat**
inhaler

das Asthma
asthma

die Krämpfe
cramps

die Übelkeit
nausea

die Windpocken
chickenpox

der Hautausschlag
rash

Vokabular • vocabulary

der Herzinfarkt heart attack	**die Allergie** allergy	**das Ekzem** eczema	**die Verkühlung** chill	**die Epilepsie** epilepsy	**der Durchfall** diarrhoea
der Blutdruck blood pressure	**der Mumps** mumps	**der Virus** virus	**die Migräne** migraine	**sich übergeben** vomit (v)	**die Masern** measles
der Schlaganfall stroke	**die Zucker krankheit** diabetes	**die Infektion** infection	**die Magenschmerzen** stomach ache	**in Ohnmacht fallen** faint (v)	**der Heuschnupfen** hayfever

der Arzt • doctor
die Konsultation • consultation

die Kranken
schwester
nurse

der
Röntgenbildbetrachter
x-ray viewer

der Arzt
doctor

das Rezept
prescription

die Patientin
patient

die
Personenwaage
scales

die
Luftmanschette
cuff

das elektrische
Blutdruckmessgerät
electric blood pressure
monitor

Vokabular • vocabulary

der Termin appointment	**die Impfung** inoculation
das Sprechzimmer surgery	**die Untersuchung** medical examination
der Warteraum waiting room	**das Thermometer** thermometer

Ich muss mit einem Arzt sprechen.
I need to see a doctor.

Es tut hier weh.
It hurts here.

die Verletzung • injury

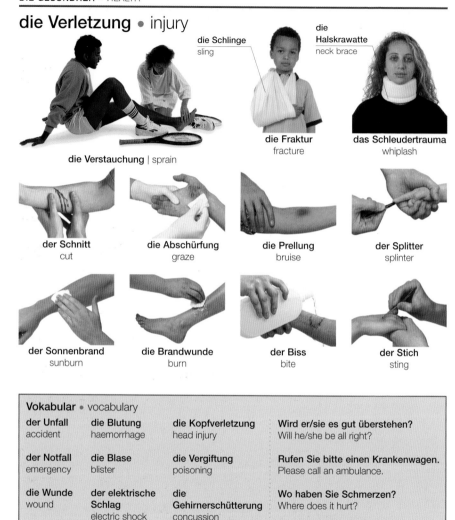

die Schlinge
sling

die Halskrawatte
neck brace

die Verstauchung | sprain

die Fraktur
fracture

das Schleudertrauma
whiplash

der Schnitt
cut

die Abschürfung
graze

die Prellung
bruise

der Splitter
splinter

der Sonnenbrand
sunburn

die Brandwunde
burn

der Biss
bite

der Stich
sting

Vokabular • vocabulary

der Unfall accident	**die Blutung** haemorrhage	**die Kopfverletzung** head injury	**Wird er/sie es gut überstehen?** Will he/she be all right?
der Notfall emergency	**die Blase** blister	**die Vergiftung** poisoning	**Rufen Sie bitte einen Krankenwagen.** Please call an ambulance.
die Wunde wound	**der elektrische Schlag** electric shock	**die Gehirnerschütterung** concussion	**Wo haben Sie Schmerzen?** Where does it hurt?

---

die erste Hilfe • first aid

die Salbe
ointment

das Pflaster
plaster

die Sicherheitsnadel
safety pin

die Bandage
bandage

die Schmerz tabletten
painkillers

das Desinfektionstuch
antiseptic wipe

die Pinzette
tweezers

die Schere
scissors

das Antiseptikum
antiseptic

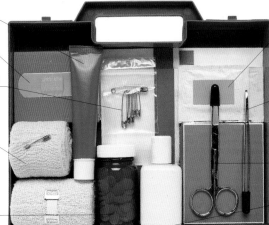

der Erste-Hilfe-Kasten | first aid box

die Gaze
gauze

der Verband
dressing

die Schiene | splint

das Leukoplast
adhesive tape

die Wiederbelebung
resuscitation

Vokabular • vocabulary

der Schock shock	**der Puls** pulse	**ersticken** choke (v)
bewusstlos unconscious	**die Atmung** breathing	**steril** sterile

Können Sie mir helfen?
Can you help?

Beherrschen Sie die Erste Hilfe?
Do you know first aid?

das Krankenhaus • hospital

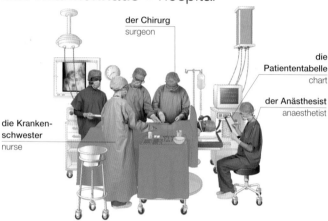

der Chirurg
surgeon

die Krankenschwester
nurse

der Operationssaal
operating theatre

die
Paticntentabelle
chart

der Anästhesist
anaesthetist

die Blutuntersuchung
blood test

die Spritze
injection

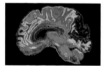

die Röntgenaufnahme
x-ray

die
fahrbare Liege
trolley

die Notaufnahme
emergency room

der Rufknopf
call button

die Krankenhausstation
ward

der Rollstuhl
wheelchair

der CT-Scan
scan

Vokabular • vocabulary

die Operation operation	**entlassen** discharged	**die Besuchszeiten** visiting hours	**die Entbindungsstation** maternity ward	**die Intensivstation** intensive care unit
aufgenommen admitted	**die Klinik** clinic	**die Kinderstation** children's ward	**das Privatzimmer** private room	**der ambulante Patient** outpatient

---

die Abteilungen • departments

die HNO-Abteilung
ENT

die Kardiologie
cardiology

die Orthopädie
orthopaedy

die Gynäkologie
gynaecology

die Physiotherapie
physiotherapy

die Dermatologie
dermatology

die Pädiatrie
paediatrics

die Radiologie
radiology

die Chirurgie
surgery

die Entbindungsstation
maternity

die Psychiatrie
psychiatry

die Ophthalmologie
ophthalmology

Vokabular • vocabulary

die Neurologie neurology	**die Urologie** urology	**die plastische Chirurgie** plastic surgery	**die Pathologie** pathology	**das Ergebnis** result
die Onkologie oncology	**die Endokrinologie** endocrinology	**die Überweisung** referral	**die Untersuchung** test	**der Facharzt** consultant

---

der Zahnarzt • dentist

der Zahn • tooth

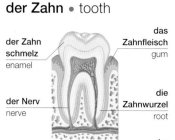

der Zahn
schmelz
enamel

das
Zahnfleisch
gum

der Nerv
nerve

die
Zahnwurzel
root

der vordere
Backenzahn
premolar

der
Schneidezahn
incisor

der
Backen-
zahn
molar

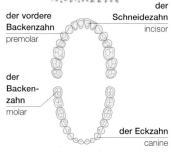

der Eckzahn
canine

Vokabular • vocabulary

der Zahnbelag plaque	**der Bohrer** drill
die Karies decay	**die Zahnseide** dental floss
die Zahnfüllung filling	**die Extraktion** extraction
die Zahnschmerzen toothache	**die Krone** crown

der Check-up • check-up

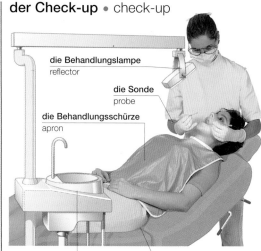

die Behandlungslampe
reflector

die Sonde
probe

die Behandlungsschürze
apron

das Speibecken
basin

der Patientenstuhl
dentist's chair

mit Zahnseide
reinigen
floss (v)

bürsten
brush

die Zahnspange
brace

die Röntgen-
aufnahme
dental x-ray

das Röntgenbild
x-ray film

die
Zahnprothese
dentures

der Augenoptiker • optician

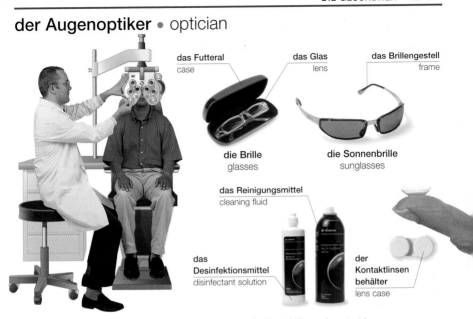

das Futteral
case

das Glas
lens

das Brillengestell
frame

die Brille
glasses

die Sonnenbrille
sunglasses

das Reinigungsmittel
cleaning fluid

das Desinfektionsmittel
disinfectant solution

der Kontaktlinsen behälter
lens case

der Sehtest | eye test

die Kontaktlinsen | contact lenses

das Auge • eye

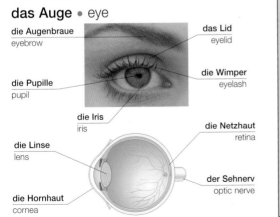

die Augenbraue
eyebrow

das Lid
eyelid

die Wimper
eyelash

die Pupille
pupil

die Iris
iris

die Netzhaut
retina

die Linse
lens

der Sehnerv
optic nerve

die Hornhaut
cornea

Vokabular • vocabulary

die Sehkraft vision	**der Astigmatismus** astigmatism
die Dioptrie diopter	**die Weitsichtigkeit** long sight
die Träne tear	**die Kurzsichtigkeit** short sight
der graue Star cataract	**Bifokal-** bifocal

die Schwangerschaft • pregnancy

der Schwangerschaftstest
pregnancy test

die Ultraschallaufnahme
scan

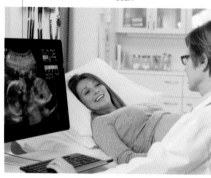

der Ultraschall | ultrasound

die
Nabelschnur
umbilical cord

die Plazenta
placenta

der
Gebärmutterhals
cervix

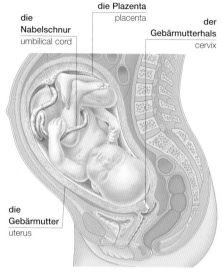

die
Gebärmutter
uterus

der Fetus | foetus

Vokabular • vocabulary

der Eisprung ovulation	**vorgeburtlich** antenatal	**das Fruchtwasser** amniotic fluid	**die Erweiterung** dilation	**die Naht** stitches	**Steiß-** breech
schwanger pregnant	**der Embryo** embryo	**die Amniozentese** amniocentesis	**der Kaiserschnitt** caesarean section	**die Geburt** birth	**vorzeitig** premature
die Empfängnis conception	**die Gebärmutter** womb	**das Fruchtwasser geht ab** break waters (v)	**die Periduralanästhesie** epidural	**die Entbindung** delivery	**der Gynäkologe** gynaecologist
schwanger expectant	**das Trimester** trimester	**die Wehe** contraction	**der Dammschnitt** episiotomy	**die Fehlgeburt** miscarriage	**der Geburtshelfer** obstetrician

---

die Geburt • childbirth

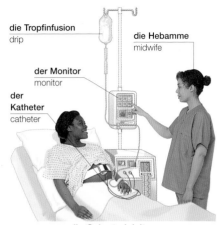

die Tropfinfusion
drip

die Hebamme
midwife

der Monitor
monitor

der Katheter
catheter

die Geburt einleiten
induce labour (v)

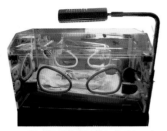

der Brutkasten | incubator

das Geburtsgewicht
birth weight

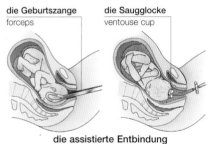

die Geburtszange
forceps

die Saugglocke
ventouse cup

die assistierte Entbindung
assisted delivery

das Erkennungsetikett
identity tag

das Neugeborene
newborn baby

das Stillen • nursing

die Brustpumpe
breast pump

der Stillbüstenhalter
nursing bra

stillen
breastfeed (v)

die Einlagen
pads

die Alternativtherapien • alternative therapy

das T-Shirt
t-shirt

die Matte
mat

das Yoga | yoga

die Massage
massage

das Shiatsu
shiatsu

die Chiropraktik
chiropractic

die Osteopathie
osteopathy

die Reflexzonenmassage
reflexology

die Meditation
meditation

der Berater
counsellor

die Gruppentherapie
group therapy

das Reiki
reiki

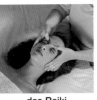

die Akupunktur
acupuncture

das Ayurveda
ayurveda

die Hypnotherapie
hypnotherapy

die ätherischen Öle
essential oils

die Kräuterheilkunde
herbalism

die Aromatherapie
aromatherapy

die Homöopathie
homeopathy

die Akupressur
acupressure

die Therapeutin
therapist

die Psychotherapie
psychotherapy

Vokabular • vocabulary

die Kristalltherapie crystal healing	**die Naturheilkunde** naturopathy	**die Entspannung** relaxation	**das Heilkraut** herb
die Wasserbehandlung hydrotherapy	**das Feng Shui** feng shui	**der Stress** stress	**die Ergänzung** supplement

das Haus
home

das Haus • house

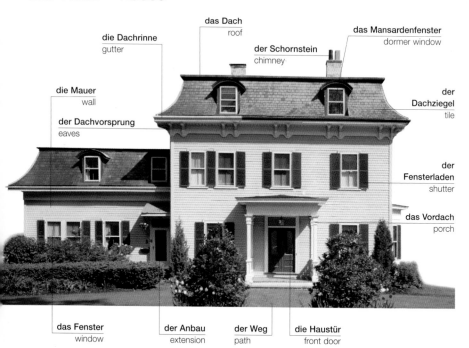

das Dach
roof

die Dachrinne
gutter

das Mansardenfenster
dormer window

der Schornstein
chimney

die Mauer
wall

der
Dachziegel
tile

der Dachvorsprung
eaves

der
Fensterladen
shutter

das Vordach
porch

das Fenster
window

der Anbau
extension

der Weg
path

die Haustür
front door

Vokabular • vocabulary					
Einzel(haus) detached	Reihen(haus) terraced	die Garage garage	das Stockwerk floor	die Alarmanlage burglar alarm	mieten rent (v)
Doppel(haus) semidetached	der Bungalow bungalow	das Zimmer room	der Hof courtyard	der Briefkasten letterbox	die Miete rent
das dreistöckige Haus townhouse	das Kellergeschoss basement	der Dachboden attic	die Haustürlampe porch light	der Vermieter landlord	der Mieter tenant

der Eingang • entrance

das
Geländer
hand rail

der **Treppen-
absatz**
landing

das **Treppen-
geländer**
banister

die **Treppe**
staircase

die Diele
hallway

die Türklingel
doorbell

der Fußabtreter
doormat

der Türklopfer
door knocker

die Türkette
door chain

der Schlüssel
key

das Schloss
lock

der Türriegel
bolt

die Wohnung •
flat

der **Balkon**
balcony

der Wohnblock
block of flats

die Sprechanlage
intercom

der Fahrstuhl
lift

die Hausanschlüsse • internal systems

der Flügel
blade

der Ventilator
fan

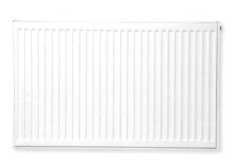

der Heizkörper
radiator

der Heizofen
heater

der Heizlüfter
convector heater

die Elektrizität • electricity

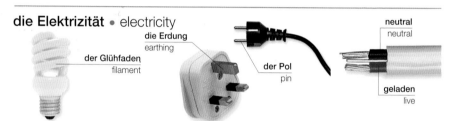

die Erdung
earthing

der Glühfaden
filament

neutral
neutral

der Pol
pin

geladen
live

die Energiesparbirne
energy-saving bulb

der Stecker
plug

die Leitung
wires

Vokabular • vocabulary				
die Spannung voltage	**die Sicherung** fuse	**die Steckdose** socket	**der Gleichstrom** direct current	**der Transformator** transformer
das Ampère amp	**der Generator** generator	**der Schalter** switch	**der Stromzähler** electricity meter	**das Stromnetz** mains supply
der Strom power	**der Sicherungskasten** fuse box	**der Wechselstrom** alternating current	**der Stromausfall** power cut	

die Installation • plumbing

die Spüle • sink

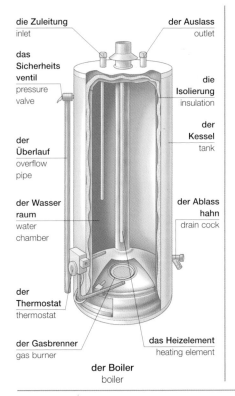

der Auslass
outlet

die Zuleitung
inlet

das Sicherheits ventil
pressure valve

die Isolierung
insulation

der Kessel
tank

der Überlauf
overflow pipe

der Ablass hahn
drain cock

der Wasser raum
water chamber

der Thermostat
thermostat

der Gasbrenner
gas burner

das Heizelement
heating element

der Boiler
boiler

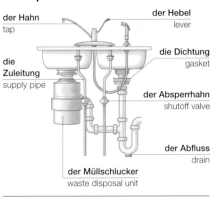

der Hahn
tap

der Hebel
lever

die Zuleitung
supply pipe

die Dichtung
gasket

der Absperrhahn
shutoff valve

der Abfluss
drain

der Müllschlucker
waste disposal unit

das WC • water closet

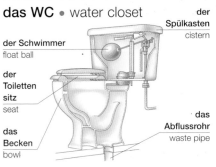

der Spülkasten
cistern

der Schwimmer
float ball

der Toiletten sitz
seat

das Becken
bowl

das Abflussrohr
waste pipe

die Abfallentsorgung • waste disposal

die Flasche
bottle

der Deckel
lid

der Trethebel
pedal

der Recyclingbehälter
recycling bin

der Abfalleimer
rubbish bin

die Abfallsortiereinheit
sorting unit

der Bio-Abfall
organic waste

das Wohnzimmer • living room

die **Wandlampe**
wall light

der **Kamin**
fireplace

die **Decke**
ceiling

die **Vase**
vase

das
Sofakissen
cushion

die **Lampe**
lamp

der
Couchtisch
coffee table

das **Sofa**
sofa

der
Fußboden
floor

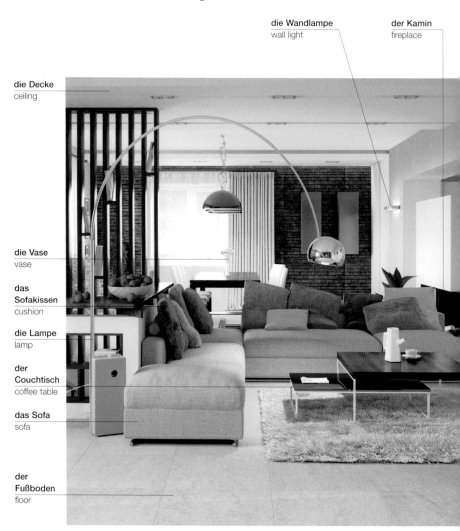

der
Bilderrahmen
frame

das Gemälde
painting

der Vorhang
curtain

die Gardine
net curtain

die Jalousie
venetian blind

das Rollo
roller blind

der Stuck
moulding

der Sessel
armchair

das Bücherregal
bookshelf

die Bettcouch
sofabed

der Teppich
rug

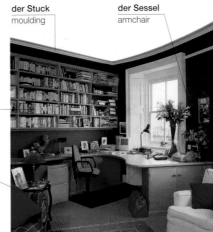

das Arbeitszimmer | study

das Esszimmer • dining room

der Pfeffer
pepper

das Salz
salt

der Tisch
table

das
Geschirr
crockery

das
Besteck
cutlery

der Stuhl
chair

die Lehne
back

die Sitzfläche
seat

das Bein
leg

Vokabular • vocabulary

die Tischdecke tablecloth	**die Gastgeberin** hostess	**die Portion** portion	**den Tisch decken** lay the table (v)	**das Frühstück** breakfast
das Set place mat	**der Gast** guest	**hungrig** hungry	**servieren** serve (v)	**das Mittagessen** lunch
das Essen meal	**der Gastgeber** host	**satt** full	**essen** eat (v)	**das Abendessen** dinner

Könnte ich bitte noch ein bisschen haben?
Can I have some more, please?

Ich bin satt, danke.
I've had enough, thank you.

Das war lecker.
That was delicious.

das Geschirr und das Besteck • crockery and cutlery

der Teelöffel
teaspoon

der Becher
mug

die Kaffeetasse
coffee cup

die Teetasse
teacup

der Teller
plate

die Schüssel
bowl

die Cafetière
cafetière

die Teekanne
teapot

das Kännchen
jug

der Eierbecher
egg cup

das Weinglas
wine glass

das Wasserglas
tumbler

die Glaswaren
glassware

der Serviettenring
napkin ring

der Beilagenteller
side plate

der Essteller
dinner plate

der Suppenteller
soup bowl

der Suppenlöffel
soup spoon

die Gabel
fork

die Serviette
napkin

das Gedeck
place setting

der Löffel
spoon

das Messer
knife

die Küche • kitchen

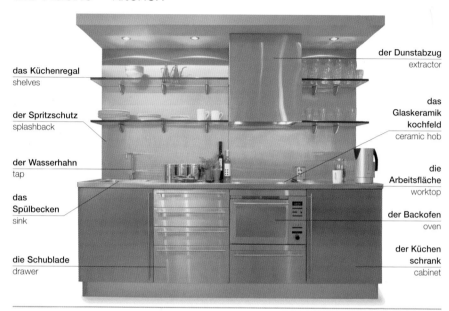

der Dunstabzug
extractor

das Küchenregal
shelves

das
Glaskeramik
kochfeld
ceramic hob

der Spritzschutz
splashback

der Wasserhahn
tap

die
Arbeitsfläche
worktop

das
Spülbecken
sink

der Backofen
oven

der Küchen
schrank
cabinet

die Schublade
drawer

die Küchengeräte • appliances

die
Mixerschüssel
mixing bowl

der Deckel
lid

die Mikrowelle
microwave oven

das
Messer
blade

**der
Elektrokessel**
kettle

der Toaster
toaster

**die
Küchenmaschine**
food processor

der Mixer
blender

die Spülmaschine
dishwasher

das
Eisfach
ice maker

der
Kühlschrank
refrigerator

der Rost
shelf

das
Gefrierfach
freezer

das
Gemüsefach
crisper

der Gefrier-Kühlschrank | fridge-freezer

Vokabular • vocabulary

das Kochfeld	**einfrieren**
hob	freeze (v)
das Abtropfbrett	**auftauen**
draining board	defrost (v)
der Brenner	**dämpfen**
burner	steam (v)
der Mülleimer	**anbraten**
rubbish bin	sauté (v)

das Kochen • cooking

schälen
peel (v)

schneiden
slice (v)

reiben
grate (v)

gießen
pour (v)

verrühren
mix (v)

schlagen
whisk (v)

kochen
boil (v)

braten
fry (v)

ausrollen
roll (v)

rühren
stir (v)

köcheln lassen
simmer (v)

pochieren
poach (v)

backen
bake (v)

braten
roast (v)

grillen
grill (v)

die Küchengeräte • kitchenware

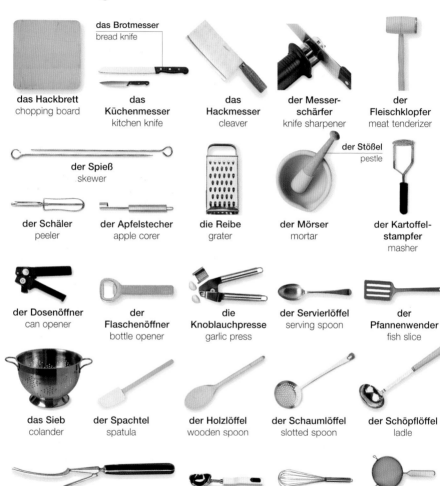

das Brotmesser
bread knife

das Hackbrett
chopping board

das Küchenmesser
kitchen knife

das Hackmesser
cleaver

der Messerschärfer
knife sharpener

der Fleischklopfer
meat tenderizer

der Spieß
skewer

der Stößel
pestle

der Schäler
peeler

der Apfelstecher
apple corer

die Reibe
grater

der Mörser
mortar

der Kartoffelstampfer
masher

der Dosenöffner
can opener

der Flaschenöffner
bottle opener

die Knoblauchpresse
garlic press

der Servierlöffel
serving spoon

der Pfannenwender
fish slice

das Sieb
colander

der Spachtel
spatula

der Holzlöffel
wooden spoon

der Schaumlöffel
slotted spoon

der Schöpflöffel
ladle

die Tranchiergabel
carving fork

der Portionierer
scoop

der Schneebesen
whisk

das Sieb
sieve

der Deckel
lid

kunststoffbeschichtet
non-stick

die Bratpfanne
frying pan

der Kochtopf
saucepan

das Grillblech
grill pan

der Wok
wok

der Schmortopf
earthenware dish

Glas-
glass

feuerfest
ovenproof

**die
Rührschüssel**
mixing bowl

die Souffléform
soufflé dish

die Auflaufform
gratin dish

**das
Auflaufförmchen**
ramekin

die Kasserolle
casserole dish

das Kuchenbacken • baking cakes

**die
Haushaltswaage**
scales

der Messbecher
measuring jug

die Kuchenform
cake tin

**die
Pastetenform**
pie tin

**die Obstkuchen-
form**
flan tin

der Backpinsel
pastry brush

das Nudelholz
rolling pin

der Spritzbeutel
piping bag

**die Törtchen-
form**
muffin tray

**das
Kuchenblech**
baking tray

das Abkühlgitter
cooling rack

**der
Topfhandschuh**
oven glove

die Schürze
apron

das Schlafzimmer • bedroom

der Kleiderschrank
wardrobe

die Nachttisch lampe
bedside lamp

das Kopfende
headboard

der Nachttisch
bedside table

die Kommode
chest of drawers

die Schublade
drawer

das Bett
bed

die Matratze
mattress

die Tagesdecke
bedspread

das Kopfkissen
pillow

die Wärmflasche
hot-water bottle

der Radiowecker
clock radio

der Wecker
alarm clock

die Papiertaschen tuchschachtel
box of tissues

der Kleiderbügel
coat hanger

die Bettwäsche • bed linen

der Kissenbezug
pillowcase

der Spiegel
mirror

das Bettlaken
sheet

der Volant
valance

der
Frisiertisch
dressing
table

die Bettdecke
duvet

die Steppdecke
quilt

der
Fußboden
floor

die Decke
blanket

Vokabular • vocabulary

das Einzelbett single bed	**das Fußende** footboard	**die Schlaflosigkeit** insomnia	**aufwachen** wake up (v)	**den Wecker stellen** set the alarm (v)
das Doppelbett double bed	**die Sprungfeder** spring	**ins Bett gehen** go to bed (v)	**aufstehen** get up (v)	**schnarchen** snore (v)
die Heizdecke electric blanket	**der Teppich** carpet	**einschlafen** go to sleep (v)	**das Bett machen** make the bed (v)	**der Einbauschrank** built-in wardrobe

das Badezimmer • bathroom

der
Handtuchhalter
towel rail

die Duschtür
shower door

der
Kaltwasserhahn
cold tap

der
Heißwasserhahn
hot tap

der **Duschkopf**
shower head

das
Waschbecken
washbasin

die Dusche
shower

der **Stöpsel**
plug

der **Abfluss**
drain

der **Toilettensitz**
toilet seat

die **Toilette**
toilet

die
Toilettenbürste
toilet brush

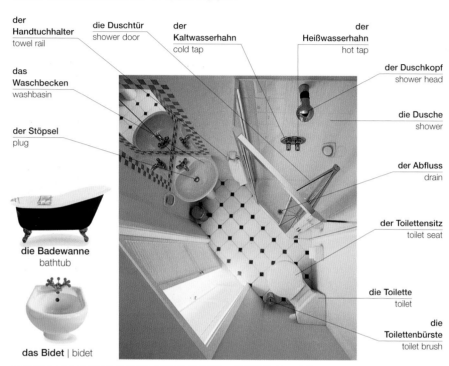

die Badewanne
bathtub

das Bidet | bidet

Vokabular • vocabulary

die Hausapotheke
medicine cabinet

die Bademphatte
bath mat

die Bademphatte
bath mat

die Rolle Toilettenpapier
toilet roll

der Duschvorhang
shower curtain

duschen
take a shower (v)

baden
take a bath
(v)

die Zahnpflege • dental hygiene

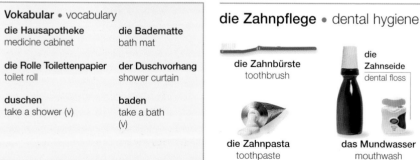

die Zahnbürste
toothbrush

die
Zahnseide
dental floss

die Zahnpasta
toothpaste

das Mundwasser
mouthwash

der Schwamm
sponge

der Bimsstein
pumice stone

die Rückenbürste
back brush

das Deo
deodorant

die
Seifenschale
soap dish

die Seife
soap

das **Duschgel**
shower gel

die Gesichtscreme
face cream

das Schaumbad
bubble bath

das Handtuch
hand towel

das
Badetuch
bath towel

die Handtücher
towels

die Körperlotion
body lotion

der Körperpuder
talcum powder

der Bademantel
bathrobe

das Rasieren • shaving

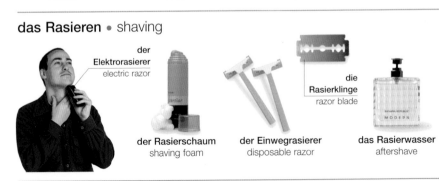

der
Elektrorasierer
electric razor

der Rasierschaum
shaving foam

der Einwegrasierer
disposable razor

die
Rasierklinge
razor blade

das Rasierwasser
aftershave

das Kinderzimmer • nursery

die Säuglingspflege • baby care

die Wundsalbe
nappy rash cream

das Erfrischungstuch
wet wipe

der Schwamm
sponge

die Babywanne
baby bath

das Töpfchen
potty

die Wickelmatte
changing mat

das Schlafen • sleeping

das Mobile
mobile

das Laken
sheet

die Decke
blanket

die Gitterstäbe
bars

die Flauschdecke
fleece

das Bettzeug
bedding

der Kopfschutz
bumper

die Matratze
mattress

das Kinderbett | cot

die Rassel
rattle

das Körbchen
moses basket

das Spielen • playing

die Puppe
doll

das Kuscheltier
soft toy

das Puppenhaus
doll's house

das Spielhaus
playhouse

die Sicherheit
• safety

die
Kindersicherung
child lock

die Babysprechanlage
baby monitor

der Teddy
teddy bear

das
Spielzeug
toy

der Spielzeugkorb
toy basket

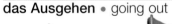

der Ball
ball

der Laufstall
playpen

das Treppengitter
stair gate

das Essen •
eating

der Kinderstuhl
high chair

der Sauger
teat

der
Babybecher
drinking cup

die Babyflasche
bottle

das Ausgehen • going out

der Sportwagen
pushchair

das Verdeck
hood

der Kinderwagen
pram

die Windel
nappy

das Tragebettchen
carrycot

die Babytasche
changing bag

die Babytrageschlinge
baby sling

der Allzweckraum • utility room

die Wäsche • laundry

die saubere Wäsche
clean clothes

die
schmutzige
Wäsche
dirty washing

der Wäschekorb
laundry basket

**die
Waschmaschine**
washing machine

**der
Waschtrockner**
washer-dryer

der Trockner
tumble dryer

**der
Wäschekorb**
linen basket

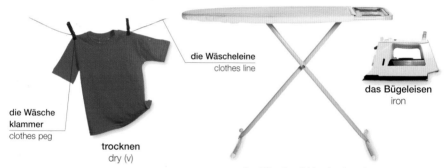

die Wäscheleine
clothes line

das Bügeleisen
iron

die Wäsche
klammer
clothes peg

trocknen
dry (v)

das Bügelbrett | ironing board

Vokabular • vocabulary

füllen load (v)	**schleudern** spin (v)	**bügeln** iron (v)	**Wie benutze ich die Waschmaschine?** How do I operate the washing machine?
spülen rinse (v)	**die Wäscheschleuder** spin dryer	**der Weichspüler** conditioner	**Welches Programm nehme ich für farbige/weiße Wäsche?** What is the setting for coloureds/whites?

---

die Reinigungsartikel • cleaning equipment

der Saugschlauch
suction hose

der Handfeger
brush

die Müllschaufel
dust pan

das Reinigungsmittel
bleach

der Eimer
bucket

das Pulver
powder

die
Flüssigkeit
liquid

das
Staubtuch
duster

der Staubsauger
vacuum cleaner

der Mopp
mop

das Waschmittel
detergent

die Politur
polish

die Tätigkeiten • activities

putzen
clean (v)

spülen
wash (v)

wischen
wipe (v)

schrubben
scrub (v)

kratzen
scrape (v)

der Besen
broom

fegen
sweep (v)

Staub wischen
dust (v)

polieren
polish (v)

die Heimwerkstatt • workshop

das Bohrfutter
chuck

der Bohrer
drill bit

die Batterie
battery pack

die Stichsäge
jigsaw

der Bohrer mit Batteriebetrieb
rechargeable drill

der Elektrobohrer
electric drill

die Leimpistole
glue gun

die Zwinge
clamp

das Blatt
blade

der Schraubstock
vice

die Schleifmaschine
sander

die Kreissäge
circular saw

die Werkbank
workbench

der Holzleim
wood glue

das Werkzeuggestell
tool rack

der Grundhobel
router

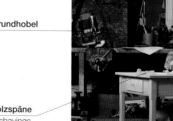

die Bohrwinde
bit brace

die Holzspäne
wood shavings

die Verlängerungsschnur
extension lead

die Fertigkeiten • techniques

schneiden
cut (v)

sägen
saw (v)

bohren
drill (v)

hämmern
hammer (v)

hobeln
plane (v)

drechseln
turn (v)

der Lötzinn
solder

schnitzen
carve (v)

löten
solder (v)

die Materialien • materials

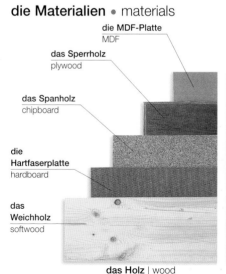

die MDF-Platte
MDF

das Sperrholz
plywood

das Spanholz
chipboard

die Hartfaserplatte
hardboard

das Weichholz
softwood

das Holz | wood

das Hartholz
hardwood

der Lack
varnish

die Beize
woodstain

der Draht
wire

das Kabel
cable

der rostfreie Stahl
stainless steel

galvanisiert
galvanised

das Metall | metal

der Werkzeugkasten • toolbox

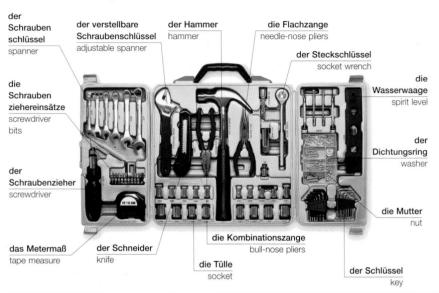

der
Schrauben
schlüssel
spanner

der verstellbare
Schraubenschlüssel
adjustable spanner

der Hammer
hammer

die Flachzange
needle-nose pliers

der Steckschlüssel
socket wrench

die
Schrauben
ziehereinsätze
screwdriver
bits

der
Schraubenzieher
screwdriver

die
Wasserwaage
spirit level

der
Dichtungsring
washer

das Metermaß
tape measure

der Schneider
knife

die Kombinationszange
bull-nose pliers

die Tülle
socket

die Mutter
nut

der Schlüssel
key

die Bohrer • drill bits

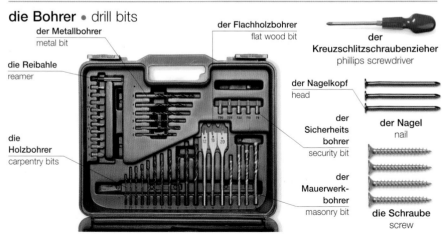

der Metallbohrer
metal bit

der Flachholzbohrer
flat wood bit

der
Kreuzschlitzschraubenzieher
phillips screwdriver

die Reibahle
reamer

der Nagelkopf
head

die
Holzbohrer
carpentry bits

der
Sicherheits
bohrer
security bit

der Nagel
nail

der
Mauerwerk-
bohrer
masonry bit

die Schraube
screw

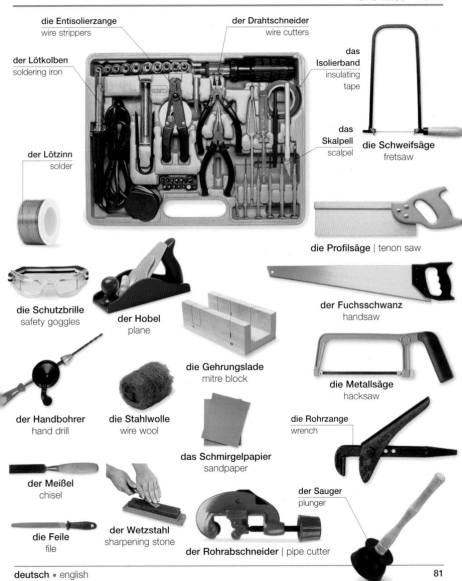

die Entisolierzange
wire strippers

der Drahtschneider
wire cutters

das
Isolierband
insulating
tape

der Lötkolben
soldering iron

das
Skalpell
scalpel

die Schweifsäge
fretsaw

der Lötzinn
solder

die Profilsäge | tenon saw

die Schutzbrille
safety goggles

der Hobel
plane

der Fuchsschwanz
handsaw

die Gehrungslade
mitre block

die Metallsäge
hacksaw

der Handbohrer
hand drill

die Stahlwolle
wire wool

die Rohrzange
wrench

der Meißel
chisel

das Schmirgelpapier
sandpaper

der Sauger
plunger

die Feile
file

der Wetzstahl
sharpening stone

der Rohrabschneider | pipe cutter

das Tapezieren • decorating

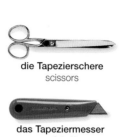

die Tapezierschere
scissors

das Tapeziermesser
craft knife

das Senkblei
plumb line

der
Tapezierer
decorator

die
Tapezierbürste
wallpaper brush

die Tapete
wallpaper

die Trittleiter
stepladder

der
Tapeziertisch
pasting table

die
Kleisterbürste
pasting brush

der
Tapetenkleister
wallpaper paste

der Eimer
bucket

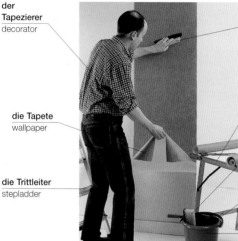

der Spachtel
scraper

tapezieren | wallpaper (v)

abziehen
strip (v)

spachteln
fill (v)

schmirgeln
sand (v)

verputzen | plaster (v)

anbringen | hang (v)

kacheln | tile (v)

deutsch • english

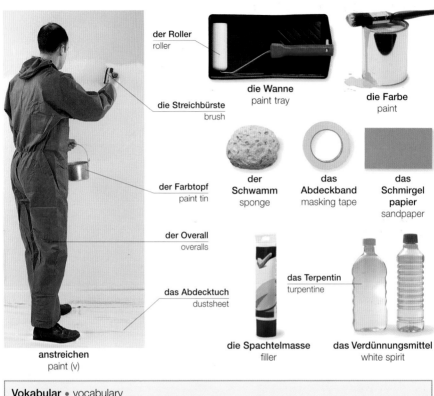

der Roller
roller

die Wanne
paint tray

die Farbe
paint

die Streichbürste
brush

der
Schwamm
sponge

das
Abdeckband
masking tape

das
Schmirgel
papier
sandpaper

der Farbtopf
paint tin

der Overall
overalls

das Terpentin
turpentine

das Abdecktuch
dustsheet

die Spachtelmasse
filler

das Verdünnungsmittel
white spirit

anstreichen
paint (v)

Vokabular • vocabulary

der Gips plaster	Glanz- gloss	das Relieftapete embossed paper	die Grundierung undercoat	das Lösungsmittel solvent
der Lack varnish	matt mat	die Grundfarbe primer	der Fugenkitt grout	der Deckanstrich top coat
die Emulsionsfarbe emulsion	die Schablone stencil	das Einsatzpapier lining paper	der Schutzanstrich preservative	das Versiegelungsmittel sealant

der Garten • garden

die Gartentypen • garden styles

die Garten ornamente • garden features

der Patio
patio garden

der Dachgarten
roof garden

die Blumenampel
hanging basket

der architektonische Garten | formal garden

der Steingarten
rock garden

das Spalier
trellis

der Hof
courtyard

der Bauerngarten
cottage garden

der Kräutergarten
herb garden

der Wassergarten
water garden

die Pergola
pergola

die Platten
paving

der Weg
path

der Kompost
haufen
compost heap

das Tor
gate

das
Blumenbeet
flowerbed

der
Schuppen
shed

das
Gewächshaus
greenhouse

der Zaun
fence

der Rasen
lawn

der Teich
pond

die Hecke
hedge

der Bogen
arch

der
Gemüsegarten
vegetable
garden

die Staudenrabatte
herbaceous border

der Boden
● soil

die Erde
topsoil

der Sand
sand

der Kalk
chalk

der Schlick
silt

der Lehm
clay

die Planken
decking

der Springbrunnen | fountain

die Gartenpflanzen • garden plants

die Pflanzenarten • types of plants

einjährig
annual

zweijährig
biennial

mehrjährig
perennial

die Zwiebel
bulb

der Farn
fern

die Binse
rush

der Bambus
bamboo

das Unkraut
weeds

das Kraut
herb

die Wasserpflanze
water plant

der Baum
tree

der Laubbaum
deciduous

die Palme
palm

der Nadelbaum
conifer

immergrün
evergreen

der Formschnitt
topiary

die Alpenpflanze
alpine

die Fettpflanze
succulent

der Kaktus
cactus

die Topfpflanze
potted plant

die Schattenpflanze
shade plant

die Kletterpflanze
climber

der Zierstrauch
flowering shrub

der Bodendecker
ground cover

die Kriechpflanze
creeper

Zier-
ornamental

das Gras
grass

die Gartengeräte • garden tools

der Laubrechen
lawn rake

die Komposterde
compost

die Samen
seeds

**die
Knochenasche**
bone meal

der Spaten
spade

die Gabel
fork

die Schere
long-handled shears

der Rechen
rake

die Hacke
hoe

der Kies
gravel

der Grasfangsack
grass bag

der Motor
motor

der Griff
handle

der Gartenkorb
trug

der Schutz
shield

der Ständer
stand

der Schneider
trimmer

der Rasenmäher
lawnmower

der Schubkarren
wheelbarrow

die Handgabel
hand fork

die Pflanzschaufel
trowel

das Messer
blade

die Heckenschere
shears

die Handsäge
hand saw

die Rosenschere
secateurs

der Setzkasten
seed tray

das Pestizid
pesticide

die Gartenhandschuhe
gardening gloves

der Zwirn
twine

**die Garten
stöcke**
canes

das Sieb
sieve

der Blumentopf
plant pot

die
Pflanzenschildchen
labels

die
Befestigungen
twist ties

die
Ringbefestigungen
ring ties

die Gummistiefel
rubber boots

das Gießen • watering

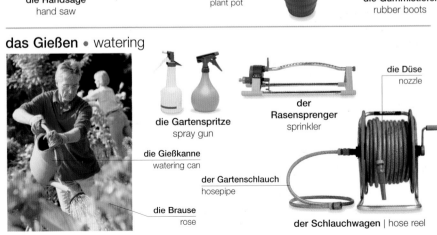

die Gartenspritze
spray gun

**der
Rasensprenger**
sprinkler

die Düse
nozzle

die Gießkanne
watering can

der Gartenschlauch
hosepipe

die Brause
rose

der Schlauchwagen | hose reel

die Gartenarbeit • gardening

der Rasen
lawn

das
Blumenbeet
flowerbed

der
Rasenmäher
lawnmower

die Hecke
hedge

die Stange
stake

mähen | mow (v)

mit Rasen bedecken
turf (v)

stechen
spike (v)

harken
rake (v)

stutzen
trim (v)

graben
dig (v)

säen
sow (v)

**mit Kopfdünger
düngen**
top dress (v)

gießen
water (v)

ziehen
train (v)

köpfen
deadhead (v)

sprühen
spray (v)

der Stock
cane

pfropfen
graft (v)

der Ableger
cutting

vermehren
propagate (v)

beschneiden
prune (v)

hochbinden
stake (v)

umpflanzen
transplant (v)

jäten
weed (v)

mulchen
mulch (v)

ernten
harvest (v)

Vokabular • vocabulary

züchten cultivate (v)	**gestalten** landscape (v)	**düngen** fertilize (v)	**sieben** sieve (v)	**biodynamisch** organic	**die Entwässerung** drainage	**der Dünger** fertilizer
hegen tend (v)	**eintopfen** pot up (v)	**pflücken** pick (v)	**auflockern** aerate (v)	**der Untergrund** subsoil	**der Unkrautvernichter** weedkiller	**der Sämling** seedling

die Dienstleistungen
services

die Dienstleistungen • emergency services

die Notdienste • ambulance

die Tragbahre
stretcher

der Krankenwagen
ambulance

der Rettungssanitäter
paramedic

die Polizei • police

die Kenn-marke
badge

die Uniform
uniform

die Sirene
siren

das Licht
lights

der Gummiknüppel
nightstick

das Polizeiauto
police car

die Polizeiwache
police station

die Pistole
gun

die Handschellen
handcuffs

der Polizist
police officer

Vokabular • vocabulary

der Inspektor inspector	**das Verbrechen** crime	**die Beschwerde** complaint	**die Festnahme** arrest
der Kriminal-beamte detective	**der Einbruch-diebstahl** burglary	**die Ermittlung** investigation	**die Anklage** charge
die Polizeizelle cell	**die Körperver-rletzung** assault	**der Verdächtige** suspect	**der Finger abdruck** fingerprint

die Feuerwehr • fire department

der Schutzhelm
helmet

der Rauch
smoke

der Schlauch
hose

der Auslegerkorb
basket

die Feuerwehrleute
firefighters

der Wasserstrahl
water jet

die Fahrerkabine
cab

der Ausleger
boom

die Leiter
ladder

der Brand | fire

die Feuerwache
fire station

die Feuertreppe
fire escape

das Löschfahrzeug
fire engine

der Rauchmelder
smoke alarm

der Feuermelder
fire alarm

das Beil
ax

der Feuerlöscher
fire extinguisher

der Hydrant
hydrant

Die Polizei/die Feuerwehr/einen Krankenwagen, bitte.
I need the police/fire department/ambulance.

Es brennt in…
There's a fire at…

Es ist ein Unfall passiert.
There's been an accident.

Rufen Sie die Polizei!
Call the police!

---

die Bank • bank

der Kunde
customer

der Schalter
window

der Kassierer
cashier

die Broschüren
leaflets

der Schalter
counter

**die Einzahlungs
scheine**
paying-in slips

die EC-Karte
debit card

**der
Abschnitt**
stub

**die
Kontonummer**
account number

**die
Unterschrift**
signature

der Betrag
amount

der Filialleiter
bank manager

die Kreditkarte
credit card

das Scheckheft
chequebook

der Scheck
cheque

Vokabular • vocabulary

die Steuer tax	**die Hypothek** mortgage	**die Zahlung** payment	**einzahlen** pay in (v)	**das Girokonto** current account
das Darlehen loan	**der Zinssatz** interest rate	**der Einzugsauftrag** direct debit	**die Bankgebühr** bank charge	**das Sparkonto** savings account
die Spareinlagen savings	**die Kontoüberziehung** overdraft	**das Abhebungsformular** withdrawal slip	**die Banküberweisung** bank transfer	**der PIN-Kode** pin number

---

die Münze
coin

der Schein
note

der Bildschirm
screen

das Tastenfeld
key pad

der Kartenschlitz
card slot

das Geld
money

der Geldautomat
cash machine

die Währung • currency

die Wechselstube
bureau de change

der Reisescheck
traveller's cheque

der Wechselkurs
exchange rate

---

die Geldwirtschaft • finance

der Aktienpreis
share price

der Börsenmakler
stockbroker

die Finanzberaterin
financial advisor

die Börse | stock exchange

Vokabular • vocabulary

einlösen
cash (v)

die Aktien
shares

der Nennwert
denomination

die Gewinnanteile
dividends

die Provision
commission

das Portefeuille
portfolio

die Wertpapiere
stocks

die Stammaktie
equity

die Kapitalanlage
investment

der Wirtschaftsprüfer
accountant

die ausländische Währung
foreign currency

Könnte ich das bitte wechseln?
Can I change this please?

Wie ist der heutige Wechselkurs?
What's today's exchange rate?

die Kommunikation • communications

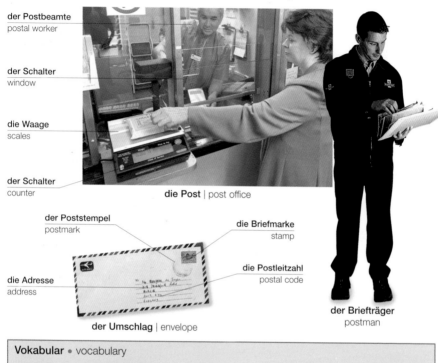

der Postbeamte
postal worker

der Schalter
window

die Waage
scales

der Schalter
counter

die Post | post office

der Poststempel
postmark

die Briefmarke
stamp

die Adresse
address

die Postleitzahl
postal code

der Umschlag | envelope

der Briefträger
postman

Vokabular • vocabulary

der Brief letter	**der Absender** return address	**die Zustellung** delivery	**zerbrechlich** fragile	**nicht falten** do not bend (v)
per Luftpost by airmail	**die Unterschrift** signature	**die Postgebühr** postage	**der Postsack** mailbag	**oben** this way up
das Einschreiben registered post	**die Leerung** collection	**die Postanweisung** postal ordery	**das Telegramm** telegram	**das Fax** fax

der Briefkasten
postbox

der Hausbriefkasten
letterbox

das Paket
parcel

der Kurierdienst
courier

das Telefon • telephone

der Hörer
handset

der Anrufbeantworter
answering machine

die Basis
base station

das schnurlose Telefon
cordless phone

das Fernsehtelefon
video phone

die Telefonzelle
telephone box

das Smartphone
smartphone

das Handy
mobile phone

das Tastenfeld
keypad

der Hörer
receiver

die Münzrückgabe
coin return

der Münzfernsprecher
payphone

Vokabular • vocabulary

abheben answer (v)	**die App** app	**der Passcode** passcode	**Können Sie mir die Nummer für…geben?** Can you give me the number for…?
wählen dial (v)	**die SMS** text (SMS)	**besetzt** engaged/busy	**Was ist die Vorwahl für…?** What is the dialling code for…?
das R-Gespräch reverse charge call	**die Sprachmit-teilung** voice message	**unterbrochen** disconnected	**Schick mir eine SMS!** Text me!
die Auskunft directory enquiries		**die Vermittlung** operator	

das Hotel • hotel
die Empfangshalle • lobby

die Nachrichten
messages

der Gast
guest

der Zimmerschlüssel
room key

das Fach
pigeonhole

die Empfangsdame
receptionist

das Gästebuch
register

der Schalter
counter

der Empfang | reception

das Gepäck
luggage

der Kofferkuli
trolley

der Hoteldiener
porter

der Fahrstuhl
lift

die Zimmernummer
room number

die Zimmer • rooms

das Einzelzimmer
single room

das Doppelzimmer
double room

das Zweibettzimmer
twin room

das Privatbadezimmer
private bathroom

die Dienstleistungen • services

die Zimmerreinigung
maid service

der Wäschedienst
laundry service

das Frühstückstablett
breakfast tray

der Zimmerservice | room service

die Minibar
mini bar

das Restaurant
restaurant

der Fitnessraum
gym

das Schwimmbad
swimming pool

Vokabular • vocabulary

die Vollpension
full board

die Halbpension
half board

die Übernachtung mit Frühstück
bed and breakfast

Haben Sie ein Zimmer frei?
Do you have any vacancies?

Ich möchte ein Einzelzimmer.
I'd like a single room.

Ich habe ein Zimmer reserviert.
I have a reservation.

Ich möchte ein Zimmer für drei Nächte.
I'd like a room for three nights.

Was kostet das Zimmer pro Nacht?
What is the charge per night?

Wann muss ich das Zimmer räumen?
When do I have to vacate the room?

der Einkauf
shopping

das Einkaufszentrum • shopping centre

das Atrium
atrium

die zweite
Etage
second floor

das Schild
sign

die erste
Etage
first floor

die Rolltreppe
escalator

der
Fahrstuhl
lift

das
Erdgeschoss
ground floor

der Kunde
customer

Vokabular • vocabulary

die Kinderabteilung children's department	**der Kundendienst** customer services	**die Anprobe** changing rooms	**Was kostet das?** How much is this?
die Gepäckabteilung luggage department	**die Anzeigetafel** store directory	**der Wickelraum** baby changing facilities	**Kann ich das umtauschen?** May I exchange this?
die Schuhabteilung shoe department	**der Verkäufer** sales assistant	**die Toiletten** toilets	

das Kaufhaus • department store

die Herrenbekleidung
men's wear

die Damenoberbekleidung
women's wear

die Damenwäsche
lingerie

die Parfümerie
perfumery

die Schönheitspflege
beauty

die Wäsche
linen

die Möbel
home furnishings

die Kurzwaren
haberdashery

die Küchengeräte
kitchenware

das Porzellan
china

die Elektroartikel
electrical goods

die Lampen
lighting

die Sportartikel
sports

die Spielwaren
toys

die Schreibwaren
stationery

die Lebensmittelabteilung
food hall

der Supermarkt • supermarket

der Gang
aisle

das Warenregal
shelf

das Laufband
conveyer belt

der Kassierer
cashier

die Angebote
offers

die Kasse | checkout

der Kunde
customer

die Kasse
till

die Einkaufstasche
shopping bag

die Lebensmittel
groceries

der Henkel
handle

der Strichkode
bar code

der Einkaufswagen
trolley

der Einkaufskorb
basket

der Scanner
scanner

die Backwaren
bakery

die Milchprodukte
dairy

die Getreideflocken
cereals

die Konserven
tinned food

die Süßwaren
confectionery

das Gemüse
vegetables

das Obst
fruit

das Fleisch und das Geflügel
meat and poultry

der Fisch
fish

die Feinkost
deli

die Gefrierware
frozen food

die Fertiggerichte
convenience food

die Getränke
drinks

die Haushaltswaren
household products

die Toilettenartikel
toiletries

die Babyprodukte
baby products

die Elektroartikel
electrical goods

das Tierfutter
pet food

die Zeitschriften | magazines

die Apotheke • chemist

die Zahnpflege
dental care

die Monats-
hygiene
feminine
hygiene

die Deos
deodorants

die
Vitamintabletten
vitamins

die Apotheke
dispensary

der Apotheker
pharmacist

das
Hustenmedikament
cough medicine

das Kräuterheilmittel
herbal remedies

die Hautpflege
skin care

die Sonnenschutzcreme
sunscreen

die After-
Sun-Lotion
aftersun

der Sonnenblock
sunblock

das
Insektenschutzmittel
insect repellent

das Reinigungstuch
wet wipe

das Papiertaschentuch
tissue

die Damenbinde
sanitary towel

der Tampon
tampon

die Slipeinlage
panty liner

der Messlöffel
measuring spoon

die Gebrauchs-
anweisung
instructions

die Kapsel
capsule

die Pille
pill

der Saft
syrup

der Inhalierstift
inhaler

die Creme
cream

die Salbe
ointment

das Gel
gel

das Zäpfchen
suppository

der Tropfer
dropper

die Nadel
needle

die Tropfen
drops

die Spritze
syringe

der Spray
spray

der Puder
powder

Vokabular • vocabulary

das Eisen iron	**das Multivitaminmittel** multivitamins	**Wegwerf-** disposable	**das Medikament** medicine	**das Schmerzmittel** painkiller
das Kalzium calcium	**die Nebenwirkungen** side-effects	**löslich** soluble	**der Durchfall** diarrhoea	**das Beruhigungsmittel** sedative
das Insulin insulin	**das Verfallsdatum** expiry date	**die Dosierung** dosage	**die Halspastille** throat lozenge	**die Schlaftablette** sleeping pill
das Magnesium magnesium	**die Reisekrankheitstabletten** travel sickness pills	**die Verordnung** medication	**das Abführmittel** laxative	**der Entzündungshemmer** anti-inflammatory

das Blumengeschäft • florist

die Blumen
flowers

die Gladiole
gladiolus

die Lilie
lily

die Iris
iris

die Akazie
acacia

die Margerite
daisy

die
Chrysantheme
chrysanthemum

die Nelke
carnation

das
Schleierkraut
gypsophila

die Topfpflanze
pot plant

| **die Levkoje** | **die Gerbera** | **die Blätter** | **die Rose** | **die Freesie** |
| stocks | gerbera | foliage | rose | freesia |

deutsch • english

die
Blumenvase
vase

die Orchidee
orchid

die Pfingstrose
peony

der Strauß
bunch

der Stengel
stem

die Osterglocke
daffodil

die Knospe
bud

das Ein
wickelpapier
wrapping

die Tulpe | tulip

die Blumenarrangements • arrangements

das Band
ribbon

das Bukett
bouquet

die Trockenblumen
dried flowers

das Duftsträußchen | pot-pourri

der Kranz | wreath

die
Blumengirlande
garland

Ich möchte einen Strauß...,
bitte.
Can I have a bunch of…
please.

Wie lange halten sie?
How long will these last?

Können Sie die Blumen
bitte einwickeln?
Can I have them wrapped?

Duften sie?
Are they fragrant?

Kann ich eine Nachricht
mitschicken?
Can I attach a message?

Können Sie die Blumen
an... schicken?
Can you send them to….?

der Zeitungshändler • newsagent

die Zigaretten
cigarettes

das Päckchen Zigaretten
packet of cigarettes

die
Briefmarken
stamps

die Postkarte
postcard

das Comicheft
comic

die Zeitschrift
magazine

die Zeitung
newspaper

das Rauchen • smoking

der Tabak
tobacco

das Feuerzeug
lighter

der Stiel
stem

der Kopf
bowl

die Pfeife
pipe

die Zigarre
cigar

der Konditor • confectioner

die Schachtel Pralinen
box of chocolates

die Nascherei
snack bar

die Chips
crisps

das Süßwarengeschäft | sweet shop

Vokabular • vocabulary

die Milchschokolade
milk chocolate

der Karamell
caramel

die bittere Schokolade
plain chocolate

der Trüffel
truffle

der Keks
biscuit

die weiße Schokolade
white chocolate

die Bonbons
boiled sweets

die bunte Mischung
pick and mix

die Süßwaren • confectionery

die Praline
chocolate

die Tafel Schokolade
chocolate bar

die Bonbons
sweets

der Lutscher
lollipop

das Toffee
toffee

der Nugat
nougat

das Marshmallow
marshmallow

das Pfefferminz
mint

der Kaugummi
chewing gum

der Geleebonbon
jellybean

der Fruchtgummi
fruit gum

die Lakritze
licquorice

andere Geschäfte • other shops

die Bäckerei
baker's

die Konditorei
cake shop

die Metzgerei
butcher's

das Fischgeschäft
fishmonger's

der Gemüseladen
greengrocer's

das Lebensmittelgeschäft
grocer's

das Schuhgeschäft
shoe shop

die Eisenwaren-handlung
hardware shop

der Antiquitätenladen
antiques shop

der Geschenkartikel-laden
gift shop

das Reisebüro
travel agent's

das Juweliergeschäft
jeweller's

der Buchladen
book shop

das Plattengeschäft
record shop

die Weinhandlung
off licence

die Tierhandlung
pet shop

das Möbelgeschäft
furniture shop

die Boutique
boutique

Vokabular • vocabulary

das Gartencenter garden centre	**das Fotogeschäft** camera shop
die Reinigung dry cleaner's	**das Reformhaus** health food shop
der Waschsalon launderette	**die Kunsthandlung** art shop
der Immobilienmakler estate agent's	**der Gebrauchtwarenhändler** second-hand shop

die Schneiderei
tailor's

der Frisiersalon
hairdresser's

der Markt | market

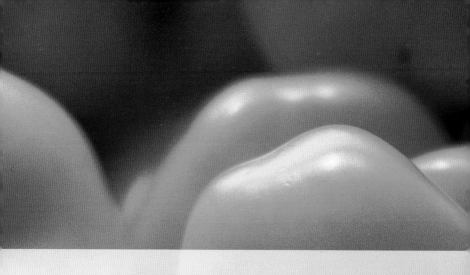

die Nahrungsmittel
food

das Fleisch • meat

das Lamm
lamb

der Metzger
butcher

der Fleischerhaken
meat hook

die Waage
scales

der Messerschärfer
knife sharpener

der Speck
bacon

die Würstchen
sausages

die Leber
liver

Vokabular • vocabulary

das Rindfleisch beef	**das Wild** venison	**die Zunge** tongue	**aus Freilandhaltung** free range	**das rote Fleisch** red meat
das Kalbfleisch veal	**das Kaninchen** rabbit	**gepökelt** cured	**biologisch kontrolliert** organic	**das magere Fleisch** lean meat
das Schweinefleisch pork	**die Innereien** offal	**geräuchert** smoked	**das weiße Fleisch** white meat	**das gekochte Fleisch** cooked meat

die Fleischsorten • cuts

der Schinken
ham

die
Schwarte
rind

die Scheibe
slice

die Speckscheibe
rasher

das Hackfleisch
mince

das Filet
fillet

das Rumpsteak
rump steak

die Niere
kidney

das Fett
fat

der
Knochen
bone

das Lendensteak
sirloin steak

das Rippenstück
rib

das Kotelett
chop

die Keule
joint

das Herz
heart

das Geflügel • poultry

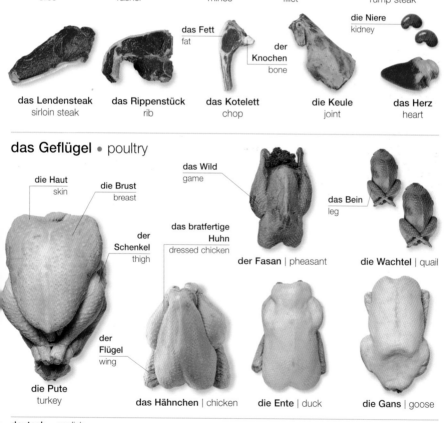

die Haut
skin

die Brust
breast

das Wild
game

das Bein
leg

der
Schenkel
thigh

das bratfertige
Huhn
dressed chicken

der Fasan | pheasant

die Wachtel | quail

der
Flügel
wing

die Pute
turkey

das Hähnchen | chicken

die Ente | duck

die Gans | goose

der Fisch • fish

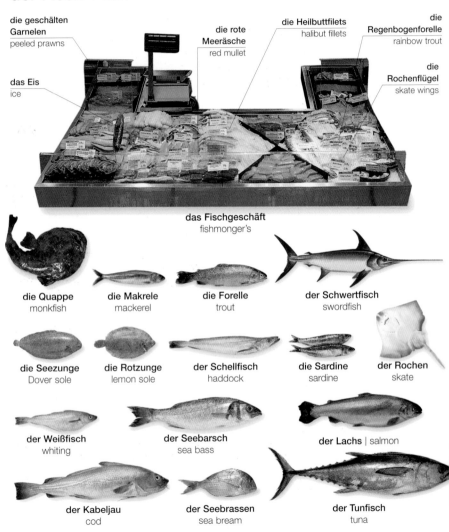

die geschälten Garnelen
peeled prawns

das Eis
ice

die rote Meeräsche
red mullet

die Heilbuttfilets
halibut fillets

die Regenbogenforelle
rainbow trout

die Rochenflügel
skate wings

das Fischgeschäft
fishmonger's

die Quappe
monkfish

die Makrele
mackerel

die Forelle
trout

der Schwertfisch
swordfish

die Seezunge
Dover sole

die Rotzunge
lemon sole

der Schellfisch
haddock

die Sardine
sardine

der Rochen
skate

der Weißfisch
whiting

der Seebarsch
sea bass

der Lachs | salmon

der Kabeljau
cod

der Seebrassen
sea bream

der Tunfisch
tuna

die Meeresfrüchte • seafood

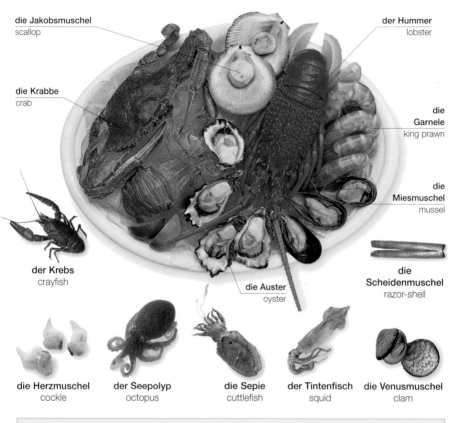

die Jakobsmuschel
scallop

der Hummer
lobster

die Krabbe
crab

die Garnele
king prawn

die Miesmuschel
mussel

der Krebs
crayfish

die Auster
oyster

die Scheidenmuschel
razor-shell

die Herzmuschel
cockle

der Seepolyp
octopus

die Sepie
cuttlefish

der Tintenfisch
squid

die Venusmuschel
clam

Vokabular • vocabulary

tiefgefroren	**gesalzen**	**zubereitet**	**entschuppt**	**enthäutet**	**die Lende**	**die Gräte**	**das Filet**
frozen	salted	cleaned	descaled	skinned	loin	bone	fillet

frisch	**geräuchert**	**filetiert**	**entgrätet**	**die Schuppe**	**der Schwanz**	**die Schnitte**	
fresh	smoked	filleted	boned	scale	tail	steak	

das Gemüse 1 • vegetables 1

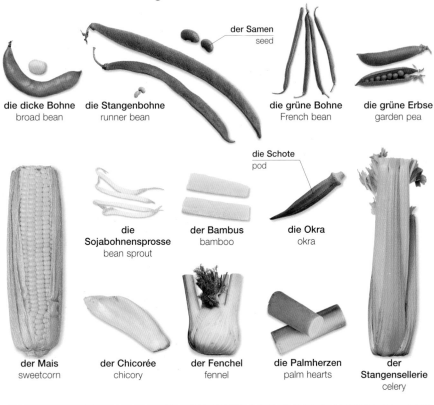

der Samen
seed

die dicke Bohne
broad bean

die Stangenbohne
runner bean

die grüne Bohne
French bean

die grüne Erbse
garden pea

die Schote
pod

**die
Sojabohnensprosse**
bean sprout

der Bambus
bamboo

die Okra
okra

der Mais
sweetcorn

der Chicorée
chicory

der Fenchel
fennel

die Palmherzen
palm hearts

**der
Stangensellerie**
celery

Vokabular • vocabulary				
das Blatt leaf	**das Röschen** floret	**die Spitze** tip	**biodynamisch** organic	**Verkaufen Sie Biogemüse?** Do you sell organic vegetables?
der Strunk stalk	**der Kern** kernel	**das Herz** heart	**die Plastiktüte** plastic bag	**Werden sie in dieser Gegend angebaut?** Are these grown locally?

die Rauke
rocket

die Brunnenkresse
watercress

der Radicchio
radicchio

der Rosenkohl
brussel sprout

der Mangold
swiss chard

der Grünkohl
kale

der Garten-Sauerampfer
sorrel

die Endivie
endive

der Löwenzahn
dandelion

der Spinat
spinach

der Kohlrabi
kohlrabi

der Chinakohl
pak-choi

der Salat
lettuce

der Brokkoli
broccoli

der Kohl
cabbage

der Frühkohl
spring greens

das Gemüse 2 • vegetables 2

die Rübe
turnip

die Artischocke
artichoke

das Radieschen
radish

der Blumenkohl
cauliflower

die Kartoffel
potato

der Spargel
asparagus

der Gartenkürbis
marrow

die Zwiebel
onion

die Paprika
pepper

die Peperoni
chilli

der Mais
sweetcorn

Vokabular • vocabulary

die Kirschtomate cherry tomato	**der Sellerie** celeriac	**tiefgefroren** frozen	**bitter** bitter	**Könnte ich bitte ein Kilo Kartoffeln haben?** Can I have one kilo of potatoes please?
die Karotte carrot	**die Tarowurzel** taro root	**roh** raw	**fest** firm	**Was kostet ein Kilo?** What's the price per kilo?
die Brotfrucht breadfruit	**der Maniok** cassava	**scharf** hot (spicy)	**das Fleisch** flesh	**Wie heißen diese?** What are those called?
die neue Kartoffel new potato	**die Wasserkastanie** water chestnut	**süß** sweet	**die Wurzel** root	

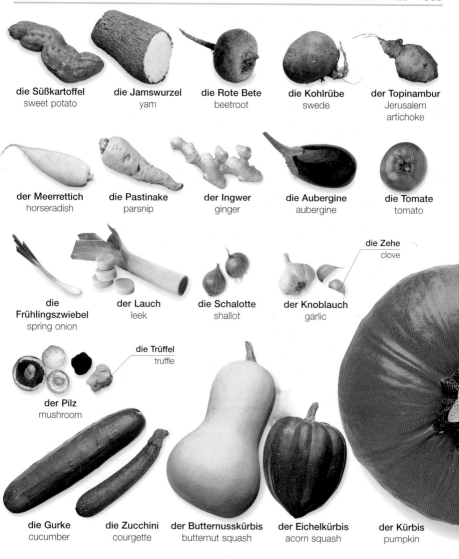

die Süßkartoffel
sweet potato

die Jamswurzel
yam

die Rote Bete
beetroot

die Kohlrübe
swede

der Topinambur
Jerusalem
artichoke

der Meerrettich
horseradish

die Pastinake
parsnip

der Ingwer
ginger

die Aubergine
aubergine

die Tomate
tomato

**die
Frühlingszwiebel**
spring onion

der Lauch
leek

die Schalotte
shallot

der Knoblauch
garlic

die Zehe
clove

die Trüffel
truffle

der Pilz
mushroom

die Gurke
cucumber

die Zucchini
courgette

der Butternusskürbis
butternut squash

der Eichelkürbis
acorn squash

der Kürbis
pumpkin

das Obst 1 • fruit 1

die Zitrusfrüchte • citrus fruit

die Orange
orange

die Klementine
clementine

die weiße
Haut
pith

die Tangelo
ugli fruit

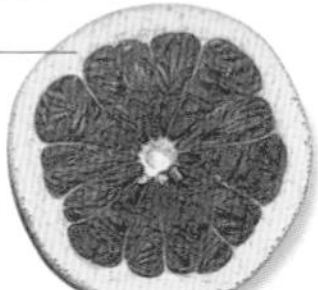

die Grapefruit
grapefruit

der Schnitt
segment

die Satsuma
satsuma

die Mandarine
tangerine

die Schale
zest

die Limone
lime

die Zitrone
lemon

die Kumquat
kumquat

das Steinobst • stoned fruit

der Pfirsich
peach

die Nektarine
nectarine

die Aprikose
apricot

die Pflaume
plum

die Kirsche
cherry

der Apfel
apple

die Birne
pear

der Obstkorb | basket of fruit

das Beerenobst und die Melonen • berries and melons

die Erdbeere
strawberry

die Himbeere
raspberry

die Melone
melon

die Weintrauben
grapes

die Brombeere
blackberry

die Johannisbeere
redcurrant

die Preiselbeere
cranberry

**die schwarze
Johannisbeere**
blackcurrant

die Schale
rind

der Kern
seed

die Heidelbeere
blueberry

**das
Fruchtfleisch**
flesh

die weiße Johannisbeere
white currant

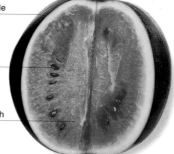
die Wassermelone
watermelon

die Loganbeere
loganberry

die Stachelbeere
gooseberry

Vokabular • vocabulary

saftig juicy	**sauer** sour	**knackig** crisp	**kernlos** seedless
die Faser fibre	**frisch** fresh	**faul** rotten	**der Saft** juice
süß sweet	**der Rhabarber** rhubarb	**das Fruchtmark** pulp	**das Kerngehäuse** core

Sind sie reif?
Are they ripe?

Könnte ich eine probieren?
Can I try one?

Wie lange halten sie sich?
How long will they keep?

das Obst 2 • fruit 2

die Mango
mango

die Ananas
pineapple

die Avocado
avocado

die Papaya
papaya

der Pfirsich
peach

die Litschi
lychee

die Kiwi
kiwifruit

die Kapstachelbeere
cape gooseberry

der Kern
pip

die Schale
skin

die Quitte
quince

die Passionsfrucht
passion fruit

die Banane
banana

die Guave
guava

der Granatapfel
pomegranate

die Kaki
persimmon

die Feijoa
feijoa

die Kaktusfeige
prickly pear

die Sternfrucht
starfruit

die Tamarillo
tamarillo

die Nüsse und das Dörrobst • nuts and dried fruit

die Piniennuss
pine nut

die Pistazie
pistachio

die Cashewnuss
cashewnut

die Erdnuss
peanut

die Haselnuss
hazelnut

die Paranuss
brazilnut

die Pecannuss
pecan

die Mandel
almond

die Walnuss
walnut

die Esskastanie
chestnut

die Macadamianuss
macadamia

die Feige
fig

die Dattel
date

die Backpflaume
prune

die Schale
shell

die Sultanine
sultana

die Rosine
raisin

die Korinthe
currant

das
Fruchtfleisch
flesh

die Kokosnuss
coconut

Vokabular • vocabulary

grün	hart	der Kern	gesalzen	geröstet	die Südfrüchte	geschält
green	hard	kernel	salted	roasted	tropical fruit	shelled
reif	**weich**	**getrocknet**	**roh**	**Saison-**	**die kandierten Früchte**	**ganz**
ripe	soft	desiccated	raw	seasonal	candied fruit	whole

die Getreidearten und die Hülsenfrüchte •
grains and pulses

das Getreide • grains

der Weizen
wheat

der Hafer
oats

die Gerste
barley

die Hirse
millet

der Mais
corn

die Reismelde
quinoa

Vokabular • vocabulary		
trocken dry	**frisch** fresh	**Vollkorn** wholegrain
die Hülse husk	**aromatisch** fragranced	**Langkorn** long-grain
der Kern kernel	**einweichen** soak (v)	**Rundkorn** short-grain
der Samen seed	**die Getreideflocken** cereal	**leicht zu kochen** easy cook

der Reis • rice

der weiße Reis
white rice

der Naturreis
brown rice

der Wasserreis
wild rice

der Milchreis
pudding rice

die verarbeiteten Getreidearten •
processed grains

der Kuskus
couscous

der Weizenschrot
cracked wheat

der Grieß
semolina

die Kleie
bran

die Bohnen und die Erbsen • beans and peas

die Mondbohnen
butter beans

die weißen Bohnen
haricot beans

die roten Bohnen
red kidney beans

die Adzuki-bohnen
aduki beans

die Saubohnen
broad beans

die Sojabohnen
soya beans

die Teparybohnen
black-eyed beans

die Pintobohnen
pinto beans

die Mungbohnen
mung beans

die französischen Bohnen
flageolet beans

die braunen Linsen
brown lentils

die roten Linsen
red lentils

die grünen Erbsen
green peas

die Kichererbsen
chick peas

die getrockneten Erbsen
split peas

die Körner • seeds

der Kürbiskern
pumpkin seed

das Senfkorn
mustard seed

der Kümmel
caraway

das Sesamkorn
sesame seed

der Sonnenblumenkern
sunflower seed

die Kräuter und Gewürze • herbs and spices

die Gewürze • spices

die Vanille
vanilla

die Muskatnuss
nutmeg

die Muskatblüte
mace

die Kurkuma
turmeric

der Kreuzkümmel
cumin

die Kräutermischung
bouquet garni

der Piment
allspice

das Pfefferkorn
peppercorn

der Bockshornklee
fenugreek

der Chili
chilli

ganz
whole

zerstoßen
crushed

der Safran
saffron

der Kardamom
cardamom

das Currypulver
curry powder

gemahlen
ground

der Paprika
paprika

geraspelt
flakes

der Knoblauch
garlic

deutsch • english

die Kräuter • herbs

die Stangen
sticks

der Zimt
cinnamon

der Fenchel
fennel

die
Fenchelsamen
fennel seeds

das Lorbeerblatt
bay leaf

die Petersilie
parsley

das
Zitronengras
lemon grass

der Schnittlauch
chives

die Minze
mint

der Thymian
thyme

der Salbei
sage

die Gewürznelke
cloves

der Estragon
tarragon

der Majoran
marjoram

das Basilikum
basil

der Sternanis
star anise

der Ingwer
ginger

der Oregano
oregano

der Koriander
coriander

der Dill
dill

der Rosmarin
rosemary

die Nahrungsmittel in Flaschen • bottled foods

der Korken
cork

das Sonnenblumenöl
sunflower oil

das Walnussöl
walnut oil

das Traubenkernöl
grapeseed oil

das Mandelöl
almond oil

das Sesamöl
sesame seed oil

das Haselnussöl
hazelnut oil

das Olivenöl
olive oil

die Kräuter
herbs

das aromatische Öl
flavoured oil

die Öle
oils

der süße Aufstrich • sweet spreads

das Glas
jar

die Honigwabe
honeycomb

der feste Honig
set honey

der Zitronenaufstrich
lemon curd

die Himbeerkonfitüre
raspberry jam

die Orangenmarmelade
marmalade

der flüssige Honig
clear honey

der Ahornsirup
maple syrup

die Würzen • condiments and spreads

der
Apfelweinessig
cider vinegar

die Majonäse
mayonnaise

der
Gewürzessig
balsamic vinegar

die Flasche
bottle

das Chutney
chutney

der Malzessig
malt vinegar

der Weinessig
wine vinegar

der Essig
vinegar

der Ketchup
ketchup

die Soße
sauce

**der englische
Senf**
English mustard

**der französische
Senf**
French mustard

der grobe Senf
wholegrain
mustard

---

das Einmachglas
sealed jar

**die
Erdnussbutter**
peanut butter

**der
Schokoladenaufstrich**
chocolate spread

**das eingemachte
Obst**
preserved fruit

Vokabular • vocabulary

das Pflanzenöl vegetable oil	**das Rapsöl** rapeseed oil
das Maiskeimöl corn oil	**das kaltgepresste Öl** cold-pressed oil
das Erdnussöl groundnut oil	

die Milchprodukte • dairy produce

der Käse • cheese

die Rinde
rind

der mittelharte Käse
semi-hard cheese

der geriebene Käse
grated cheese

der Hartkäse
hard cheese

der halbfeste Käse
semi-soft cheese

der Hüttenkäse
cottage cheese

der Rahmkäse
cream cheese

der Blauschim melkäse
blue cheese

der Weichkäse
soft cheese

der Frischkäse | fresh cheese

die Milch • milk

die Vollmilch
whole milk

die Halbfettmilch
semi-skimmed milk

die Magermilch
skimmed milk

die Milchtüte
milk carton

die Kuhmilch | cow's milk

die Ziegenmilch
goat's milk

die Kondensmilch
condensed milk

die Butter
butter

die Margarine
margarine

die Sahne
cream

die fettarme Sahne
single cream

die Schlagsahne
double cream

die Schlagsahne
whipped cream

die saure Sahne
sour cream

der Joghurt
yoghurt

das Eis
ice-cream

die Eier • eggs

das Eigelb
yolk

das Eiweiß
egg white

die Eierschale
shell

der Eier becher
egg cup

das gekochte Ei
boiled egg

das Gänseei
goose egg

das Hühnerei
hen's egg

das Wachtelei
quail egg

das Entenei
duck egg

Vokabular • vocabulary

pasteurisiert pasteurized	**fettfrei** fat free	**gesalzen** salted	**die Schafmilch** sheep's milk	**die Laktose** lactose	**der Milchshake** milkshake
unpasteurisiert unpasteurized	**das Milchpulver** powdered milk	**ungesalzen** unsalted	**die Buttermilch** buttermilk	**homogenisiert** homogenised	**der gefrorene Joghurt** frozen yoghurt

---

das Brot und das Mehl • breads and flours

das
Scheibenbrot
sliced bread

der Mohn
poppy seeds

das Roggenbrot
rye bread

das Baguette
baguette

die Bäckerei | bakery

Brot backen • making bread

das Weizenmehl
white flour

das Roggenmehl
brown flour

das Vollkornmehl
wholemeal flour

die Hefe
yeast

sieben | sift (v)

verrühren | mix (v)

der Teig
dough

Kneten | knead (v)

backen | bake (v)

deutsch • english

die Kruste
crust

der Laib
loaf

die Scheibe
slice

das Weißbrot
white bread

das Graubrot
brown bread

das Vollkornbrot
wholemeal bread

das Mehrkornbrot
granary bread

das Maisbrot
corn bread

das Sodabrot
soda bread

das Sauerteigbrot
sourdough bread

das Fladenbrot
flatbread

das Hefebrötchen
bagel

das weiche Brötchen
bap

das Brötchen
roll

das Rosinenbrot
fruit bread

das Körnerbrot
seeded bread

der Naan
naan bread

das Pitabrot
pitta bread

das Knäckebrot
crispbread

Vokabular • vocabulary

das angereicherte Mehl strong flour	**das Paniermehl** breadcrumbs	**gehen lassen** prove (v)	**aufgehen** rise (v)	**der Brotschneider** slicer
das Mehl mit Backpulver self-raising flour	**das Mehl ohne Backpulver** plain flour	**glasieren** glaze (v)	**die Flöte** flute	**der Bäcker** baker

Kuchen und Nachspeisen • cakes and desserts

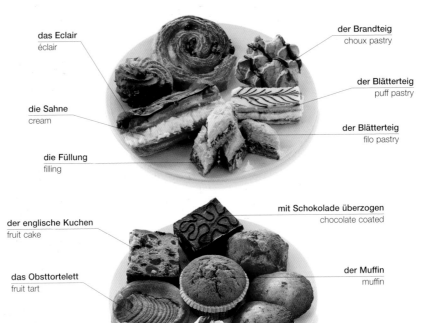

das Eclair
éclair

der Brandteig
choux pastry

der Blätterteig
puff pastry

die Sahne
cream

der Blätterteig
filo pastry

die Füllung
filling

der englische Kuchen
fruit cake

mit Schokolade überzogen
chocolate coated

das Obsttortelett
fruit tart

der Muffin
muffin

das Baiser
meringue

das Biskuittörtchen
sponge cake

das Gebäck | cakes

Vokabular • vocabulary

die Konditorcreme crème patisserie	das Teilchen bun	der Teig pastry	der Milchreis rice pudding	**Könnte ich bitte ein Stück haben?** May I have a slice please?
die Schokoladentorte chocolate cake	der Vanillepudding custard	das Stück slice	die Feier celebration	

das Schokoladen-stückchen
chocolate chip

die Löffelbiskuits
sponge fingers

der Florentiner
florentine

das Trifle
trifle

die Kekse | biscuits

die Mousse
mousse

das Sorbett
sorbet

die Sahnetorte
cream pie

der Karamellpudding
crème caramel

die festlichen Kuchen • celebration cakes

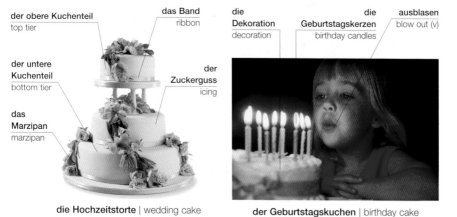

der obere Kuchenteil
top tier

das Band
ribbon

der untere Kuchenteil
bottom tier

der Zuckerguss
icing

das Marzipan
marzipan

die Hochzeitstorte | wedding cake

die Dekoration
decoration

die Geburtstagskerzen
birthday candles

ausblasen
blow out (v)

der Geburtstagskuchen | birthday cake

die Feinkost • delicatessen

die pikante Wurst
spicy sausage

die Quiche
flan

der Essig
vinegar

das Öl
oil

das frische Fleisch
uncooked meat

die Theke
counter

die Salami
salami

die Pepperoniwurst
pepperoni

die Pastete
pâté

der Mozzarella
mozzarella

der Brie
brie

der Ziegenkäse
goat's cheese

der Cheddar
cheddar

der Parmesan
parmesan

der Camembert
camembert

die Rinde
rind

der Edamer
edam

der Manchego
manchego

die Pasteten
pies

die schwarze Olive
black olive

die
Peperoni
chili

die Soße
sauce

das Brötchen
bread roll

das gekochte
Fleisch
cooked meat

die grüne Olive
green olive

der Schinken
ham

die Sandwichtheke
sandwich counter

der Räucherfisch
smoked fish

die Kapern
capers

die Chorizo
chorizo

der Prosciutto
prosciutto

die gefüllte Olive
stuffed olive

Vokabular • vocabulary

in Öl	mariniert	geräuchert
in oil	marinated	smoked
in Lake	gepökelt	getrocknet
in brine	salted	cured

Nehmen Sie bitte eine Nummer.
Take a number please.

Kann ich bitte etwas davon probieren?
Can I try some of that please?

Ich hätte gerne sechs Scheiben davon, bitte.
May I have six slices of that please?

die Getränke • drinks

das Wasser • water

das
Flaschenwasser
bottled water

mit Kohlensäure
sparkling

das Leitungswasser
tap water

ohne Kohlensäure
still

das Tonicwater
tonic water

das Mineralwasser
mineral water

das Sodawasser
soda water

die heißen Getränke • hot drinks

der Teebeutel
teabag

die Teeblätter
loose leaf tea

der Tee
tea

die Bohnen
beans

der gemahlene Kaffee
ground coffee

der Kaffee
coffee

die heiße Schokolade
hot chocolate

das Malzgetränk
malted drink

die alkoholfreien Getränke • soft drinks

der Strohhalm
straw

der Tomatensaft
tomato juice

der Traubensaft
grape juice

die Limonade
lemonade

die Orangeade
orangeade

die Cola
cola

die alkoholischen Getränke • alcoholic drinks

der Gin
gin

das Bier
beer

die Dose
can

der Apfelwein
cider

das halbdunkle Bier
bitter

der Stout
stout

der Wodka
vodka

der Whisky
whisky

der Rum
rum

der Weinbrand
brandy

der Portwein
port

trocken
dry

der Sherry
sherry

der Campari
campari

rosé
rosé

weiß
white

rot
red

der Likör
liqueur

der Tequila
tequila

der Champagner
champagne

der Wein
wine

auswärts essen
eating out

das Café • café

die Markise
awning

die
Speisekarte
menu

der
Sonnenschirm
umbrella

das Terrassencafé
terrace café

der
Kellner
waiter

die Kaffeemaschine
coffee machine

der Tisch
table

das Straßencafé | pavement café

die Snackbar | snack bar

der Kaffee • coffee

der Kaffee mit Milch
white coffee

der schwarze
Kaffee
black coffee

das
Kakaopulver
cocoa powder

der Schaum
froth

der Filterkaffee
filter coffee

der Espresso
espresso

der Cappuccino
cappuccino

der Eiskaffee
iced coffee

der Tee • tea

der Kräutertee
herbal tea

der Kamillentee
camomile tea

der grüne Tee
green tea

der Tee mit Milch
tea with milk

der schwarze Tee
black tea

der Tee mit
Zitrone
tea with lemon

der Pfefferminztee
mint tea

der Eistee
iced tea

die Säfte und Milchshakes • juices and milkshakes

der
Schokoladenmilchshake
chocolate milkshake

der
Erdbeermilchshake
strawberry milkshake

der
Orangensaft
orange juice

der
Apfelsaft
apple juice

der
Ananassaft
pineapple juice

der
Tomatensaft
tomato juice

der
Kaffeemilchshake
coffee milkshake

das Essen • food

das Graubrot
brown bread

die Kugel
scoop

der getoastete Sandwich
toasted sandwich

der Salat
salad

das Eis
ice cream

das Gebäck
pastry

die Bar • bar

die Gläser
glasses

das Maß
optic

die Kasse
till

der Barkeeper
bartender

der Zapfhahn
beer tap

die Kaffeemaschine
coffee machine

der Eiskübel
ice bucket

der Barhocker
bar stool

der Aschbecher
ashtray

der Untersetzer
coaster

die Theke
bar counter

der Flaschenöffner
bottle opener

der Hebel
lever

der Korkenzieher | corkscrew

die Eiszange
tongs

der Cocktailrührer
stirrer

der Messbecher
measure

der Cocktailshaker | cocktail shaker

der Gin Tonic
gin and tonic

der Krug
pitcher

der Scotch mit Wasser
scotch and water

der Eiswürfel
ice cube

der Rum mit Cola
rum and coke

der Wodka mit Orangensaft
vodka and orange

der Martini
martini

der Cocktail
cocktail

der Wein
wine

das Bier | beer

einfach
single

doppelt
double

ein Schuss
a shot

das Maß
measure

ohne Eis
without ice

Eis und Zitrone
ice and lemon

mit Eis
with ice

die Knabbereien • bar snacks

die Kartoffelchips | crisps

die Cashewnüsse
cashewnuts

die Mandeln
almonds

die Erdnüsse
peanuts

die Nüsse | nuts

die Oliven | olives

das Restaurant • restaurant

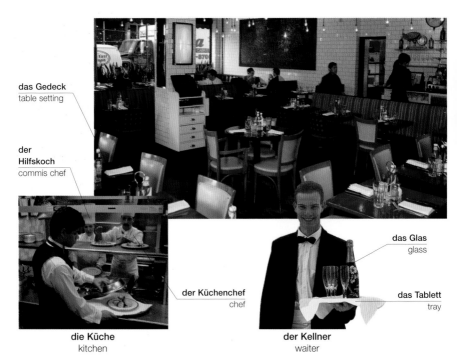

das Gedeck
table setting

der Hilfskoch
commis chef

das Glas
glass

der Küchenchef
chef

das Tablett
tray

die Küche
kitchen

der Kellner
waiter

Vokabular • vocabulary

das Abendmenü evening menu	**die Spezialitäten** specials	**der Preis** price	**das Trinkgeld** tip	**das Buffet** buffet	**der Kunde** customer
die Weinkarte wine list	**à la carte** à la carte	**die Quittung** receipt	**ohne Bedienung** service not included	**die Bar** bar	**der Pfeffer** pepper
das Mittagsmenü lunch menu	**der Dessertwagen** sweet trolley	**die Rechnung** bill	**Bedienung inbegriffen** service included	**das Salz** salt	

---

die **Speisekarte**
menu

die **Kinderportion**
child's meal

bestellen
order (v)

bezahlen
pay (v)

die Gänge • courses

der **Aperitif**
apéritif

die **Vorspeise**
starter

die **Suppe**
soup

das **Hauptgericht**
main course

die **Beilage**
side order

der **Nachtisch** | dessert

der **Kaffee** | coffee

Ein Tisch für zwei Personen bitte.
A table for two please.

Könnte ich bitte die Speisekarte/Weinliste sehen?
Can I see the menu/winelist please?

Gibt es ein Festpreismenü?
Is there a fixed price menu?

Haben Sie vegetarische Gerichte?
Do you have any vegetarian dishes?

Könnte ich die Rechnung/Quittung haben?
Could I have the bill/a receipt please?

Könnten wir getrennt zahlen?
Can we pay separately?

Wo sind die Toiletten bitte ?
Where are the toilets, please?

der Schnellimbiss • fast food

der Strohhalm
straw

der Hamburger
burger

das alkoholfreie Getränk
soft drink

die Pommes frites
french fries

die Papierserviette
paper napkin

das Tablett
tray

der Hamburger mit Pommes frites
burger meal

die Pizza
pizza

die Preisliste
price list

das Dosengetränk
canned drink

die Lieferung ins Haus
home delivery

der Imbissstand
street stall

Vokabular • vocabulary

die Pizzeria
pizza parlour

die Imbissstube
burger bar

die Speisekarte
menu

hier essen
eat-in

zum Mitnehmen
take-away

aufwärmen
re-heat (v)

der Tomatenketchup
tomato sauce

Ich möchte das mitnehmen.
Can I have that to go please?

Liefern Sie ins Haus?
Do you deliver?

der Hamburger
hamburger

der Chickenburger
chicken burger

das
Brötchen
bun

der vegetarische Hamburger
veggie burger

der Senf
mustard

die Wurst
sausage

das Hot Dog
hot dog

der Sandwich
sandwich

der Klubsandwich
club sandwich

das belegte Brot
open sandwich

die Füllung
filling

das gefüllte Fladenbrot
wrap

die Soße
sauce

der Kebab
kebab

die Hähnchenstückchen
chicken nuggets

salzig
savoury

die Crêpes | crêpes

süß
sweet

der Pizzabelag
topping

der Bratfisch mit Pommes frites
fish and chips

die Rippen
ribs

das gebratene Hähnchen
fried chicken

die Pizza
pizza

das Frühstück • breakfast

die **Milch**
milk

die **Getreide flocken**
cereal

die **Konfitüre**
jam

das **Dörrobst**
dried fruit

der **Schinken**
ham

der **Käse**
cheese

das **Knäckebrot**
crispbread

das **Frühstücksbuffet**
breakfast buffet

die **Orangenmarmelade**
marmalade

die **Pastete**
pâté

die **Butter**
butter

der **Obstsaft**
fruit juice

der **Kaffee**
coffee

die **Schokolade**
hot chocolate

das **Croissant**
croissant

der **Tee**
tea

der **Frühstückstisch** | breakfast table

die **Getränke** | drinks

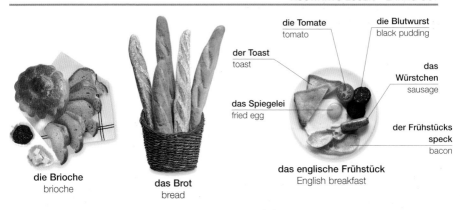

die Tomate
tomato

die Blutwurst
black pudding

der Toast
toast

das Würstchen
sausage

das Spiegelei
fried egg

der Frühstücks speck
bacon

das englische Frühstück
English breakfast

die Brioche
brioche

das Brot
bread

die Räucherheringe
kippers

das in Ei gebratene Brot
french toast

das Eigelb
yolk

das gekochte Ei
boiled egg

das Rührei
scrambled eggs

die Sahne
cream

die Pfannkuchen
pancakes

die Waffeln
waffles

der Früchtejoghurt
fruit yoghurt

der Porridge
porridge

das Obst
fresh fruit

die Hauptmahlzeit • dinner

die Suppe | soup

die Brühe | broth

der Eintopf | stew

das Curry | curry

der Braten
roast

die Pastete
pie

das Soufflé
soufflé

der Schaschlik
kebab

die Fleischklöße
meatballs

das Omelett
omelette

die Nudeln
noodles

das Schnellbratgericht
stir fry

die Nudeln | pasta

der Reis
rice

der gemischte Salat
mixed salad

der grüne Salat
green salad

die Salatsoße
dressing

die Zubereitung • techniques

gefüllt | stuffed

in Soße | in sauce

gegrillt | grilled

mariniert | marinated

pochiert | poached

püriert | mashed

gebacken | baked

kurzgebraten | pan fried

gebraten
fried

eingelegt
pickled

geräuchert
smoked

frittiert
deep fried

in Saft
in syrup

angemacht
dressed

gedämpft
steamed

getrocknet
cured

das Lernen
study

die Schule • school

die Tafel
blackboard

die Lehrerin
teacher

das Klassenzimmer | classroom

die Schultasche
school bag

der Schüler
pupil

das Pult
desk

die Kreide
chalk

das Schulmädchen   **der Schuljunge**
schoolgirl   schoolboy

Vokabular • vocabulary

die Literatur literature	**die Kunst** art	**die Physik** physics
die Sprachen languages	**die Musik** music	**die Chemie** chemistry
die Erdkunde geography	**die Mathematik** maths	**die Biologie** biology
die Geschichte history	**die Naturwiss-enschaft** science	**der Sport** physical education

die Aktivitäten • activities

lesen | read (v)

schreiben | write (v)

buchstabieren
spell (v)

zeichnen
draw (v)

die Feder
nib

der Buntstift
colouring pencil

der Spitzer
pencil
sharpener

der Digitalprojektor
digital projector

der Füller
pen

der Bleistift
pencil

das Heft
notebook

der Radiergummi
rubber

das Schulbuch | textbook

das Federmäppchen
pencil case

das Lineal
ruler

fragen
question (v)

antworten
answer (v)

diskutieren
discuss (v)

lernen
learn (v)

Vokabular • vocabulary

der Schulleiter head teacher	**die Antwort** answer	**die Note** grade
die Stunde lesson	**der Aufsatz** essay	**die Klasse** year
die Frage question	**die Prüfung** examination	**das Lexikon** encyclopedia
Notizen machen take notes (v)	**die Hausaufgabe** homework	**das Wörterbuch** dictionary

die Mathematik • maths

die Formen • shapes

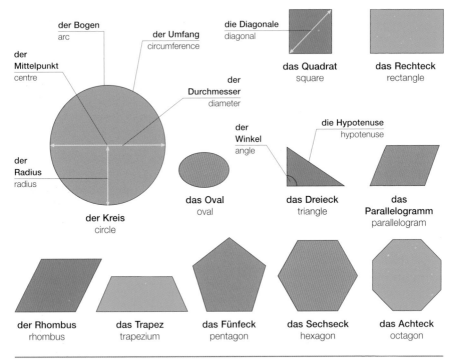

der Bogen
arc

der Umfang
circumference

die Diagonale
diagonal

der Mittelpunkt
centre

der Durchmesser
diameter

das Quadrat
square

das Rechteck
rectangle

der Radius
radius

der Winkel
angle

die Hypotenuse
hypotenuse

das Oval
oval

der Kreis
circle

das Dreieck
triangle

das Parallelogramm
parallelogram

der Rhombus
rhombus

das Trapez
trapezium

das Fünfeck
pentagon

das Sechseck
hexagon

das Achteck
octagon

die Körper • solids

die Seite
side

die Spitze
apex

die Grundfläche
base

der Kegel
cone

der Zylinder
cylinder

der Würfel
cube

die Pyramide
pyramid

die Kugel
sphere

die Linien • lines

gerade
straight

parallel
parallel

senkrecht
perpendicular

gekrümmt
curved

die Maße • measurements

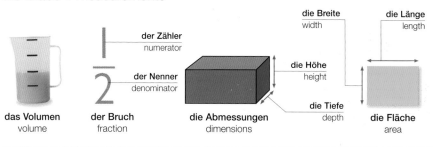

die Breite
width

die Länge
length

der Zähler
numerator

der Nenner
denominator

die Höhe
height

die Tiefe
depth

das Volumen
volume

der Bruch
fraction

die Abmessungen
dimensions

die Fläche
area

die Ausrüstung • equipment

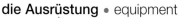

**das
Zeichendreieck**
set square

der Winkelmesser
protractor

das Lineal
ruler

der Zirkel
compass

**der
Taschenrechner**
calculator

Vokabular • vocabulary

die Geometrie geometry	**plus** plus	**mal** times	**gleich** equals	**addieren** add (v)	**multiplizieren** multiply (v)	**die Gleichung** equation
die Arithmetik arithmetic	**minus** minus	**geteilt durch** divided by	**zählen** count (v)	**subtrahieren** subtract (v)	**dividieren** divide (v)	**der Prozentsatz** percentage

die Wissenschaft • science

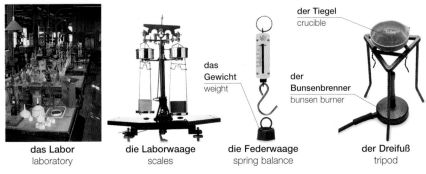

das Labor
laboratory

die Laborwaage
scales

das
Gewicht
weight

die Federwaage
spring balance

der Tiegel
crucible

der
Bunsenbrenner
bunsen burner

der Dreifuß
tripod

die Glasflasche
glass bottle

das Stativ
lamp stand

das Reagenzglas
test tube

das Gestell
rack

die Klammer
clamp

der Stöpsel
stopper

der Trichter
funnel

der Zeitmesser
timer

der Kolben
flask

die Petrischale
petri dish

der Versuch | experiment

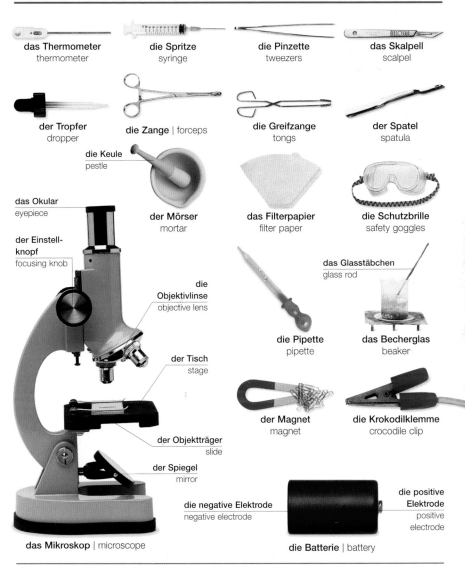

das Thermometer
thermometer

die Spritze
syringe

die Pinzette
tweezers

das Skalpell
scalpel

der Tropfer
dropper

die Zange | forceps

die Greifzange
tongs

der Spatel
spatula

die Keule
pestle

der Mörser
mortar

das Filterpapier
filter paper

die Schutzbrille
safety goggles

das Okular
eyepiece

der Einstell-knopf
focusing knob

die Objektivlinse
objective lens

das Glasstäbchen
glass rod

die Pipette
pipette

das Becherglas
beaker

der Tisch
stage

der Magnet
magnet

die Krokodilklemme
crocodile clip

der Objektträger
slide

der Spiegel
mirror

die negative Elektrode
negative electrode

die positive Elektrode
positive electrode

das Mikroskop | microscope

die Batterie | battery

die Hochschule • college

das Sekretariat
admissions

der Sportplatz
sports field

die Mensa
refectory

das Studenten-heim
hall of residence

die Gesundheits-fürsorge
health centre

der Campus | campus

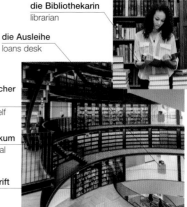

die Bibliothekarin
librarian

die Ausleihe
loans desk

das Bücher regal
bookshelf

das Periodikum
periodical

die Zeitschrift
journal

die Bibliothek | library

Vokabular • vocabulary

der Leserausweis library card	**die Auskunft** enquiries	**verlängern** renew (v)
der Lesesaal reading room	**ausleihen** borrow (v)	**das Buch** book
die Literaturliste reading list	**vorbestellen** reserve (v)	**der Titel** title
das Rückgabedatum return date	**die Ausleihe** loan	**der Gang** aisle

der Student
undergraduate

der Dozent
lecturer

die Graduierte
graduate

die Robe
robe

der Hörsaal
lecture theatre

die Graduierungsfeier
graduation ceremony

die Fachhochschulen • schools

das Model
model

die Kunsthochschule
art college

die Musikhochschule
music school

die Tanzakademie
dance academy

Vokabular • vocabulary

das Stipendium scholarship	**die Forschung** research	**die Examensarbeit** dissertation	**die Medizin** medicine	**die Philosophie** philosophy
postgraduiert postgraduate	**der Magister** masters	**der Fachbereich** department	**die Zoologie** zoology	**die Politologie** politics
das Diplom diploma	**die Promotion** doctorate	**der Maschinenbau** engineering	**die Physik** physics	**die Literatur** literature
der akademische Grad degree	**die Dissertation** thesis	**die Kunstgeschichte** history of art	**die Rechtswissenschaft** law	
			die Wirtschaftswissenschaft economics	

die Arbeit
work

das Büro 1 • office 1

der Bildschirm
monitor

der Stifthalter
desktop organizer

der Laptop
laptop

das Notizbuch
notebook

die Ablage für Ausgänge
out-tray

die Ablage für Eingänge
in-tray

die Schublade
drawer

der Schreibtisch
desk

der Drehstuhl
swivel chair

der Papierkorb
wastebasket

der Aktenschrank
filing cabinet

die Büroausstattung • office equipment

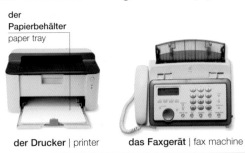

der Papierbehälter
paper tray

der Drucker | printer

das Faxgerät | fax machine

Vokabular • vocabulary

drucken
print (v)

vergrößern
enlarge (v)

kopieren
copy (v)

verkleinern
reduce (v)

Ich möchte fotokopieren.
I need to make some copies.

der Bürobedarf • office supplies

der Empfehlungszettel
compliments slip

der Geschäftsbogen
letterhead

der Briefumschlag
envelope

der Aktenordner
box file

der Kartenreiter
tab

der Teiler
divider

das Klemmbrett
clipboard

der Notizblock
note pad

der Hängeordner
hanging file

der Fächerordner
concertina file

der Leitz-Ordner
lever arch file

die Klammern
staples

der Tesafilm
sticky tape

das Stempelkissen
ink pad

der Terminkalender
personal organizer

der Hefter
stapler

der Tesafilmhalter
tape dispenser

der Locher
hole punch

der Stempel
rubber stamp

der Reißnagel
drawing pin

das Gummiband
rubber band

die Papierklammer
bulldog clip

die Büroklammer
paper clip

die Pinnward | notice board

das Büro 2 • office 2

das Flipchart
flipchart

das Gestell
easel

das Protokoll
minutes

der **Bericht**
report

der **Manager**
manager

das Angebot
proposal

der leitende **Angestellte**
executive

die Sitzung | meeting

Vokabular • vocabulary

der Sitzungsraum meeting room	**teilnehmen** attend (v)
die Tagesordnung agenda	**den Vorsitz führen** chair (v)

Um wieviel Uhr ist die Sitzung?
What time is the meeting?

Was sind Ihre Geschäftszeiten?
What are your office hours?

die Sprecherin
speaker

die Präsentation | presentation

das Geschäft • business

der Geschäftsmann
businessman

die Geschäftsfrau
businesswoman

das Arbeitsessen
business lunch

die Geschäftsreise
business trip

der Termin
appointment

die Kundin
client

der Terminkalender | diary

der
Generaldirektor
managing
director

das Geschäftsabkommen
business deal

Vokabular • vocabulary

die Firma company	**das Personal** staff	**die Buchhaltung** accounts department	**die Rechtsabteilung** legal department
die Zentrale head office	**die Lohnliste** payroll	**die Marketingabteilung** marketing department	**die Kundendienstabteilung** customer service department
die Zweigstelle branch	**das Gehalt** salary	**die Verkaufsabteilung** sales department	**die Personalabteilung** personnel department

der Computer • computer

der Drucker
printer

der Scanner
scanner

der Bildschirm
screen

der Laptop
laptop

die Taste
key

die Tastatur
keyboard

die Maus
mouse

der Lautsprecher
speaker

die Hardware
hardware

der Memorystick
memory stick

die externe Festplatte
external hard drive

Vokabular • vocabulary		
das RAM RAM	**die Software** software	**der Server** server
die Bytes bytes	**das Programm** program	**der Port** port
das System system	**das Netzwerk** network	**der Prozessor** processor
der Speicher memory	**die Anwendung** application	**das Stromkabel** power cable

das iPad
iPad

das Smartphone
smartphone

das Desktop • desktop

der Menübalken
menubar

die Werkzeugleiste
toolbar

die Tapete
wallpaper

die Schriftart
font

das Symbol
icon

der Scrollbalken
scrollbar

das Fenster
window

die Datei
file

der Ordner
folder

der Papierkorb
trash

das Internet • internet

der Browser
browser

browsen
browse (v)

die E-Mail • email

die E-Mail-Adresse
email address

die Inbox
inbox

die Web-Site
website

Vokabular • vocabulary

verbinden connect (v)	**der Serviceprovider** service provider	**einloggen** log on (v)	**herunterladen** download (v)	**senden** send (v)	**sichern** save (v)
installieren instal (v)	**das E-Mail-Konto** email account	**online** on-line	**der Anhang** attachment	**erhalten** receive (v)	**suchen** search (v)

die Medien • media

das Fernsehstudio • television studio

die
Studioeinrichtung
set

der
Moderator
presenter

die
Beleuchtung
light

die **Kamera**
camera

der **Kamerakran**
camera crane

der **Kameramann**
cameraman

Vokabular • vocabulary

der Kanal channel	**die Nachrichten** news	**die Presse** press	**senden** broadcast (v)	**live** live	**der Zeichentrickfilm** cartoon
die Programm–gestaltung programming	**der Dokumentarfilm** documentary	**die Fernsehserie** television series	**die Spielshow** game show	**vorher aufgezeichnet** prerecorded	**die Seifenoper** soap

---

deutsch • english

der Interviewer
interviewer

die Reporterin
reporter

der Teleprompter
autocue

die Nachrichtensprecherin
newsreader

die Schauspieler
actors

der Mikrophongalgen
sound boom

die Klappe
clapper board

das Set
film set

das Radio • radio

der Tonmeister
sound technician

das Mischpult
mixing desk

das Mikrophon
microphone

das Tonstudio | recording studio

Vokabular • vocabulary	
der DJ DJ	**die Mittelwelle** medium wave
die Sendung broadcast	**die Frequenz** frequency
die Wellenlänge wavelength	**die Lautstärke** volume
die Langwelle long wave	**analog** analog
die Rundfunkstation radio station	**digital** digital
die Kurzwelle short wave	**einstellen** tune (v)

das Recht • law

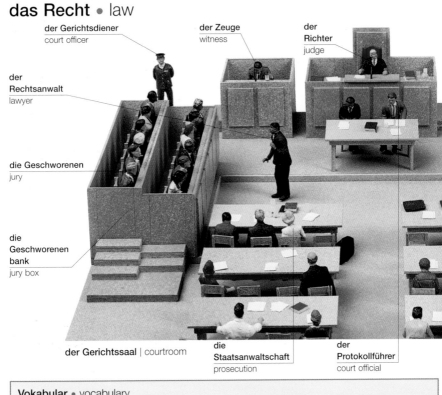

der Gerichtsdiener
court officer

der Zeuge
witness

der Richter
judge

der Rechtsanwalt
lawyer

die Geschworenen
jury

die Geschworenen bank
jury box

der Gerichtssaal | courtroom

die Staatsanwaltschaft
prosecution

der Protokollführer
court official

Vokabular • vocabulary

das Anwaltsbüro lawyer's office	**die Vorladung** summons	**die Verfügung** writ	**der Rechtsfall** court case
die Rechtsberatung legal advice	**die Aussage** statement	**der Gerichtstermin** court date	**die Anklage** charge
der Klient client	**der Haftbefehl** warrant	**das Plädoyer** plea	**der Angeklagte** accused

---

der
Gerichtsstenograf
stenographer

der
Straftäter
criminal

der **Verdächtige**
suspect

der **Angeklagte**
defendant

die **Verteidigung**
defence

das Phantombild
photofit

das Strafregister
criminal record

der Gefängniswärter
prison guard

die Gefängniszelle
cell

das Gefängnis
prison

Vokabular • vocabulary

das Beweismittel evidence	**schuldig** guilty	**die Kaution** bail	**Ich möchte mit einem Anwalt sprechen.** I want to see a lawyer.
das Urteil verdict	**freigesprochen** acquitted	**die Berufung** appeal	**Wo ist das Gericht?** Where is the courthouse?
unschuldig innocent	**das Strafmaß** sentence	**die Haftentlassung auf Bewährung** parole	**Kann ich die Kaution leisten?** Can I post bail?

---

der Bauernhof 1 • farm 1

das Ackerland
farmland

der Hof
farmyard

das Nebengebäude
outbuilding

das Bauernhaus
farmhouse

das Feld
field

die Scheune
barn

der Bauer
farmer

der Gemüse-garten
vegetable plot

die Hecke
hedge

das Tor
gate

der Zaun
fence

die Weide
pasture

das Vieh
livestock

der Kultivator
cultivator

der Traktor | tractor

der Mähdrescher | combine harvester

die landwirtschaftlichen Betriebe • types of farm

die Feldfrucht
crop

der Ackerbaubetrieb
arable farm

**der Betrieb für
Milchproduktion**
dairy farm

die Herde
flock

die Schaffarm
sheep farm

die Hühnerfarm
poultry farm

die Schweinefarm
pig farm

die Fischzucht
fish farm

der Obstanbau
fruit farm

der Weinstock
vine

der Weinberg
vineyard

die Tätigkeiten • actions

die
Furche
furrow

pflügen
plough (v)

säen
sow (v)

melken
milk (v)

füttern
feed (v)

bewässern | water (v)

ernten | harvest (v)

Vokabular • vocabulary

das Herbizid herbicide	**die Herde** herd	**der Trog** trough
das Pestizid pesticide	**der Silo** silo	**pflanzen** plant (v)

der Bauernhof 2 • farm 2

die Feldfrüchte • crops

der Weizen
wheat

der Mais
corn

die Gerste
barley

der Raps
rapeseed

die Sonnenblume
sunflower

der Ballen
bale

das Heu
hay

die Luzerne
alfalfa

der Tabak
tobacco

der Reis
rice

der Tee
tea

der Kaffee
coffee

der Flachs
flax

das Zuckerrohr
sugarcane

die Baumwolle
cotton

die Vogelscheuche
scarecrow

das Vieh • livestock

das Ferkel
piglet

das Kalb
calf

das Schwein
pig

die Kuh
cow

der Stier
bull

das Schaf
sheep

das Lamm
lamb

das Zicklein
kid

die Ziege
goat

das Fohlen
foal

das Pferd
horse

der Esel
donkey

das Küken
chick

das Huhn
chicken

der Hahn
cockerel

der Truthahn
turkey

das Entenküken
duckling

die Ente
duck

der Stall
stable

der Pferch
pen

der Hühnerstall
chicken coop

der Schweinestall
pigsty

der Bau • construction

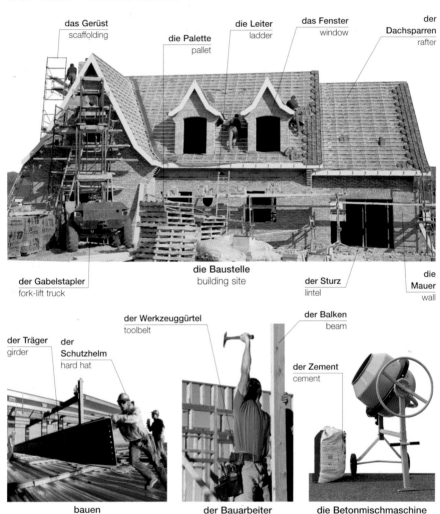

das Gerüst
scaffolding

die Palette
pallet

die Leiter
ladder

das Fenster
window

der Dachsparren
rafter

der Gabelstapler
fork-lift truck

die Baustelle
building site

der Sturz
lintel

die Mauer
wall

der Träger
girder

der Schutzhelm
hard hat

der Werkzeuggürtel
toolbelt

der Balken
beam

der Zement
cement

bauen
build (v)

der Bauarbeiter
builder

die Betonmischmaschine
cement mixer

das Material • materials

der Ziegelstein
brick

das Bauholz
timber

der Dachziegel
roof tile

der Betonblock
concrete block

die Werkzeuge • tools

der Mörtel
mortar

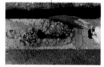
die Kelle
trowel

die Wasserwaage
spirit level

der Stiel
handle

der Vorschlaghammer
sledgehammer

die Spitzhacke
pickaxe

die Schaufel
shovel

die Maschinen • machinery

die Walze
roller

der Kipper
dumper truck

die Stütze
support

der Haken
hook

der Kran | crane

die Straßenarbeiten • roadworks

der Asphalt
tarmac

der Leitkegel
cone

der Pressluftbohrer
pneumatic drill

der Neubelag
resurfacing

der Bagger
mechanical digger

die Berufe 1 • occupations 1

der Schreiner
carpenter

der Elektriker
electrician

der Klempner
plumber

der Bauhandwerker
builder

der Gärtner
gardener

der Staubsauger
vacuum cleaner

der Gebäudereiniger
cleaner

der Mechaniker
mechanic

der Metzger
butcher

die Fischhändlerin
fishmonger

der Gemüsehändler
greengrocer

die Floristin
florist

der Friseur
hairdresser

der Friseur
barber

der Juwelier
jeweller

die Verkäuferin
shop assistant

die Immobilienmaklerin
estate agent

der Optiker
optician

die Maske
mask

die Zahnärztin
dentist

der Arzt
doctor

die Apothekerin
pharmacist

die Krankenschwester
nurse

die Tierärztin
vet

der Bauer
farmer

der Fischer
fisherman

das
Maschinen-
gewehr
machine-
gun

die Uniform
uniform

das Abzeichen
identity badge

der Wächter
security guard

der Seemann
sailor

der Soldat
soldier

der Polizist
policeman

der Feuerwehrmann
fireman

die Berufe 2 • occupations 2

das Modell
model

der Rechtsanwalt
lawyer

der Wirtschaftsprüfer
accountant

der Architekt
architect

die Wissenschaftlerin
scientist

die Lehrerin
teacher

der Bibliothekar
librarian

die Empfangsdame
receptionist

die
Posttasche
mailbag

der Briefträger
postman

der Busfahrer
bus driver

der Lastwagenfahrer
lorry driver

der Taxifahrer
taxi driver

der Pilot
pilot

die Flugbegleiterin
air stewardess

die Reisebürokauffrau
travel agent

die
Kochmütze
chef's hat

der Koch
chef

das
Ballett
röckchen
tutu

der Musiker
musician

die Tänzerin
dancer

die Schauspielerin
actress

die Sängerin
singer

die Kellnerin
waitress

der Barkeeper
barman

der Sportler
sportsman

der Bildhauer
sculptor

die Notizen
notes

die Malerin
painter

der Fotograf
photographer

die Nachrichtensprecherin
newsreader

der Journalist
journalist

die Redakteurin
editor

der Designer
designer

die Damenschneiderin
seamstress

der Schneider
tailor

der Verkehr
transport

die Straßen • roads

die Autobahn
motorway

die Mautstelle
toll booth

die Straßen-
markierungen
road markings

die
Zufahrtsstraße
slip road

Einbahn-
one-way

die Verkehrsinsel
divider

die Kreuzung
junction

die
Verkehrs-
ampel
traffic light

der
Lastwagen
lorry

die rechte Spur
inside lane

die mittlere Spur
middle lane

die Überholspur
outside lane

die Ausfahrt
exit ramp

der Verkehr
traffic

die
Überführung
flyover

der Seitenstreifen
hard shoulder

der Mittelstreifen
central reservation

die Unterführung
underpass

die Notrufsäule
emergency phone

der Behindertenparkplatz
disabled parking

der Verkehrsstau
traffic jam

der Fußgängerüberweg
pedestrian crossing

das Navi
satnav

die Parkuhr
parking meter

der Verkehrspolizist
traffic policeman

Vokabular • vocabulary

parken park (v)	**die Umleitung** diversion	**der Kreisverkehr** roundabout
überholen overtake (v)	**die Leitplanke** crash barrier	**Ist dies die Straße nach...?** Is this the road to...?
rückwärts fahren reverse (v)	**die Straßenbaustelle** roadworks	**Wo kann ich parken?** Where can I park?
fahren drive (v)	**die Schnellstraße** dual carriageway	
die abschleppen tow away (v)		

die Verkehrsschilder • road signs

keine Einfahrt
no entry

die Geschwindig-keitsbegrenzung
speed limit

Gefahr
hazard

Halten verboten
no stopping

rechts abbiegen verboten
no right turn

der Bus • bus

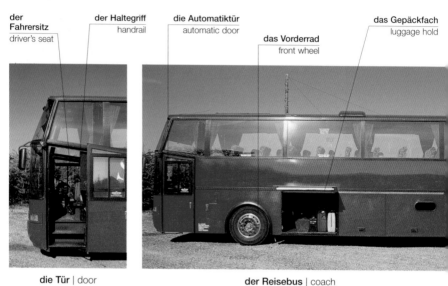

der Fahrersitz
driver's seat

der Haltegriff
handrail

die Automatiktür
automatic door

das Vorderrad
front wheel

das Gepäckfach
luggage hold

die Tür | door

der Reisebus | coach

die Bustypen • types of buses

die Liniennummer
route number

der Fahrer
driver

der Doppeldecker
double-decker bus

die Straßenbahn
tram

der Obus
trolley bus

der Schulbus | school bus

das Fenster
window

der Halteknopf
stop button

das Hinterrad
rear wheel

der Fahrschein
bus ticket

die Klingel
bell

der Busbahnhof
bus station

die Bushaltestelle
bus stop

Vokabular • vocabulary

der Fahrpreis
fare

der Rollstuhlzugang
wheelchair access

der Fahrplan
timetable

das Wartehäuschen
bus shelter

Halten Sie am…?
Do you stop at…?

Welcher Bus fährt nach…?
Which bus goes to…?

der Kleinbus
minibus

der Touristenbus | tourist bus

der Zubringer | shuttle bus

das Auto 1 · car 1

das Äußere · exterior

der Rückspiegel
rearview mirror

der Scheibenwischer
windscreen wiper

die Autotür
door

der Seitenspiegel
wing mirror

die Windschutz scheibe
windscreen

die Motorhaube
bonnet

der Kofferraum
boot

der Blinker
indicator

die Stoßstange
bumper

das Nummernschild
licence plate

der Scheinwerfer
headlight

das Rad
wheel

der Reifen
tyre

das Gepäck
luggage

der Dachgepäckträger
roofrack

die Hecktür
tailgate

der Sicherheitsgurt
seat belt

der Kindersitz
child seat

die Wagentypen • types

das Elektroauto
electric car

die Fließhecklimousine
hatchback

die Limousine
saloon

der Kombiwagen
estate

das Kabriolett
convertible

das Sportkabriolett
sports car

**die Großraum-
limousine**
people carrier

der Geländewagen
four-wheel drive

das Vorkriegsmodell
vintage

die verlängerte Limousine
limousine

die Tankstelle • petrol station

die Zapfsäule
petrol pump

der Benzinpreis
price

der Tankstellenplatz
forecourt

Vokabular • vocabulary

das Benzin	**verbleit**	**die Autowaschanlage**
petrol	leaded	car wash
bleifrei	**das Öl**	**das Frostschutzmittel**
unleaded	oil	antifreeze
die Werkstatt	**der Diesel**	**die Scheibenwasch anlage**
garage	diesel	screenwash

Voll tanken, bitte.
Fill the tank, please.

das Auto 2 • car 2

die Innenausstattung • interior

der Rücksitz
back seat

die Armstütze
armrest

die Kopfstütze
headrest

die
Türverriegelung
door lock

der Türgriff
handle

Vokabular • vocabulary

zweitürig two-door	**viertürig** four-door	**die Zündung** ignition	**die Bremse** brake	**das Gaspedal** accelerator
dreitürig three-door	**mit** **Handschaltung** manual	**mit** **Automatik** automatic	**die** **Kupplung** clutch	**die Klimaanlage** air conditioning

Wie komme ich nach…?
Can you tell me the way to…?

Wo ist hier ein Parkplatz?
Where is the car park?

Kann ich hier parken?
Can I park here?

die Armaturen • controls

das Lenkrad
steering wheel

die Hupe
horn

das Armaturenbrett
dashboard

die Warnlichter
hazard lights

das GPS-System
satellite navigation

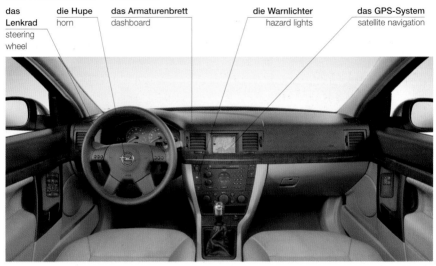

die Linkssteuerung | left-hand drive

die Temperaturanzeige
temperature gauge

der Drehzahlmesser
rev counter

der Tachometer
speedometer

die Kraftstoffanzeige
fuel gauge

die Autostereoanlage
car stereo

der Lichtschalter
lights switch

der Heizungsregler
heater controls

der Kilometerzähler
odometer

der Schalthebel
gearstick

der Airbag
air bag

die Rechtssteuerung | right-hand drive

das Auto 3 • car 3

die Mechanik • mechanics

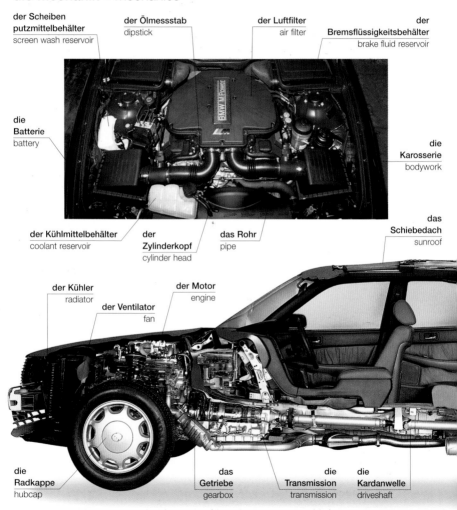

der Scheiben putzmittelbehälter
screen wash reservoir

der Ölmessstab
dipstick

der Luftfilter
air filter

der Bremsflüssigkeitsbehälter
brake fluid reservoir

die Batterie
battery

die Karosserie
bodywork

der Kühlmittelbehälter
coolant reservoir

der Zylinderkopf
cylinder head

das Rohr
pipe

das Schiebedach
sunroof

der Kühler
radiator

der Motor
engine

der Ventilator
fan

die Radkappe
hubcap

das Getriebe
gearbox

die Transmission
transmission

die Kardanwelle
driveshaft

die Reifenpanne • puncture

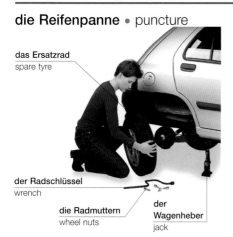

das Ersatzrad
spare tyre

der Radschlüssel
wrench

die Radmuttern
wheel nuts

der Wagenheber
jack

ein Rad wechseln
change a wheel (v)

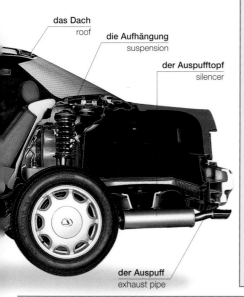

das Dach
roof

die Aufhängung
suspension

der Auspufftopf
silencer

der Auspuff
exhaust pipe

Vokabular • vocabulary

der Autounfall car accident	**der Nockenriemen** cam belt
die Panne breakdown	**der Turbolader** turbocharger
die Versicherung insurance	**der Verteiler** distributor
der Abschleppwagen tow truck	**die Einstellung** timing
der Mechaniker mechanic	**das Chassis** chassis
der Reifendruck tyre pressure	**die Handbremse** handbrake
der Sicherungskasten fuse box	**die Lichtmaschine** alternator
die Zündkerze spark plug	**Ich habe eine Panne.** I've broken down.
der Keilriemen fan belt	**Mein Auto springt nicht an.** My car won't start.
der Benzintank petrol tank	

das Motorrad • motorbike

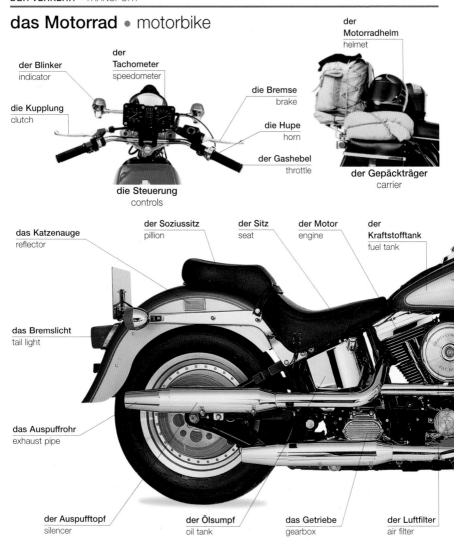

der
Motorradhelm
helmet

der Blinker
indicator

der
Tachometer
speedometer

die Bremse
brake

die Kupplung
clutch

die Hupe
horn

der Gashebel
throttle

die Steuerung
controls

der Gepäckträger
carrier

das Katzenauge
reflector

der Soziussitz
pillion

der Sitz
seat

der Motor
engine

der
Kraftstofftank
fuel tank

das Bremslicht
tail light

das Auspuffrohr
exhaust pipe

der Auspufftopf
silencer

der Ölsumpf
oil tank

das Getriebe
gearbox

der Luftfilter
air filter

die Typen • types

das Visier
visor

der Lederanzug
leathers

der
Leuchtstreifen
reflector strap

der
Knieschützer
knee pad

die Kleidung | clothing

der Scheinwerfer
headlight

die
Aufhängung
suspension

das
Schutzblech
mudguard

das Bremspedal
brake pedal

die Achse
axle

der Reifen
tyre

die Rennmaschine | racing bike

die Windschutzscheibe
windshield

der Tourer | tourer

das Geländemotorrad | dirt bike

der Motor
radständer
stand

der Roller | scooter

das Fahrrad • bicycle

das Tandem
tandem

das Rennrad
racing bike

das Mountainbike
mountain bike

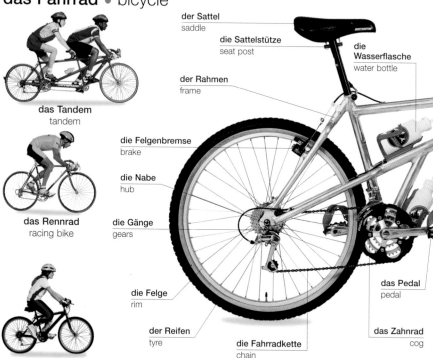

der Sattel
saddle

die Sattelstütze
seat post

die Wasserflasche
water bottle

der Rahmen
frame

die Felgenbremse
brake

die Nabe
hub

die Gänge
gears

die Felge
rim

der Reifen
tyre

die Fahrradkette
chain

das Pedal
pedal

das Zahnrad
cog

der Fahrradhelm
helmet

das Tourenfahrrad
touring bike

das Straßenrad
road bike

der Fahrradweg | cycle lane

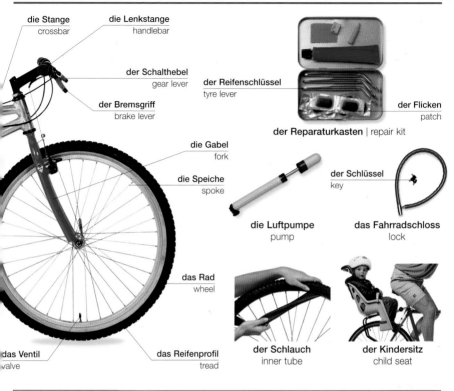

die Stange
crossbar

die Lenkstange
handlebar

der Schalthebel
gear lever

der Reifenschlüssel
tyre lever

der Bremsgriff
brake lever

der Flicken
patch

der Reparaturkasten | repair kit

die Gabel
fork

die Speiche
spoke

der Schlüssel
key

die Luftpumpe
pump

das Fahrradschloss
lock

das Rad
wheel

das Ventil
valve

das Reifenprofil
tread

der Schlauch
inner tube

der Kindersitz
child seat

Vokabular • vocabulary

das Rücklicht rear light	**die Stützräder** stabilisers	**das Kabel** cable	**der Korb** basket	**der Riemen** toe strap	**bremsen** brake (v)
die Fahrradlampe lamp	**der Fahrradständer** kickstand	**die Bremsbacke** brake block	**die Reifenpanne** puncture	**der Rennbügel** toe clip	**schalten** change gear (v)
der Rückstrahler reflector	**der Fahrradständer** bike rack	**das Kettenzahnrad** sprocket	**der Dynamo** dynamo	**treten** pedal (v)	**Rad fahren** cycle (v)

der Zug • train

der
Wagen
carriage

die
Gleisnummer
platform number

der
Bahnsteig
platform

der **Pendler**
commuter

der
Kofferkuli
trolley

der Bahnhof | train station

die Zugtypen • types of train

die
Lokomotive
engine

der **Führerstand**
driver's cab

die **Schiene**
rail

die Dampflokomotive
steam train

die Diesellokomotive | diesel train

die Elektrolokomotive
electric train

der Hochgeschwindigkeitszug
high-speed train

die Einschienenbahn
monorail

die U-Bahn
underground train

die Straßenbahn
tram

der Güterzug
freight train

die Gepäckablage
luggage rack

das Zugfenster
window

das Gleis
track

die Tür   der Sitz
door   seat

die Eingangssperre
ticket barrier

das Abteil
compartment

der Lautsprecher
public address system

der
Fahrplan
timetable

die Fahrkarte
ticket

der Speisewagen | dining car

das Schlafabteil
sleeping compartment

die Bahnhofshalle | concourse

Vokabular • vocabulary

das Bahnnetz rail network	**der U-Bahnplan** underground map	**der Fahrkartenschalter** ticket office	**die stromführende Schiene** live rail
der Intercity inter-city train	**die Verspätung** delay	**der Schaffner** ticket inspector	**das Signal** signal
die Stoßzeit rush hour	**der Fahrpreis** fare	**umsteigen** change (v)	**der Nothebel** emergency lever

das Flugzeug • aircraft

das Verkehrsflugzeug • airliner

der Bug
nose

das Cockpit
cockpit

das Triebwerk
engine

der Rumpf
fuselage

die Tragfläche
wing

das Heck
tail

das Seitenruder
rudder

der Ausgang
exit

das Bugfahrwerk
nosewheel

das Hauptfahrwerk
landing gear

das Querruder
aileron

das Seiten leitwerk
fin

das Höhen leitwerk
tailplane

die Kabine • cabin

der Notausgang
emergency exit

die Flugbegleiterin
flight attendant

das Gepäckfach
overhead locker

das Fenster
window

die Luftdüse
air vent

die Leselampe
reading light

der Sitz
seat

die Reihe
row

der Klapptisch
tray-table

die Armlehne
armrest

der Gang
aisle

die Rückenlehne
seat back

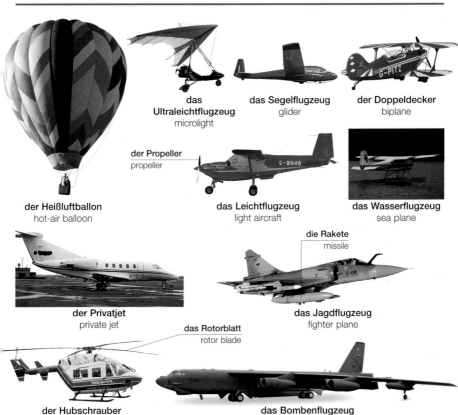

das Ultraleichtflugzeug
microlight

das Segelflugzeug
glider

der Doppeldecker
biplane

der Propeller
propeller

der Heißluftballon
hot-air balloon

das Leichtflugzeug
light aircraft

das Wasserflugzeug
sea plane

die Rakete
missile

der Privatjet
private jet

das Jagdflugzeug
fighter plane

das Rotorblatt
rotor blade

der Hubschrauber
helicopter

das Bombenflugzeug
bomber

Vokabular • vocabulary				
der Pilot pilot	**starten** take off (v)	**landen** land (v)	**die Economyclass** economy class	**das Handgepäck** hand luggage
der Kopilot co-pilot	**fliegen** fly (v)	**die Höhe** altitude	**die Businessclass** business class	**der Sicherheitsgurt** seat belt

der Flughafen • airport

das Vorfeld
apron

der
Gepäckanhänger
baggage trailer

der Terminal
terminal

das Versorgungsfahrzeug
service vehicle

die Fluggastbrücke
walkway

das Verkehrsflugzeug | airliner

Vokabular • vocabulary

das Gepäckband carousel	**die Flugnummer** flight number	**die Start- und Landebahn** runway	**der Urlaub** holiday
der Auslandsflug international flight	**die Passkontrolle** immigration	**die Sicherheitsvorkehrungen** security	**einen Flug buchen** book a flight (v)
der Inlandsflug domestic flight	**der Zoll** customs	**die Gepäckröntgenmaschine** X-ray machine	**einchecken** check in (v)
die Flugverbindung connection	**das Übergepäck** excess baggage	**der Urlaubsprospekt** holiday brochure	**der Kontrollturm** control tower

das
Handgepäck
hand luggage

das **Gepäck**
luggage

der **Kofferkuli**
trolley

der **Abfertigungsschalter**
check-in desk

das **Visum**
visa

der **Pass** | passport

die **Passkontrolle**
passport control

die **Bordkarte**
boarding pass

das **Flugticket**
ticket

die **Gatenummer**
gate number

der **Abflug**
departures

die **Abflughalle**
departure lounge

das **Reiseziel**
destination

die **Ankunft**
arrivals

die **Fluginformationsanzeige**
information screen

der **Duty-free-Shop**
duty-free shop

die **Gepäckausgabe**
baggage reclaim

der **Taxistand**
taxi rank

der **Autoverleih**
car hire

das Schiff • ship

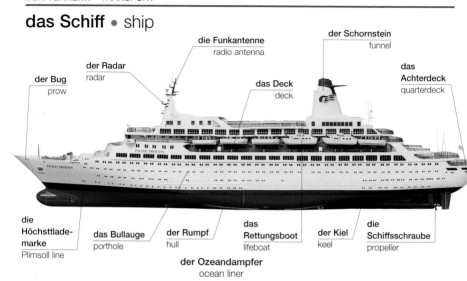

die Funkantenne
radio antenne

der Schornstein
funnel

der Radar
radar

der Bug
prow

das Deck
deck

das
Achterdeck
quarterdeck

die
Höchsttlade-
marke
Plimsoll line

das Bullauge
porthole

der Rumpf
hull

das
Rettungsboot
lifeboat

der Kiel
keel

die
Schiffsschraube
propeller

der Ozeandampfer
ocean liner

die Kommandobrücke
bridge

der Maschinenraum
engine room

die Kabine
cabin

die Kombüse
galley

Vokabular • vocabulary

das Dock dock	**die Ankerwinde** windlass
der Hafen port	**der Kapitän** captain
die Landungsbrücke gangway	**das Rennboot** speedboat
der Anker anchor	**das Ruderboot** rowing boat
der Poller bollard	**das Kanu** canoe

andere Schiffe • other ships

die Fähre
ferry

der
Außenbordmotor
outboard motor

das Schlauchboot
inflatable dinghy

das Tragflügelboot
hydrofoil

die Jacht
yacht

der Katamaran
catamaran

der Schleppdampfer
tug boat

das Luftkissenboot
hovercraft

die Takelung
rigging

der
Frachtraum
hold

das Containerschiff
container ship

das Segelboot
sailboat

das Frachtschiff
freighter

der Öltanker
oil tanker

der Flugzeugträger
aircraft carrier

das Kriegsschiff
battleship

der
Kommandoturm
conning tower

das U-Boot
submarine

der Hafen • port

das **Warenlager**
warehouse

der **Kran**
crane

der **Gabelstapler**
fork-lift truck

die **Zufahrtßsstraße**
access road

das **Zollamt**
customs house

das **Dock**
dock

der **Container**
container

der **Kai**
quay

die **Fracht**
cargo

der **Fährterminal**
ferry terminal

die **Fähre**
ferry

der **Fahrkartenschalter**
ticket office

der **Passagier**
passenger

der Containerhafen | container port

der Passagierhafen | passenger port

das Netz
net

das Fischerboot
fishing boat

die Verankerung
mooring

die Marina
marina

der Fischereihafen
fishing port

der Hafen
harbour

der Pier
pier

der Landungssteg
jetty

die Werft
shipyard

die Laterne
lamp

der Leuchtturm
lighthouse

die Boje
buoy

Vokabular • vocabulary

die Küstenwache coastguard	**festmachen** moor (v)	**an Bord gehen** board (v)
der Hafenmeister harbour master	**anlegen** dock (v)	**von Bord gehen** disembark (v)
das Trockendock dry dock	**den Anker werfen** drop anchor (v)	**auslaufen** set sail (v)

deutsch • english

217

der **Sport**
sports

der Football • American football

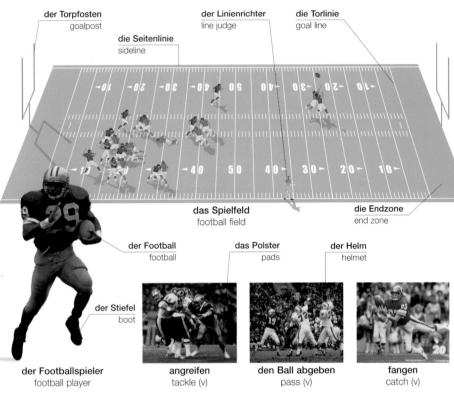

der Torpfosten
goalpost

die Seitenlinie
sideline

der Linienrichter
line judge

die Torlinie
goal line

das Spielfeld
football field

die Endzone
end zone

der Football
football

das Polster
pads

der Helm
helmet

der Stiefel
boot

der Footballspieler
football player

angreifen
tackle (v)

den Ball abgeben
pass (v)

fangen
catch (v)

Vokabular • vocabulary

die Auszeit time out	**die Mannschaft** team	**die Verteidigung** defence	**der Cheerleader** cheerleader	**Wie ist der Stand?** What is the score?
das unsichere Fangen des Balls fumble	**der Angriff** attack	**der Spielstand** score	**der Touchdown** touchdown	**Wer gewinnt?** Who is winning?

---

das Rugby • rugby

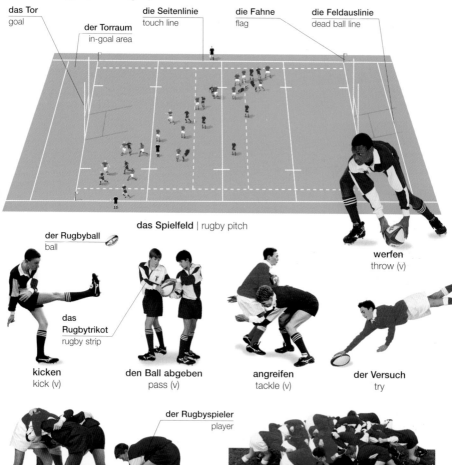

das Tor
goal

der Torraum
in-goal area

die Seitenlinie
touch line

die Fahne
flag

die Feldauslinie
dead ball line

das Spielfeld | rugby pitch

der Rugbyball
ball

das Rugbytrikot
rugby strip

werfen
throw (v)

kicken
kick (v)

den Ball abgeben
pass (v)

angreifen
tackle (v)

der Versuch
try

der Rugbyspieler
player

das offene Gedränge | ruck

das Gedränge | scrum

der Fußball • soccer

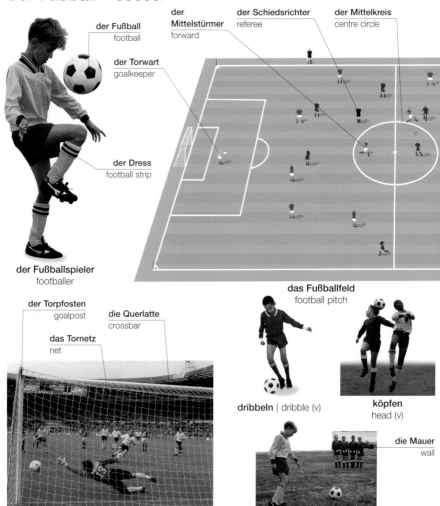

der Fußball
football

der Torwart
goalkeeper

der Dress
football strip

der Fußballspieler
footballer

der Mittelstürmer
forward

der Schiedsrichter
referee

der Mittelkreis
centre circle

der Torpfosten
goalpost

die Querlatte
crossbar

das Tornetz
net

das Tor | goal

das Fußballfeld
football pitch

dribbeln | dribble (v)

köpfen
head (v)

die Mauer
wall

der Freistoß | free kick

der Strafraum
penalty area

die Torlinie
goal line

der Torraum
goal area

das Tor
goal

der Verteidiger
defender

der Linienrichter
linesman

die Eckfahne
corner flag

der Einwurf
throw-in

kicken
kick (v)

der Fußballschuh
boot

den Ball abgeben
pass (v)

schießen
shoot (v)

halten
save (v)

angreifen
tackle (v)

Vokabular • vocabulary

das Stadion stadium	**das Foul** foul	**die gelbe Karte** yellow card	**die Liga** league	**die Verlängerung** extra time
der Elfmeter penalty	**der Eckball** corner	**das Abseits** off-side	**die Halbzeit** half time	**der Ersatzspieler** substitute
ein Tor schießen score a goal (v)	**die rote Karte** red card	**der Platzverweis** send off	**das Unentschieden** draw	**die Auswechslung** substitution

das Hockey • hockey

das Eishockey • ice hockey

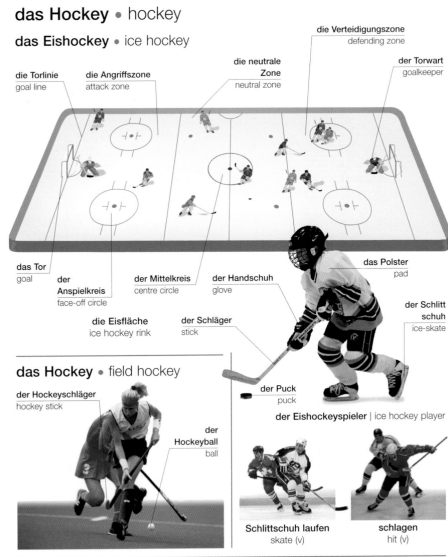

die Verteidigungszone
defending zone

die neutrale
Zone
neutral zone

der Torwart
goalkeeper

die Torlinie
goal line

die Angriffszone
attack zone

das Tor
goal

der
Anspielkreis
face-off circle

der Mittelkreis
centre circle

der Handschuh
glove

das Polster
pad

der Schlitt
schuh
ice-skate

die Eisfläche
ice hockey rink

der Schläger
stick

das Hockey • field hockey

der Hockeyschläger
hockey stick

der
Hockeyball
ball

der Puck
puck

der Eishockeyspieler | ice hockey player

Schlittschuh laufen
skate (v)

schlagen
hit (v)

das Kricket • cricket

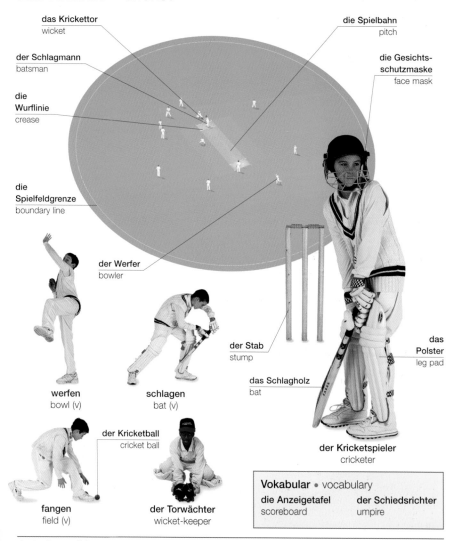

das Krickettor
wicket

die Spielbahn
pitch

der Schlagmann
batsman

die Gesichts-schutzmaske
face mask

die Wurflinie
crease

die Spielfeldgrenze
boundary line

der Werfer
bowler

der Stab
stump

das Polster
leg pad

das Schlagholz
bat

werfen
bowl (v)

schlagen
bat (v)

der Kricketspieler
cricketer

der Kricketball
cricket ball

fangen
field (v)

der Torwächter
wicket-keeper

Vokabular • vocabulary

die Anzeigetafel	**der Schiedsrichter**
scoreboard	umpire

der Basketball • basketball

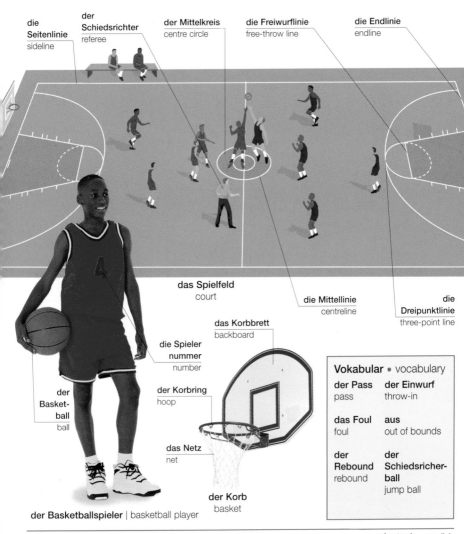

die
Seitenlinie
sideline

der
Schiedsrichter
referee

der Mittelkreis
centre circle

die Freiwurflinie
free-throw line

die Endlinie
endline

das Spielfeld
court

die Mittellinie
centreline

die
Dreipunktlinie
three-point line

das Korbbrett
backboard

die **Spieler
nummer**
number

der
**Basket-
ball**
ball

der Korbring
hoop

das Netz
net

der Korb
basket

der Basketballspieler | basketball player

Vokabular • vocabulary

der Pass
pass

der Einwurf
throw-in

das Foul
foul

aus
out of bounds

**der
Rebound**
rebound

**der
Schiedsricher-
ball**
jump ball

die Aktionen • actions

werfen
throw (v)

fangen
catch (v)

schießen
shoot (v)

springen
jump (v)

decken
mark (v)

blocken
block (v)

springen lassen
bounce (v)

einen Dunk spielen
dunk (v)

der Volleyball • volleyball

blocken
block (v)

das Netz
net

baggern
dig (v)

der Schiedsrichter
referee

der Knieschützer
knee support

das Spielfeld | court

der Baseball • baseball

das Spielfeld • field

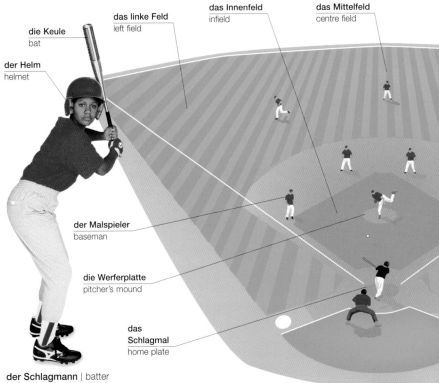

die Keule
bat

der Helm
helmet

das linke Feld
left field

das Innenfeld
infield

das Mittelfeld
centre field

der Malspieler
baseman

die Werferplatte
pitcher's mound

das Schlagmal
home plate

der Schlagmann | batter

der Baseball
ball

der Handschuh
mitt

die Schutzmaske
mask

Vokabular • vocabulary		
das Inning inning	**aus** out	**der Schlagfehler** strike
der Lauf run	**in Sicherheit** safe	**der ungültige Schlag** foul ball

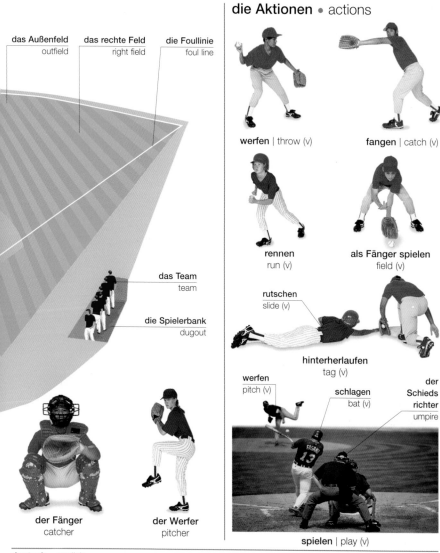

die Aktionen • actions

das Außenfeld
outfield

das rechte Feld
right field

die Foullinie
foul line

werfen | throw (v)

fangen | catch (v)

rennen
run (v)

als Fänger spielen
field (v)

das Team
team

die Spielerbank
dugout

rutschen
slide (v)

hinterherlaufen
tag (v)

werfen
pitch (v)

schlagen
bat (v)

der Schieds richter
umpire

der Fänger
catcher

der Werfer
pitcher

spielen | play (v)

das Tennis • tennis

der Griff
handle

der Kopf
head

die Saite
string

der Schiedsrichter
umpire

die Grundlinie
baseline

der Tennis-schläger
racquet

die Aufschlaglinie
service line

die Seitenlinie
sideline

der Tennisball
ball

das Schweißband
wristband

der Tennisplatz | tennis court

Vokabular • vocabulary

das Einzel singles	**der Satz** set	**der Einstand** deuce	**der Fehler** fault	**der Slice** slice	**der Spin** spin
das Doppel doubles	**das Match** match	**der Vorteil** advantage	**das Ass** ace	**Netz!** let!	**der Linienrichter** linesman
das Spiel game	**der Tiebreak** tiebreak	**null** love	**der Stoppball** dropshot	**der Ballwechsel** rally	**die Meisterschaft** championship

die Schläge • strokes

der Aufschlag
serve

der Volley
volley

der Return
return

der Lob
lob

die Vorhand
forehand

die Rückhand
backhand

das Netz
net

der Schmetterball
smash

der Balljunge
ballboy

aufschlagen
serve (v)

die Tennisschuhe
tennis shoes

der Tennisspieler
player

die Schlägerspiele • racquet games

der Federball
shuttlecock

der Tischtennisschläger
bat

das Badminton
badminton

das Tischtennis
table tennis

das Squash
squash

das Racquetball
racquetball

das Golf • golf

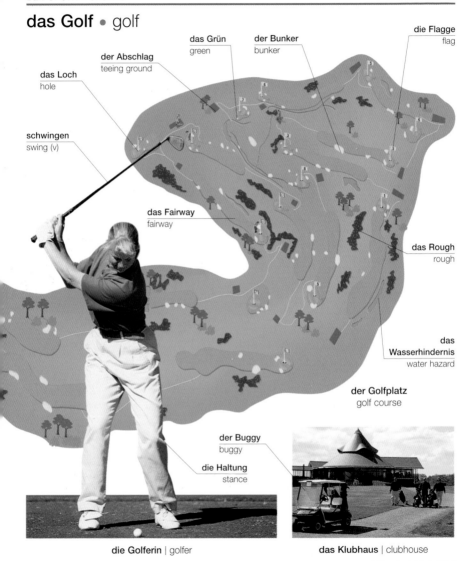

das Grün
green

der Bunker
bunker

die Flagge
flag

der Abschlag
teeing ground

das Loch
hole

schwingen
swing (v)

das Fairway
fairway

das Rough
rough

das
Wasserhindernis
water hazard

der Golfplatz
golf course

der Buggy
buggy

die Haltung
stance

die Golferin | golfer

das Klubhaus | clubhouse

deutsch • english

die Ausrüstung • equipment

der Golfball
golf ball

das Tee
tee

die Golftasche
golf bag

die Spikes
spikes

der Handschuh
glove

der Caddie
golf trolley

der Golfschuh
golf shoe

die Golf-schläger • golf clubs

das Holz
wood

der Putter
putter

das Eisen
iron

das Wedge
wedge

die Aktionen • actions

vom Abschlag spielen
tee-off (v)

driven
drive (v)

einlochen
putt (v)

chippen
chip (v)

Vokabular • vocabulary

das Par par	**über Par** over par	**das Golfturnier** tournament	**der Caddie** caddy	**der Schlag** stroke	**die Spielbahn** line of play
unter Par under par	**das Hole-in-One** hole in one	**das Handicap** handicap	**die Zuschauer** spectators	**der Übungsschwung** practice swing	**der Durchschwung** backswing

die Leichtathletik • athletics

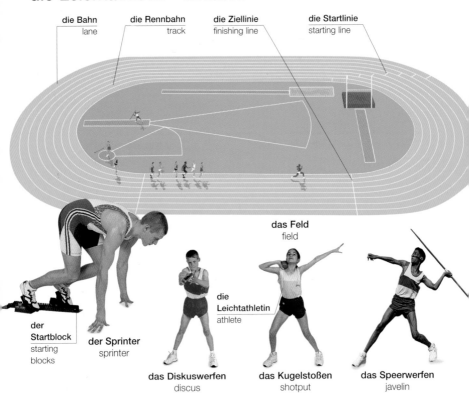

die Bahn
lane

die Rennbahn
track

die Ziellinie
finishing line

die Startlinie
starting line

das Feld
field

die Leichtathletin
athlete

der Startblock
starting blocks

der Sprinter
sprinter

das Diskuswerfen
discus

das Kugelstoßen
shotput

das Speerwerfen
javelin

Vokabular • vocabulary			
das Rennen race	**der Rekord** record	**das Fotofinish** photo finish	**der Stabhochsprung** pole vault
die Zeit time	**einen Rekord brechen** break a record (v)	**der Marathon** marathon	**die persönliche Bestleistung** personal best

die Stoppuhr
stopwatch

der Stab
baton

der Staffellauf
relay race

die Latte
crossbar

der Hochsprung
high jump

der Weitsprung
long jump

der Hürdenlauf
hurdles

das Turnen • gymnastics

das Sprungbrett
springboard

das Pferd
horse

der Salto
somersault

die Turnerin
gymnast

der Schwebebalken
beam

das Gymnastikband
ribbon

die Matte
mat

der Sprung
vault

das Bodenturnen
floor exercises

die Bodenakrobatik
tumble

die rhythmische Gymnastik
rhythmic gymnastics

Vokabular • vocabulary

das Reck horizontal bar	**der Stufenbarren** asymmetric bars	**die Ringe** rings	**die Medaillen** medals	**das Silber** silver
der Barren parallel bars	**das Seitpferd** pommel horse	**das Siegerpodium** podium	**das Gold** gold	**die Bronze** bronze

---

der Kampfsport • combat sports

der Gegner
opponent

der Kopfschutz
guard

der Handschuh
glove

der Gürtel
belt

das Taekwondo
tae-kwon-do

das Karate
karate

das Judo
judo

die Maske
mask

der Säbel
sword

das Aikido
aikido

das Kendo
kendo

das Kung-Fu
kung fu

das Kickboxen
kickboxing

das Ringen
wrestling

das Boxen
boxing

die Techniken • actions

das Fallen
fall

der Griff
hold

der Wurf
throw

das Fesseln
pin

der Seitfußstoß
kick

der Stoß
punch

der Angriff
strike

der Sprung
jump

der Block
block

der Hieb
chop

Vokabular • vocabulary

der Boxring boxing ring	**die Runde** round	**die Faust** fist	**der schwarze Gürtel** black belt	**das Capoeira** capoeira
die Boxhandschuhe boxing gloves	**der Kampf** bout	**der Knockout** knock out	**die Selbstverteidigung** self defence	**das Sumo** sumo wrestling
der Mundschutz mouth guard	**das Sparren** sparring	**der Sandsack** punch bag	**die Kampfsportarten** martial arts	**das Tai Chi** tai-chi

der Schwimmsport • swimming
die Ausrüstung • equipment

der Schwimmflügel
armband

die Schwimmbrille
goggles

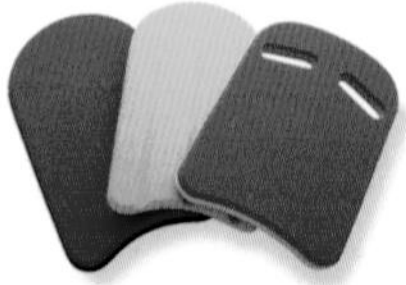

die Nasenklemme
nose clip

das Schwimmfloß
float

der Badeanzug
swimsuit

die Badekappe
cap

die Bahn
lane

das Wasser
water

der Startblock
starting block

die Badehose
trunks

das Schwimmbecken
swimming pool

der Schwimmer | swimmer

das Sprungbrett
springboard

der Springer
diver

springen | dive (v)

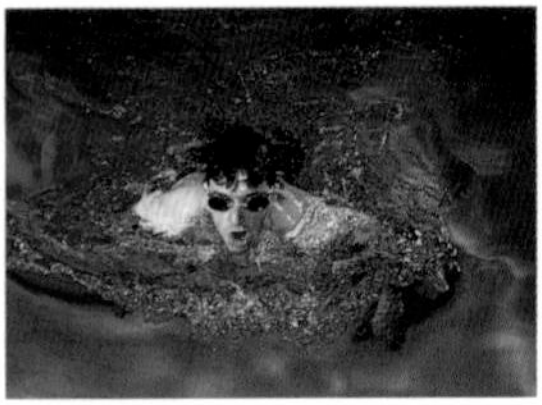

schwimmen | swim (v)

die Kehre | turn

die Schwimmstile • styles

das Kraulen
front crawl

das Brustschwimmen
breaststroke

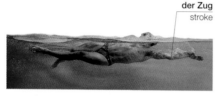

der Zug
stroke

der Stoß
kick

das Rückenschwimmen | backstroke

der Butterfly | butterfly

das Tauchen • scuba diving

die Druckluftflasche
air cylinder

der Taucheranzug
wetsuit

die
Taschermaske
mask

die
Schwimmflosse
flipper

der
Lungenautomat
regulator

der Bleigürtel
weight belt

der Schnorchel
snorkel

Vokabular • vocabulary

der Sprung dive	**Wasser treten** tread water (v)	**das tiefe Ende** deep end	**der Wasserball** water polo	**das flache Ende** shallow end	**der Krampf** cramp
der Turmsprung high dive	**der Startsprung** racing dive	**die Schließfächer** lockers	**der Bademeister** lifeguard	**das Synchronschwimmen** synchronized swimming	**ertrinken** drown (v)

der Segelsport • sailing

der Kompass
compass

der Anker
anchor

die Klampe
cleat

das Seitendeck
sidedeck

die Fock
headsail

der Bug
bow

die Pinne
tiller

der Rumpf
hull

navigieren | navigate (v)

der Mast
mast

die Takelung
rigging

das Großsegel
mainsail

der Baum
boom

das Heck
stern

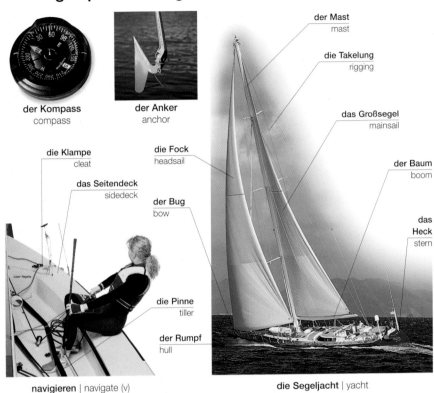

die Segeljacht | yacht

die Sicherheit • safety

die Leuchtrakete
flare

der Rettungsring
lifebuoy

die Schwimmweste
life jacket

das Rettungsboot
life raft

der Wassersport • watersports

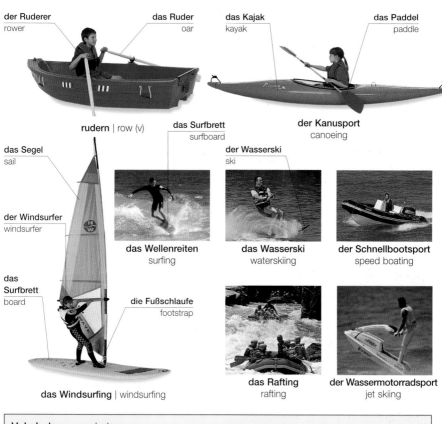

der Ruderer
rower

das Ruder
oar

das Kajak
kayak

das Paddel
paddle

rudern | row (v)

der Kanusport
canoeing

das Surfbrett
surfboard

das Segel
sail

der Wasserski
ski

der Windsurfer
windsurfer

das
Surfbrett
board

die Fußschlaufe
footstrap

das Wellenreiten
surfing

das Wasserski
waterskiing

der Schnellbootsport
speed boating

das Rafting
rafting

der Wassermotorradsport
jet skiing

das Windsurfing | windsurfing

Vokabular • vocabulary

der Surfer surfer	die Crew crew	der Wind wind	die Brandung surf	die Schot sheet	das Schwert centreboard
der Wasserskifahrer waterskier	aufkreuzen tack (v)	die Welle wave	das Wildwasser rapids	das Ruder rudder	kentern capsize (v)

---

der Reitsport • horse riding

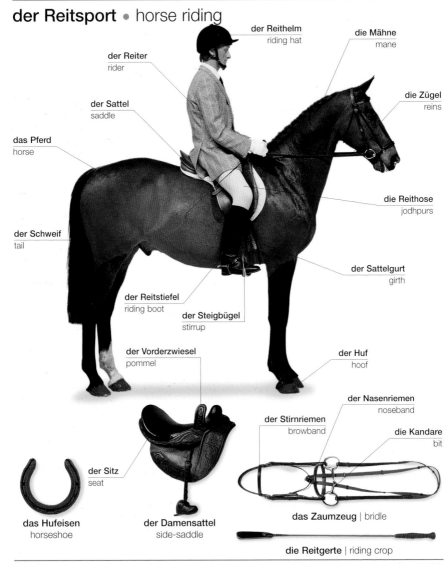

der Reithelm
riding hat

die Mähne
mane

der Reiter
rider

die Zügel
reins

der Sattel
saddle

das Pferd
horse

die Reithose
jodhpurs

der Schweif
tail

der Sattelgurt
girth

der Reitstiefel
riding boot

der Steigbügel
stirrup

der Huf
hoof

der Vorderzwiesel
pommel

der Nasenriemen
noseband

der Stirnriemen
browband

die Kandare
bit

der Sitz
seat

das Hufeisen
horseshoe

der Damensattel
side-saddle

das Zaumzeug | bridle

die Reitgerte | riding crop

die Veranstaltungen • events

das Rennpferd
racehorse

das Hindernis
fence

das Pferderennen
horse race

das Jagdrennen
steeplechase

das Trabrennen
harness race

das Rodeo
rodeo

das Springreiten
showjumping

das Zweispännerrennen
carriage race

das Trekking
trekking

das Dressurreiten
dressage

das Polo
polo

Vokabular • vocabulary

der Schritt walk	**der Kanter** canter	**der Sprung** jump	**das Halfter** halter	**die Koppel** paddock	**das Flachrennen** flat race
der Trab trot	**der Galopp** gallop	**der Stallbursche** groom	**der Pferdestall** stable	**der Turnierplatz** arena	**die Rennbahn** racecourse

der Angelsport • fishing

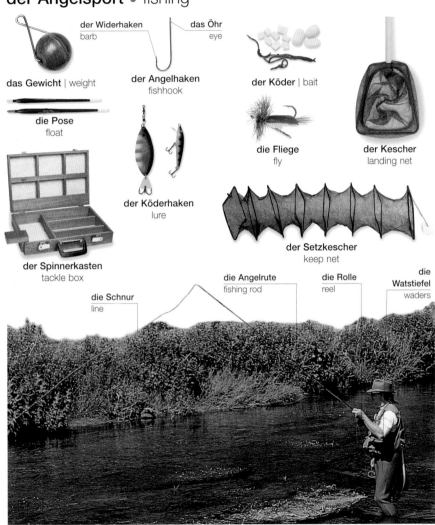

der Widerhaken
barb

das Öhr
eye

das Gewicht | weight

der Angelhaken
fishhook

der Köder | bait

die Pose
float

die Fliege
fly

der Kescher
landing net

der Köderhaken
lure

der Setzkescher
keep net

der Spinnerkasten
tackle box

die Angelrute
fishing rod

die Rolle
reel

die
Watstiefel
waders

die Schnur
line

der Angler | angler

die Fischfangarten • types of fishing

das Süßwasserangeln
freshwater fishing

das Fliegenangeln
fly fishing

das Sportangeln
sport fishing

die Hochseefischerei
deep sea fishing

das Brandungsangeln
surfcasting

die Aktivitäten • activities

auswerfen
cast (v)

fangen
catch (v)

einholen
reel in (v)

mit dem Netz fangen
net (v)

loslassen
release (v)

Vokabular • vocabulary

ködern bait (v)	**die Angelgeräte** tackle	**die Regenhaut** waterproofs	**der Angelschein** fishing permit	**der Fischkorb** creel
anbeißen bite (v)	**die Rolle** spool	**die Stake** pole	**die Seefischerei** marine fishing	**das Speerfischen** spearfishing

---

der Skisport • skiing

der Skihang
ski slope

der Sessellift
chairlift

der Kabinenlift
cable car

der Handschuh
glove

der Skistock
ski pole

die Skipiste
ski run

die Sicherheitssperre
safety barrier

die Spitze
tip

die Kante
edge

der Ski
ski

die Skijacke
ski jacket

die Skiläuferin
skier

der Skistiefel
ski boot

die Disziplinen • events

der Abfahrtslauf
downhill skiing

das Tor
gate

der Slalom
slalom

der Skisprung
ski jump

der Langlauf
cross-country skiing

der Wintersport • winter sports

das Eisklettern
ice climbing

das Eislaufen
ice-skating

der Eiskunstlauf
figure skating

die Skibrille
goggles

der
Schlittschuh
skate

das Snowboarding
snowboarding

der Bobsport
bobsleigh

das Rennrodeln
luge

das Schneemobil
snowmobile

das Schlittenfahren
sledding

Vokabular • vocabulary

die alpine Kombination alpine skiing	**das Hundeschlittenfahren** dog sledding
der Riesenslalom giant slalom	**das Eisschnelllauf** speed skating
abseits der Piste off-piste	**das Biathlon** biathlon
das Curling curling	**die Lawine** avalanche

die anderen Sportarten • other sports

das Segelflugzeug
glider

der Drachen
hang-glider

das Segelfliegen
gliding

der Fallschirm
parachute

das Drachenfliegen
hang-gliding

das Seil
rope

das Klettern
rock climbing

das Fallschirmspringen
parachuting

das Gleitschirmfliegen
paragliding

das Fallschirmspringen
skydiving

das Abseilen
abseiling

das Bungeejumping
bungee jumping

das Rallyefahren
rally driving

der
Rennfahrer
racing driver

der Rennsport
motor racing

das Motocross
motorcross

das Motorradrennen
motorbike racing

das Skateboard
skateboard

das Skateboard-
fahren
skateboarding

das Inlineskaten
inline skating

der Lacrosseschläger
stick

das Lacrosse
lacrosse

das Florett   die Maske
foil   mask

das Fechten
fencing

der Kegel
pin

die Zielscheibe
target

der Bogen
bow

der Pfeil
arrow

der Köcher
quiver

das Bogenschießen
archery

**das
Scheibenschießen**
target shooting

die
Bowlingkugel
bowling ball

das Bowling
bowling

das Poolbillard
pool

das Snooker
snooker

die Fitness • fitness

das Trainingsrad
exercise bike

das Fitnessgerät
gym machine

die Bank
bench

die
Gewichte
free weights

die Stange
bar

das Fitnesscenter | gym

die Rudermaschine
rowing machine

das Laufband
treadmill

die Langlaufmaschine
cross trainer

die private Fitness-
trainerin
personal trainer

die Tretmaschine
step machine

das Schwimmbecken
swimming pool

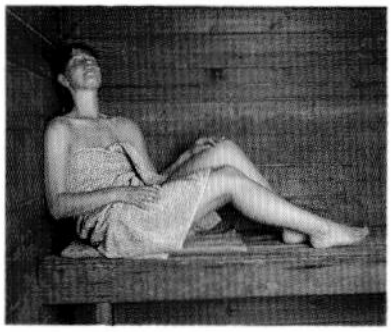

die Sauna
sauna

deutsch • english

die Übungen • exercises

die Strumpfhose
tights

das Strecken
stretch

der Ausfall
lunge

der Liegestütz
press-up

die Kniebeuge
squat

das Rumpfheben
sit-up

die Hantel
dumb bell

die Bizepsübung
bicep curl

der Beinstütz
leg press

die Brustübung
chest press

Trainings schuhe
trainers

das Krafttraining
weight training

die Gewicht hantel
weight bar

das Jogging
jogging

das Pilates
pilates

Vokabular • vocabulary

trainieren train (v)	**beugen** flex (v)	**ausstrecken** extend (v)	**die Boxgymnastik** boxercise	**das Seilspringen** skipping
sich aufwärmen warm up (v)	**auf der Stelle joggen** jog on the spot (v)	**hochziehen** pull up (v)	**das Zirkeltraining** circuit training	

die Freizeit
leisure

das Theater • theatre

der Vorhang
curtain

die Kulisse
wings

das Bühnenbild
set

das Publikum
audience

das Orchester
orchestra

die Bühne | stage

der Sitzplatz
seat

der zweite Rang
upper circle

die Reihe
row

die Loge
box

der erste Rang
circle

der Balkon
balcony

der Gang
aisle

das Parkett
stalls

die Bestuhlung | seating

Vokabular • vocabulary

das Theaterstück play	**der Regisseur** director	**die Premiere** first night
die Besetzung cast	**der Prospekt** backdrop	**die Pause** interval
der Schauspieler actor	**das Rollenheft** script	**das Programm** programme
die Schauspielerin actress	**der Regisseur** producer	**der Orchestergraben** orchestra pit

das Konzert
concert

das Musical
musical

das
Theaterkostüm
costume

das Ballett
ballet

Vokabular • vocabulary

der Platzanweiser
usher

die klassische Musik
classical music

die Noten
musical score

die Tonspur
soundtrack

applaudieren
applaud (v)

die Zugabe
encore

Ich möchte zwei Karten für die Aufführung heute Abend.
I'd like two tickets for tonight's performance.

Um wieviel Uhr beginnt die Aufführung?
What time does it start?

die Oper
opera

das Kino • cinema

das
Popcorn
popcorn

die Kasse
box office

das Foyer
lobby

das
Plakat
poster

der Kinosaal
cinema hall

die Leinwand
screen

Vokabular • vocabulary

die Komödie
comedy

der Thriller
thriller

der Horrorfilm
horror film

der Western
western

der Liebesfilm
romance

der Science-Fiction-Film
science fiction film

der Abenteuerfilm
adventure

der Zeichentrickfilm
animated film

das Orchester • orchestra

die Saiteninstrumente • strings

die Harfe
harp

der Dirigent
conductor

der Kontrabass
double bass

die Geige
violin

das Podium
podium

die Bratsche
viola

das Cello
cello

die Noten
score

der
Violinschlüssel
treble clef

die Note
note

das
Liniensystem
staff

der
Bassschlüssel
bass clef

die Notation | notation

das Klavier | piano

Vokabular • vocabulary

die Ouvertüre overture	die Sonate sonata	die Tonhöhe pitch	das Kreuz sharp	der Taktstrich bar	die Tonleiter scale
die Symphonie symphony	die Musikins- trumente instruments	das Pausen- zeichen rest	das B flat	das Auflösungs- zeichen natural	der Taktstock baton

---

die Holzblasinstrumente • woodwind

die Pikkoloflöte
piccolo

die Querflöte
flute

die Oboe
oboe

das Englischhorn
cor anglais

die Klarinette
clarinet

die Bassklarinette
bass clarinet

das Fagott
bassoon

das Kontrafagott
double bassoon

das Saxophon
saxophone

die Schlaginstrumente • percussion

das Vibraphon
vibraphone

die Kesselpauke
kettledrum

der Gong
gong

die Bongos
bongos

die kleine Trommel
snare drum

das Becken
cymbals

das Tamburin
tambourine

das Fußpedal
foot pedal

der Triangel
triangle

die Maracas
maracas

die Blechblasinstrumente • brass

die Trompete
trumpet

die Posaune
trombone

das Horn
French horn

die Tuba
tuba

das Konzert • concert

der Lautsprecher
speaker

die Fans
fans

der
Leadsänger
lead singer

der Gitarrist
guitarist

das
Mikrophon
microphone

der
Schlag-zeuger
drummer

das Rockkonzert | rock concert

die Instrumente • instruments

der
Tonabnehmer
pickup

der Hals
neck

der Bund
fret

der Wirbel
tuning peg

die Saite
string

der Steg
bridge

die
Trommel
drum

die Bassgitarre
bass guitar

das Keyboard
keyboard

die elektrische Gitarre
electric guitar

das Schlagzeug
drum kit

die Musikstile • musical styles

der Jazz
jazz

der Blues
blues

die Punkmusik
punk

der Folk
folk music

der Pop
pop

die Tanzmusik
dance

der Rap
rap

das Heavymetal
heavy metal

die klassische Musik
classical music

Vokabular • vocabulary					
das Lied	**der Text**	**die Melodie**	**der Beat**	**der Reggae**	**die Countrymusic**
song	lyrics	melody	beat	reggae	country

die Besichtigungstour • sightseeing

die Route
itinerary

mit offenem Oberdeck
open-top

der Tourist
tourist

der Stadtrundfahrtbus | tour bus

die Fremdenführerin
tour guide

die Figur
statuette

die Touristenattraktion | tourist attraction

die Führung
guided tour

die Andenken
souvenirs

Vokabular • vocabulary

geöffnet open	**der Film** film	**der Camcorder** camcorder	**links** left	**Wo ist…?** Where is…?
geschlossen closed	**die Batterien** batteries	**die Kamera** camera	**rechts** right	**Ich habe mich verlaufen.** I'm lost.
das Eintrittsgeld entrance fee	**der Reiseführer** guide book	**die Richtungsangaben** directions	**geradeaus** straight on	**Können Sie mir sagen, wie ich nach… komme?** Can you tell me the way to….?

die Sehenswürdigkeiten • attractions

das
Gemälde
painting

das
Aussellungs
stück
exhibit

die
Ausstellung
exhibition

die berühmte
Ruine
famous ruin

die Kunstgalerie
art gallery

das Monument
monument

das Museum
museum

das historische Gebäude
historic building

das Kasino
casino

der Park
gardens

der Nationalpark
national park

die Information • information

die Zeiten
times

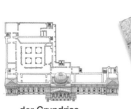

der Grundriss
floor plan

der Stadtplan
map

der Fahrplan
timetable

die Touristeninformation
tourist information

die Aktivitäten im Freien • outdoor activities

der Fußweg
footpath

die Sonnenuhr
sundial

das Café
café

der Park | park

das Gras
grass

die Bank
bench

die Gartenanlagen
formal gardens

die Berg-und-
Talbahn
roller coaster

der Jahrmarkt
fairground

der Vergnügungspark
theme park

der Safaripark
safari park

der Zoo
zoo

die Aktivitäten • activites

das Radfahren
cycling

das Jogging
jogging

das Skateboardfahren
skateboarding

das Inlinerfahren
rollerblading

der Reitweg
bridle path

das Vogelbeobachten
bird watching

das Reiten
horse riding

das Wandern
hiking

der Pick-nickkorb
hamper

das Picknick
picnic

---

der Spielplatz • playground

der Sandkasten
sandpit

das Planschbecken
paddling pool

die Schaukel
swings

die Wippe | seesaw

die Rutsche
slide

das Klettergerüst
climbing frame

der Strand • beach

das
Hotel
hotel

**der
Sonnenschirm**
beach umbrella

das
Strandhäuschen
beach hut

der Sand
sand

die Welle
wave

das Meer
sea

die Strandtasche
beach bag

der Bikini
bikini

sonnenbaden | sunbathe (v)

deutsch • english

der
Rettungsschwimmer
lifeguard

der Rettungsturm
lifeguard tower

der Windschutz
windbreak

die Promenade
promenade

der Liegestuhl
deck chair

die Sonnenbrille
sunglasses

der Sonnenhut
sunhat

die Sonnenmilch
suntan lotion

der Sonnenblock
sunblock

der Wasserball
beach ball

der Schwimmreifen
rubber ring

der Badeanzug
swimsuit

der Eimer
bucket

die Schaufel
spade

die Sandburg
sandcastle

die Muschel
shell

das Strandtuch
beach towel

das Camping • camping

die Toiletten
toilets

die Mülleimer
waste disposal

die Duschen
shower block

der Stromanschluss
electric hook-up

das Überdach
flysheet

der Hering
tent peg

die
Zeltspannleine
guy rope

der
Wohnwagen
caravan

der Campingplatz
campsite

Vokabular • vocabulary

zelten camp (v)	**der Zeltplatz** pitch	**die Picknickbank** picnic bench	**die Holzkohle** charcoal
Zeltplätze frei pitches available	**die Zeltstange** tent pole	**die Hängematte** hammock	**der Feueranzünder** firelighter
voll full	**das Faltbett** camp bed	**das Wohnmobil** camper van	**ein Feuer machen** light a fire (v)
die Campingplatzverwaltung site manager's office	**ein Zelt aufschlagen** pitch a tent (v)	**der Anhänger** trailer	**das Lagerfeuer** campfire

das
Gestänge
frame

der Zeltboden
ground sheet

der Rucksack
backpack

**die Thermos
flasche**
vacuum flask

die Wasserflasche
water bottle

das Zelt
tent

der Insektenspray
insect repellent

die Taschenlampe
torch

das Moskitonetz
mosquito net

die Thermowäsche
thermals

die Wanderschuhe
walking boots

die Regenhaut
waterproofs

der Schlafsack
sleeping bag

der Gasbrenner
camping stove

der Grill
barbecue

die Schlafmatte
sleeping mat

die Luftmatratze | air mattress

die Privatunterhaltung • home entertainment

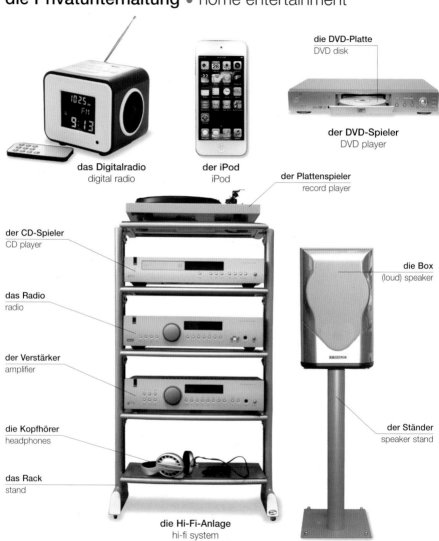

die DVD-Platte
DVD disk

der DVD-Spieler
DVD player

das Digitalradio
digital radio

der iPod
iPod

der Plattenspieler
record player

der CD-Spieler
CD player

die Box
(loud) speaker

das Radio
radio

der Verstärker
amplifier

die Kopfhörer
headphones

der Ständer
speaker stand

das Rack
stand

die Hi-Fi-Anlage
hi-fi system

der Bildschirm
screen

die Okularmuschel
eyecup

die Digitale Box
digital box

der Camcorder
camcorder

die Satellitenschüssel
satellite dish

der Flachbildfernseher
flatscreen TV

das Pult
console

der Vorlauf
fast forward

die Pause
pause

die Aufnahme
record

die Lautstärke
volume

der Steuerhebel
controller

der Rücklauf
rewind

der Stop
stop

das Abspielen
play

das Videospiel | video game

die Fernbedienung
remote control

Vokabular • vocabulary

die CD-Platte compact disc	der Spielfilm feature film	das Streaming streaming	digital digital	stereo stereo
die Kassette cassette tape	die Werbung advertisement	das Kabelfernsehen cable television	fernsehen watch television (v)	das Radio einstellen tune the radio (v)
der Kassettenrekorder cassette player	der Pay-Kanal pay per view channel	das Programm programme	den Fernseher einschalten turn the television off (v)	den Fernseher abschalten turn the television off (v)
hochauflösend high-definition	WLAN wifi	den Kanal wechseln change channel (v)		

die Fotografie • photography

der Auslöser
shutter release

der Blendenregler
aperture dial

die Linse
lens

der Filter
filter

die Schutzkappe
lens cap

die Spiegelreflexkamera | SLR camera

der Elektronenblitz
flash gun

der Belichtungsmesser
lightmeter

das Zoom
zoom lens

das Stativ
tripod

die Fotoapparattypen • types of camera

der Blitz
flash

die Polaroidkamera
polaroid camera

die Kamera für APS-Film
APS camera

das Kamera-Handy
camera phone

die Einwegkamera
disposable camera

fotografieren · photograph (v)

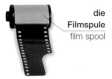

die Filmspule
film spool

der Film
film

einstellen
focus (v)

entwickeln
develop (v)

das Negativ
negative

quer
landscape

hoch
portrait

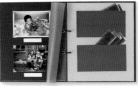

das Fotoalbum
photo album

der Fotorahmen
photo frame

das Foto | photograph

die Probleme · problems

unterbelichtet
underexposed

überbelichtet
overexposed

unscharf
out of focus

die Rotfärbung der Augen
red eye

Vokabular · vocabulary

der Bildsucher viewfinder	**der Abzug** print
die Kameratasche camera case	**matt** mat
die Belichtung exposure	**hochglanz** gloss
die Dunkelkammer darkroom	**die Vergrößerung** enlargement

Könnten Sie diesen Film entwickeln lassen?
I'd like this film processed

die Spiele • games

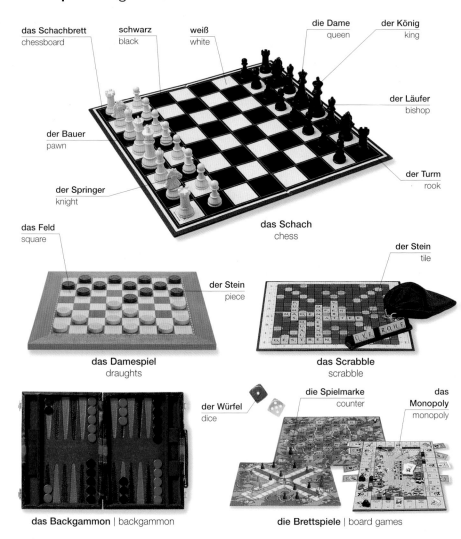

das Schachbrett	schwarz	weiß	die Dame	der König
chessboard	black	white	queen	king

der Läufer
bishop

der Bauer
pawn

der Turm
rook

der Springer
knight

das Schach
chess

das Feld
square

der Stein
tile

der Stein
piece

das Damespiel
draughts

das Scrabble
scrabble

der Würfel
dice

die Spielmarke
counter

das
Monopoly
monopoly

das Backgammon | backgammon

die Brettspiele | board games

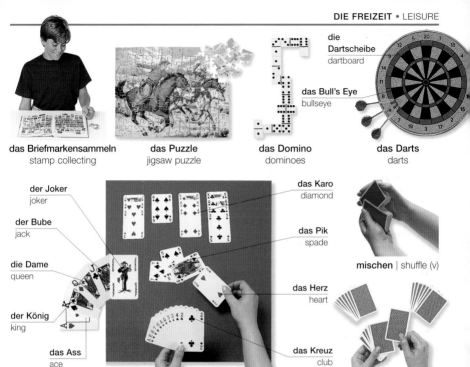

das Briefmarkensammeln
stamp collecting

das Puzzle
jigsaw puzzle

das Domino
dominoes

die Dartscheibe
dartboard

das Bull's Eye
bullseye

das Darts
darts

der Joker
joker

der Bube
jack

die Dame
queen

der König
king

das Ass
ace

die Karten
cards

das Karo
diamond

das Pik
spade

das Herz
heart

das Kreuz
club

mischen | shuffle (v)

geben | deal (v)

Vokabular • vocabulary

der Zug move	**gewinnen** win (v)	**der Verlierer** loser	**das Bridge** bridge	**der Punkt** point	**Wer ist dran?** Whose turn is it?
spielen play (v)	**der Gewinner** winner	**das Spiel** game	**das Poker** poker	**die Farbe** suit	**Du bist dran.** It's your move.
der Spieler player	**verlieren** lose (v)	**die Wette** bet	**das Kartenspiel** pack of cards	**das Spielergebnis** score	**Würfle.** Roll the dice.

---

das Kunsthandwerk 1 • arts and crafts 1

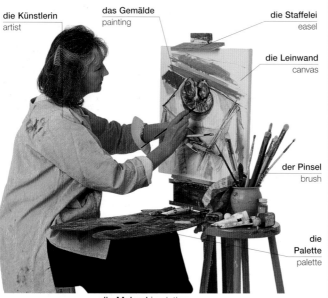

die Künstlerin
artist

das Gemälde
painting

die Staffelei
easel

die Leinwand
canvas

der Pinsel
brush

die
Palette
palette

die Malerei | painting

die Farben • colours

rot red	**blau** blue	**gelb** yellow	**grün** green
orange orange	**lila** purple	**weiß** white	**schwarz** black
grau grey	**rosa** pink	**braun** brown	**indigoblau** indigo

die Farben • paints

die Ölfarben
oil paints

die Aquarellfarbe
watercolour paint

die Pastellstifte
pastels

die Acrylfarbe
acrylic paint

die Plakatfarbe
poster paint

andere Kunstfertigkeiten • other crafts

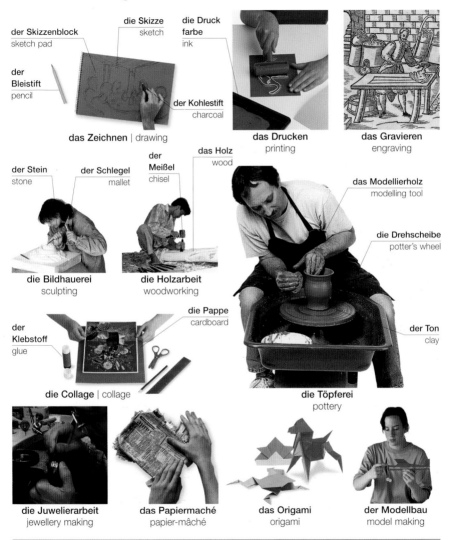

der Skizzenblock
sketch pad

die Skizze
sketch

die Druck farbe
ink

der Bleistift
pencil

der Kohlestift
charcoal

das Zeichnen | drawing

das Drucken
printing

das Gravieren
engraving

der Stein
stone

der Schlegel
mallet

der Meißel
chisel

das Holz
wood

das Modellierholz
modelling tool

die Drehscheibe
potter's wheel

die Bildhauerei
sculpting

die Holzarbeit
woodworking

der Ton
clay

der Klebstoff
glue

die Pappe
cardboard

die Collage | collage

die Töpferei
pottery

die Juwelierarbeit
jewellery making

das Papiermaché
papier-mâché

das Origami
origami

der Modellbau
model making

das Kunsthandwerk 2 • arts and crafts 2

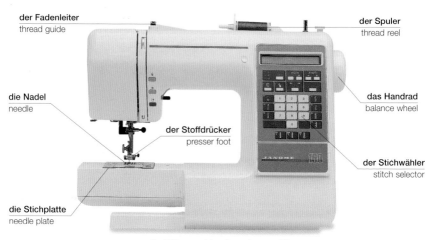

der Fadenleiter
thread guide

der Spuler
thread reel

die Nadel
needle

das Handrad
balance wheel

der Stoffdrücker
presser foot

der Stichwähler
stitch selector

die Stichplatte
needle plate

die **Nähmaschine** | sewing machine

die Schere
scissors

das Schnittmuster
pattern

das Nadelkissen
pincushion

die Stecknadel
pin

das Zentimetermaß
tape measure

der Stoff
material

der **Nähkorb** | sewing basket

das Garn
thread

die Öse
eye

die Spule
bobbin

der Haken
hook

der Fingerhut
thimble

die
Schneiderkreide
tailor's chalk

die
Schneiderpuppe
tailor's dummy

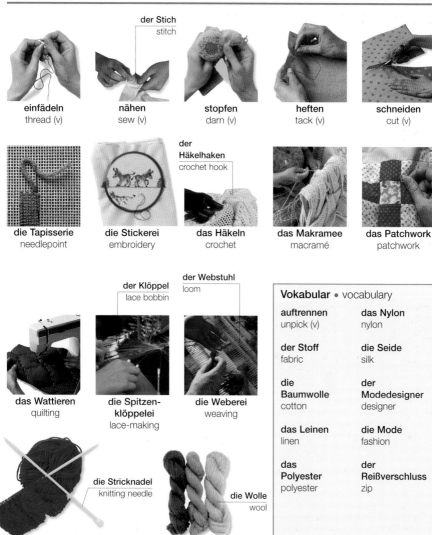

der Stich
stitch

einfädeln
thread (v)

nähen
sew (v)

stopfen
darn (v)

heften
tack (v)

schneiden
cut (v)

die Tapisserie
needlepoint

die Stickerei
embroidery

der Häkelhaken
crochet hook

das Häkeln
crochet

das Makramee
macramé

das Patchwork
patchwork

der Klöppel
lace bobbin

der Webstuhl
loom

das Wattieren
quilting

die Spitzen-klöppelei
lace-making

die Weberei
weaving

die Stricknadel
knitting needle

das Stricken | knitting

der Strang | skein

die Wolle
wool

Vokabular • vocabulary

auftrennen
unpick (v)

das Nylon
nylon

der Stoff
fabric

die Seide
silk

die Baumwolle
cotton

der Modedesigner
designer

das Leinen
linen

die Mode
fashion

das Polyester
polyester

der Reißverschluss
zip

die Umwelt
environment

der Weltraum • space

der Merkur
Mercury

die Erde
Earth

der Mars
Mars

der Jupiter
Jupiter

der Neptun
Neptune

der Uranus
Uranus

der Pluto
Pluto

die Venus
Venus

die Sonne
Sun

der Mond
Moon

das Sonnensystem
Saturn

das Sonnensystem | solar system

die Galaxie
galaxy

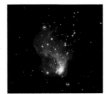

der Nebelfleck
nebula

der Asteroid
asteroid

der Schweif
tail

der Stern
star

der Komet
comet

vokabular • vocabulary

der Planet
planet

das Universum
universe

der Vollmond
full moon

der Meteor
meteor

die Umlaufbahn
orbit

der Neumond
new moon

die Schwerkraft
gravity

das schwarze Loch
black hole

die Mondsichel
crescent moon

die Finsternis | eclipse

die Raumforschung • space exploration

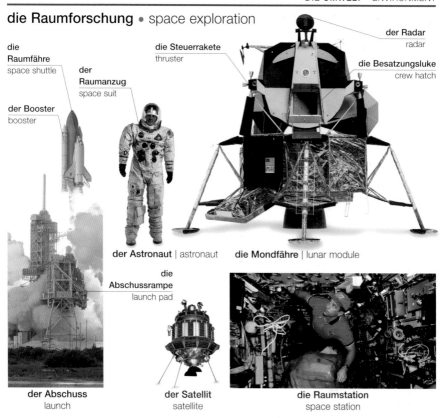

der Radar
radar

die
Raumfähre
space shuttle

die Steuerrakete
thruster

die Besatzungsluke
crew hatch

der
Raumanzug
space suit

der Booster
booster

der Astronaut | astronaut

die Mondfähre | lunar module

die
Abschussrampe
launch pad

der Abschuss
launch

der Satellit
satellite

die Raumstation
space station

die Astronomie • astronomy

das Sternbild
constellation

das Fernglas
binoculars

das
Teleskop
telescope

das Stativ
tripod

die Erde • Earth

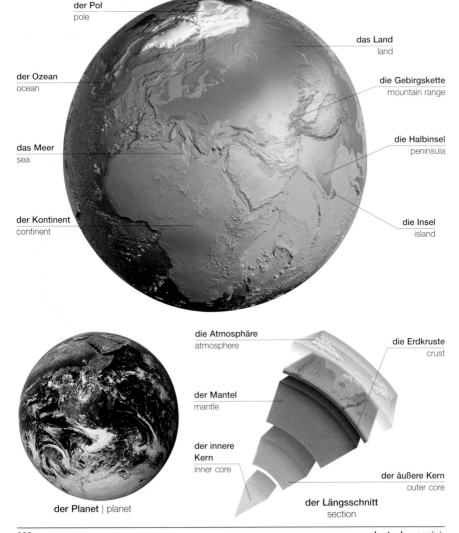

der Pol
pole

das Land
land

der Ozean
ocean

die Gebirgskette
mountain range

das Meer
sea

die Halbinsel
peninsula

der Kontinent
continent

die Insel
island

die Atmosphäre
atmosphere

die Erdkruste
crust

der Mantel
mantle

der innere Kern
inner core

der äußere Kern
outer core

der Planet | planet

der Längsschnitt
section

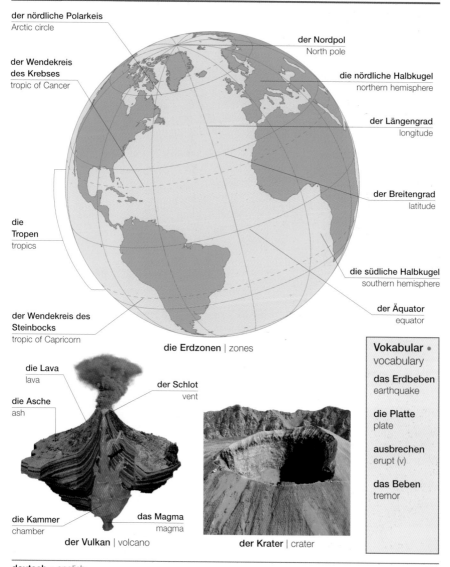

der nördliche Polarkeis
Arctic circle

der Nordpol
North pole

der Wendekreis
des Krebses
tropic of Cancer

die nördliche Halbkugel
northern hemisphere

der Längengrad
longitude

der Breitengrad
latitude

die
Tropen
tropics

die südliche Halbkugel
southern hemisphere

der Wendekreis des
Steinbocks
tropic of Capricorn

der Äquator
equator

die Erdzonen | zones

die Lava
lava

der Schlot
vent

die Asche
ash

Vokabular •
vocabulary

das Erdbeben
earthquake

die Platte
plate

ausbrechen
erupt (v)

die Kammer
chamber

das Magma
magma

das Beben
tremor

der Vulkan | volcano

der Krater | crater

die Landschaft • landscape

der Berg
mountain

der Hang
slope

das Ufer
bank

der Fluss
river

die Strom
schnellen
rapids

die Felsen
rocks

der Gletscher
glacier

das Tal | valley

der Hügel
hill

das Plateau
plateau

die Schlucht
gorge

die Höhle
cave

die Ebene | plain

die Wüste | desert

der Wald | forest

der Wald | wood

der Regenwald
rainforest

der Sumpf
swamp

die Wiese label
meadow

das Grasland
grassland

der Wasserfall
waterfall

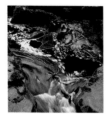
der Bach
stream

der See
lake

der Geysir
geyser

die Küste
coast

die Klippe
cliff

das Korallenriff
coral reef

die Flussmündung
estuary

das Wetter • weather

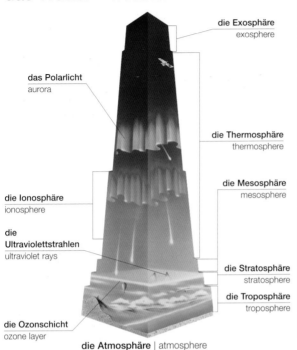

die Exosphäre
exosphere

das Polarlicht
aurora

die Thermosphäre
thermosphere

die Ionosphäre
ionosphere

die Mesosphäre
mesosphere

die
Ultraviolettstrahlen
ultraviolet rays

die Stratosphäre
stratosphere

die Troposphäre
troposphere

die Ozonschicht
ozone layer

die **Atmosphäre** | atmosphere

der **Sonnenschein**
sunshine

der **Wind**
wind

Vokabular • vocabulary

der Schneeregen sleet	**der Schauer** shower	**heiß** hot	**trocken** dry	**windig** windy	**Mir ist heiß/kalt.** I'm hot/cold.
der Hagel hail	**sonnig** sunny	**kalt** cold	**nass** wet	**der Sturm** gale	**Es regnet.** It's raining.
der Donner thunder	**bewölkt** cloudy	**warm** warm	**feucht** humid	**die Temperatur** temperature	**Es sind ... Grad.** It's ... degrees.

die Wolke
cloud

der Regen
rain

der Blitz
lightning

das Gewitter
storm

der feine Nebel
mist

der dichte Nebel
fog

der Regenbogen
rainbow

der Schnee
snow

der Raureif
frost

der Eiszapfen
icicle

das Eis
ice

der Frost
freeze

der Hurrikan
hurricane

der Tornado
tornado

der Monsun
monsoon

die Überschwemmung
flood

das Gestein • rocks

eruptiv • igneous

der Granit
granite

der Obsidian
obsidian

der Basalt
basalt

der Bimsstein
pumice

sedimentär • sedimentary

der Sandstein
sandstone

der Kalkstein
limestone

die Kreide
chalk

der Feuerstein
flint

das Konglomerat
conglomerate

die Kohle
coal

metamorph • metamorphic

der Schiefer
slate

der Glimmers
schist

der Gneis
gneiss

der Marmor
marble

die Schmucksteine • gems

der Rubin
ruby

der Aquamarin
aquamarine

der Amethyst
amethyst

der Diamant
diamond

der Jade
jade

der Jett
jet

der Smaragd
emerald

der Opal
opal

der Saphir
sapphire

der Turmalin
tourmaline

der Mondstein
moonstone

der Topas
topaz

der Granat
garnet

die Mineralien • minerals

der Quarz
quartz

der Glimmer
mica

der Schwefel
sulphur

der Hämatit
hematite

der Kalzit
calcite

der Malachit
malachite

der Türkis
turquoise

der Onyx
onyx

der Achat
agate

der Graphit
graphite

die Metalle • metals

das Gold
gold

das Silber
silver

das Platin
platinum

das Nickel
nickel

das Eisen
iron

das Kupfer
copper

das Zinn
tin

das Aluminium
aluminium

das Quecksilber
mercury

das Zink
zinc

die Tiere 1 • animals 1
die Säugetiere • mammals

die Schnurrhaare
whiskers

der Schwanz
tail

das Kaninchen
rabbit

der Hamster
hamster

die Maus
mouse

die Ratte
rat

der Igel
hedgehog

das Eichhörnchen
squirrel

die Fledermaus
bat

der Waschbär
raccoon

der Fuchs
fox

der Wolf
wolf

der Welpe
puppy

das Kätzchen
kitten

das Junge
pup

der Hund
dog

die Katze
cat

der Otter
otter

die Robbe
seal

die Flosse
flipper

das Atemloch
blowhole

der Seelöwe
sea lion

das Walross
walrus

der Wal
whale

der Delphin
dolphin

das Geweih
antler

die Mähne
mane

der Höcker
hump

der Huf
hoof

der Hirsch
deer

das Zebra
zebra

die Giraffe
giraffe

das Kamel
camel

der Rüssel
trunk

der Stoßzahn
tusk

das Horn
horn

das Nilpferd
hippopotamus

der Elefant
elephant

das Nashorn
rhinoceros

der Tiger
tiger

die Mähne
mane

der Löwe
lion

der Affe
monkey

der Gorilla
gorilla

der Koalabär
koala

der Beutel
pouch

der Pandabär
panda

die Klaue
claw

das Känguru
kangaroo

der Bär
bear

der Eisbär
polar bear

deutsch • english

die Tiere 2 • animals 2
die Vögel • birds

der Schwanz
tail

der Kanarienvogel
canary

der Spatz
sparrow

der Kolibri
hummingbird

die Schwalbe
swallow

die Krähe
crow

die Taube
pigeon

der Specht
woodpecker

der Falke
falcon

die Eule
owl

die Möwe
gull

der Adler
eagle

der Pelikan
pelican

der Flamingo
flamingo

der Storch
stork

der Kranich
crane

der Pinguin
penguin

der Strauß
ostrich

die Reptilien • reptiles

die Gans | goose

der Schwan
swan

die Schuppen
scales

der Alligator
alligator

der Pfau
peacock

der Fasan
pheasant

die Eidechse
lizard

der Leguan
iguana

der Panzer
shell

der Truthahn
turkey

die Wasserschildkröte
turtle

die Schildkröte
tortoise

die Schlange
snake

der Schnabel
bill

die Feder
feather

der
Flügel
wing

die Schnauze
snout

der Kakadu
cockatoo

die Kralle
claw

der Papagei
parrot

das Krokodil
crocodile

die Tiere 3 • animals 3

die Amphibien • amphibians

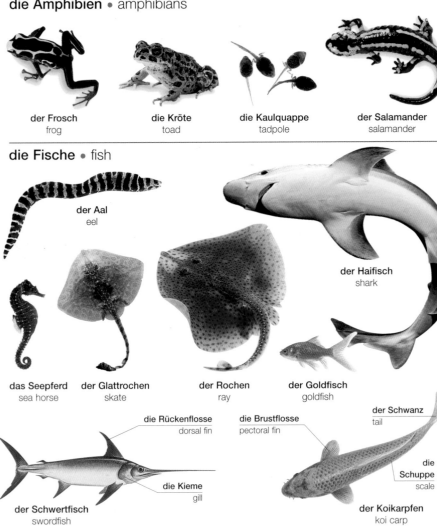

der Frosch
frog

die Kröte
toad

die Kaulquappe
tadpole

der Salamander
salamander

die Fische • fish

der Aal
eel

der Haifisch
shark

das Seepferd
sea horse

der Glattrochen
skate

der Rochen
ray

der Goldfisch
goldfish

die Rückenflosse
dorsal fin

die Brustflosse
pectoral fin

der Schwanz
tail

die Kieme
gill

die Schuppe
scale

der Schwertfisch
swordfish

der Koikarpfen
koi carp

die Wirbellosen • invertebrates

die Ameise
ant

die Termite
termite

die Biene
bee

die Wespe
wasp

der Käfer
beetle

der Kakerlak
cockroach

die Motte
moth

der Fühler
antenna
der Schmetterling
butterfly

der Kokon
cocoon

die Raupe
caterpillar

die Grille
cricket

die Heuschrecke
grasshopper

die Gottesanbeterin
praying mantis

der
Stachel
sting
der Skorpion
scorpion

**der
Tausendfüßer**
centipede

die Libelle
dragonfly

die Fliege
fly

die Stechmücke
mosquito

der Marienkäfer
ladybird

die Spinne
spider

**die
Wegschnecke**
slug

die Schnecke
snail

der Wurm
worm

der Seestern
starfish

die Muschel
mussel

der Krebs
crab

der Hummer
lobster

der Krake
octopus

der Tintenfisch
squid

die Qualle
jellyfish

die Pflanzen • plants

der Baum • tree

der Ast
branch

das Blatt
leaf

der Zweig
twig

die Rinde
bark

die Weide
willow

die Wurzel
root

der Stamm
trunk

die Eiche
oak

die Pappel
poplar

der Eukalyptus
eucalyptus

die Lärche
larch

die Buche
beech

die Birke
birch

die Kiefer
pine

die Zeder
cedar

der Ahorn
maple

die Ulme
elm

die Linde
lime

die Stechpalme
holly

die Beere
berry

die Palme
palm

die blühende Pflanze • flowering plant

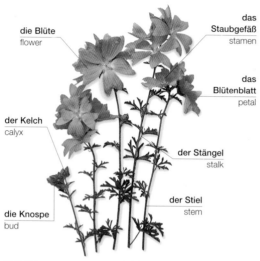

die Blüte
flower

das
Staubgefäß
stamen

das
Blütenblatt
petal

der Kelch
calyx

der Stängel
stalk

der Stiel
stem

die Knospe
bud

der Hahnenfuß
buttercup

**das
Gänseblümchen**
daisy

die Distel
thistle

der Löwenzahn
dandelion

das Heidekraut
heather

**der
Klatschmohn**
poppy

der Fingerhut
foxglove

das Geißblatt
honeysuckle

**die
Sonnenblume**
sunflower

der Klee
clover

**die
Sternhyazinthen**
bluebells

**die
Schlüsselblume**
primrose

die Lupinen
lupins

die Nessel
nettle

die Stadt • town

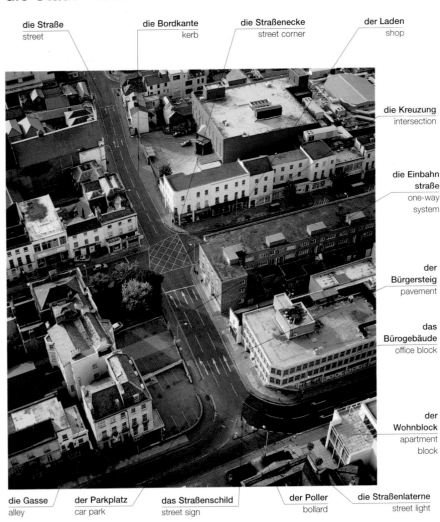

die Straße
street

die Bordkante
kerb

die Straßenecke
street corner

der Laden
shop

die Kreuzung
intersection

**die Einbahn
straße**
one-way
system

**der
Bürgersteig**
pavement

**das
Bürogebäude**
office block

**der
Wohnblock**
apartment
block

die Gasse
alley

der Parkplatz
car park

das Straßenschild
street sign

der Poller
bollard

die Straßenlaterne
street light

die Gebäude • buildings

das Rathaus
town hall

die Bibliothek
library

das Kino
cinema

das Theater
theatre

die Universität
university

der Wolkenkratzer
skyscraper

die Wohngegend • areas

das Industriegebiet
industrial estate

die Stadt
city

der Vorort
suburb

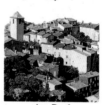
das Dorf
village

die Schule
school

Vokabular • vocabulary

die Fußgängerzone pedestrian zone	**die Seitenstraße** side street	**der Kanalschacht** manhole	**der Rinnstein** gutter	**die Kirche** church
die Allee avenue	**der Platz** square	**die Bushaltestelle** bus stop	**die Fabrik** factory	**der Kanal** drain

---

die Architektur • architecture

die Gebäude und Strukturen • buildings and structures

die
Kreuzblume
finial

die
Turmspitze
spire

der Mauerturm
turret

der Burggraben
moat

der Giebel
gable

der Wolkenkratzer
skyscraper

die Burg
castle

die Kuppel
dome

der Turm
tower

die Kirche
church

die Moschee
mosque

das Gewölbe
vault

das Gesims
cornice

der Tempel
temple

die Synagoge
synagogue

die Säule
pillar

der Staudamm
dam

die Brücke
bridge

die Kathedrale | cathedral

die Baustile • styles

gotisch
gothic

der Architrav
architrave

Renaissance
Renaissance

barock
baroque

der Bogen
arch

der Fries
frieze

der Chor
choir

Rokoko
rococo

das Giebeldreieck
pediment

der Strebepfeiler
buttress

klassizistisch
neoclassical

der Jugendstil
art nouveau

Art-déco
art deco

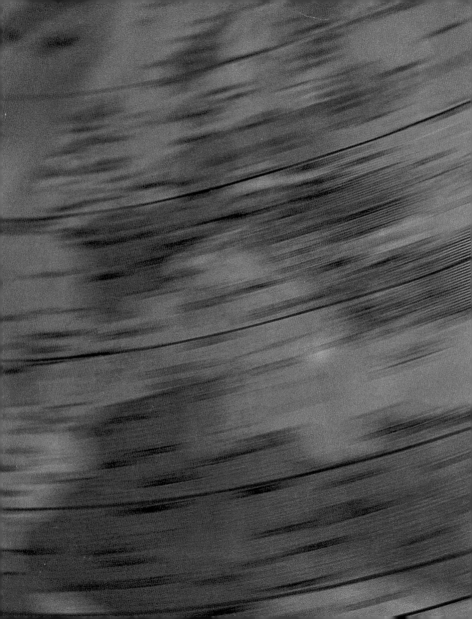

die Information
reference

die Uhrzeit • time

der Minutenzeiger
minute hand

der Stundenzeiger
hour hand

die Uhr
clock

Vokabular • vocabulary

die Stunde hour	**jetzt** now	**zwanzig Minuten** twenty minutes
die Minute minute	**später** later	**vierzig Minuten** forty minutes
die Sekunde second	**eine halbe stunde** half an hour	**eine Viertelstunde** a quarter of an hour
Wie spät ist es? What time is it?		**Es ist drei Uhr.** It's three o'clock.

fünf nach eins
five past one

zehn nach eins
ten past one

Viertel nach eins
quarter past one

zwanzig nach eins
twenty past one

der Sekundenzeiger
second hand

fünf vor halb zwei
twenty five past one

ein Uhr dreißig
one thirty

fünf nach halb zwei
twenty five to two

zwanzig vor zwei
twenty to two

Viertel vor zwei
quarter to two

zehn vor zwei
ten to two

fünf vor zwei
five to two

zwei Uhr
two o'clock

deutsch • english

die Nacht und der Tag • night and day

die Mitternacht
midnight

der Sonnenaufgang
sunrise

die Morgendämmerung
dawn

der Morgen
morning

der Sonnenuntergang
sunset

der Mittag
midday

die Abenddämmerung
dusk

der Abend
evening

der Nachmittag
afternoon

Vokabular • vocabulary

früh
early

pünktlich
on time

spät
late

Du bist früh.
You're early.

Du hast dich verspätet.
You're late.

Ich werde bald dort sein.
I'll be there soon.

Sei bitte pünktlich.
Please be on time.

Bis später.
I'll see you later.

Wann fängt es an?
What time does it start?

Wann ist es zu Ende?
What time does it finish?

Wie lange dauert es?
How long will it last?

Es ist schon spät.
It's getting late.

der Kalender • calendar

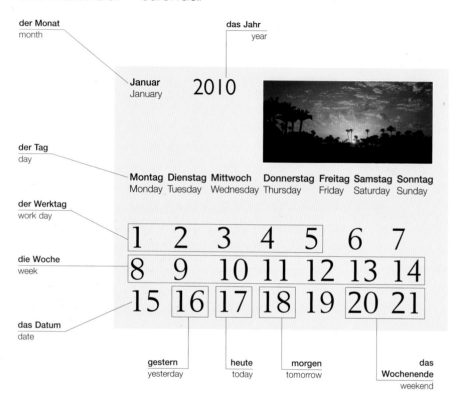

der Monat
month

das Jahr
year

Januar
January

2010

der Tag
day

der Werktag
work day

die Woche
week

das Datum
date

Montag	**Dienstag**	**Mittwoch**	**Donnerstag**	**Freitag**	**Samstag**	**Sonntag**
Monday	Tuesday	Wednesday	Thursday	Friday	Saturday	Sunday
1	2	3	4	5	6	7
8	9	10	11	12	13	14
15	16	17	18	19	20	21

gestern
yesterday

heute
today

morgen
tomorrow

das Wochenende
weekend

Vokabular • vocabulary

Januar	**März**	**Mai**	**Juli**	**September**	**November**
January	March	May	July	September	November
Februar	**April**	**Juni**	**August**	**Oktober**	**Dezember**
February	April	June	August	October	December

die Jahre • years

1900   **neunzehnhundert** • nineteen hundred

1901   **neunzehnhunderteins** • nineteen hundred and one

1910   **neunzehnhundertzehn** • nineteen ten

2000   **zweitausend** • two thousand

2001   **zweitausendeins** • two thousand and one

die Jahreszeiten • seasons

der Frühling
spring

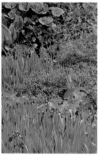

der Sommer
summer

der Herbst
autumn

der Winter
winter

Vokabular • vocabulary

das Jahrhundert century	**letzte Woche** last week	**monatlich** monthly
das Jahrzehnt decade	**nächste Woche** next week	**jährlich** annual
das Jahrtausend millennium	**vorgestern** the day before yesterday	
vierzehn Tage fortnight	**übermorgen** the day after tomorrow	**Welches Datum haben wir heute?** What's the date today?
diese Woche this week	**wöchentlich** weekly	**Heute ist der siebte Februar zweitausendzwei.** It's February seventh, two thousand and two.

die Zahlen • numbers

0 **null** • zero

1 **eins** • one

2 **zwei** • two

3 **drei** • three

4 **vier** • four

5 **fünf** • five

6 **sechs** • six

7 **sieben** • seven

8 **acht** • eight

9 **neun** • nine

10 **zehn** • ten

11 **elf** • eleven

12 **zwölf** • twelve

13 **dreizehn** • thirteen

14 **vierzehn** • fourteen

15 **fünfzehn** • fifteen

16 **sechzehn** • sixteen

17 **siebzehn** • seventeen

18 **achtzehn** • eighteen

19 **neunzehn** • nineteen

20 **zwanzig** • twenty

21 **einundzwanzig** • twenty-one

22 **zweiundzwanzig** • twenty-two

30 **dreißig** • thirty

40 **vierzig** • forty

50 **fünfzig** • fifty

60 **sechzig** • sixty

70 **siebzig** • seventy

80 **achtzig** • eighty

90 **neunzig** • ninety

100 **hundert** • one hundred

110 **hundertzehn** • one hundred and ten

200 **zweihundert** • two hundred

300 **dreihundert** • three hundred

400 **vierhundert** • four hundred

500 **fünfhundert** • five hundred

600 **sechshundert** • six hundred

700 **siebenhundert** • seven hundred

800 **achthundert** • eight hundred

900 **neunhundert** • nine hundred

1,000	**tausend** • one thousand
10,000	**zehntausend** • ten thousand
20,000	**zwanzigtausend** • twenty thousand
50,000	**fünfzigtausend** • fifty thousand
55,500	**fünfundfünfzigtausend-fünfhundert** • fifty-five thousand five hundred
100,000	**hunderttausend** • one hundred thousand
1,000,000	**eine Million** • one million
1,000,000,000	**eine Milliarde** • one billion

erster
first

zweiter
second

dritter
third

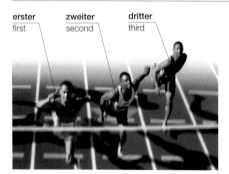

vierter • fourth

fünfter • fifth

sechster • sixth

siebter • seventh

achter • eighth

neunter • ninth

zehnter • tenth

elfter • eleventh

zwölfter • twelfth

dreizehnter • thirteenth

vierzehnter • fourteenth

fünfzehnter • fifteenth

sechzehnter
• sixteenth

siebzehnter
• seventeenth

achtzehnter
• eighteenth

neunzehnter
• nineteenth

zwanzigster
• twentieth

einundzwanzigster
• twenty-first

zweiundzwanzigster
• twenty-second

dreiundzwanzigster
• twenty-third

dreißigster
• thirtieth

vierzigster
• fortieth

fünfzigster
• fiftieth

sechzigster
• sixtieth

siebzigster
• seventieth

achtzigster
• eightieth

neunzigster
• ninetieth

hundertster
• hundredth

die Maße und Gewichte • weights and measures

die Fläche • area

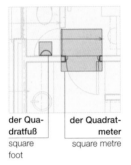

der Qua-dratfuß
square foot

der Quadrat-meter
square metre

die Entfernung • distance

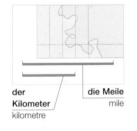

der Kilometer
kilometre

die Meile
mile

das Pfund
pound

die Unze
ounce

das Kilogramm
kilogram

das Gramm
gram

KRUPS

die Waage | scales

Vokabular • vocabulary

das Yard
yard

der Meter
metre

die Tonne
tonne

das Milligramm
milligram

messen
measure (v)

wiegen
weigh (v)

die Länge • length

der Fuß
foot

HELIX 205
Made in England

der Millimeter
millimetre

der Zentimeter
centimetre

der Zoll
inch

deutsch • english

das Fassungsvermögen • capacity

der halbe Liter
half-litre

das Pint
pint

das Volumen
volume

der Milliliter
millilitre

der Messbecher
measuring jug

das Flüssigkeitsmaß
liquid measure

Vokabular •
vocabulary

die Gallone
gallon

das Quart
quart

der Liter
litre

der Behälter • container

die Tüte
carton

das Päckchen
packet

die Flasche
bottle

der Beutel
bag

die Dose | tub

das Glas | jar

die Dose
can

die Dose | tin

die Spritze
liquid dispenser

das Stück
bar

die Tube
tube

die Rolle
roll

das Päckchen
pack

die Sprühdose
spray can

die Weltkarte • world map

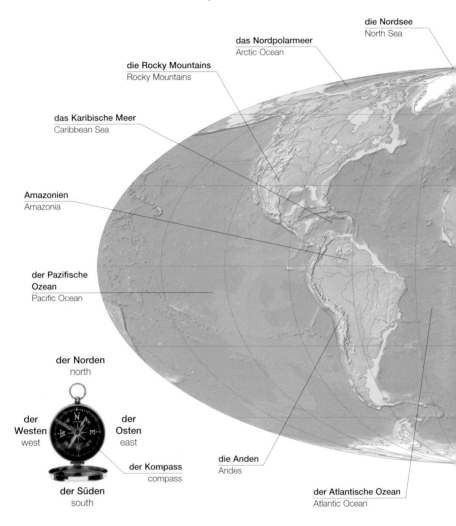

die Nordsee
North Sea

das Nordpolarmeer
Arctic Ocean

die Rocky Mountains
Rocky Mountains

das Karibische Meer
Caribbean Sea

Amazonien
Amazonia

der Pazifische
Ozean
Pacific Ocean

der Norden
north

der
Westen
west

der
Osten
east

der Kompass
compass

die Anden
Andes

der Atlantische Ozean
Atlantic Ocean

der Süden
south

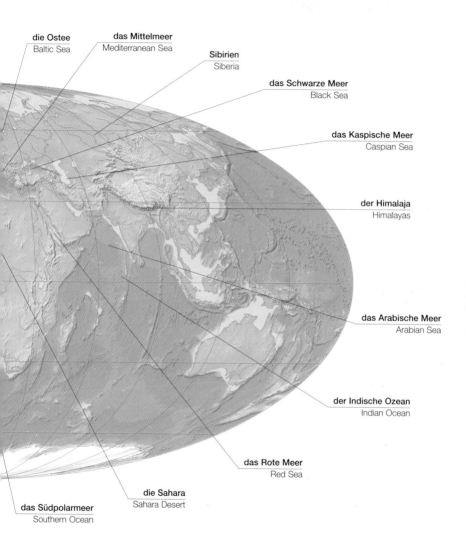

die Ostee
Baltic Sea

das Mittelmeer
Mediterranean Sea

Sibirien
Siberia

das Schwarze Meer
Black Sea

das Kaspische Meer
Caspian Sea

der Himalaja
Himalayas

das Arabische Meer
Arabian Sea

der Indische Ozean
Indian Ocean

das Rote Meer
Red Sea

die Sahara
Sahara Desert

das Südpolarmeer
Southern Ocean

Nord- und Mittelamerika • North and Central America

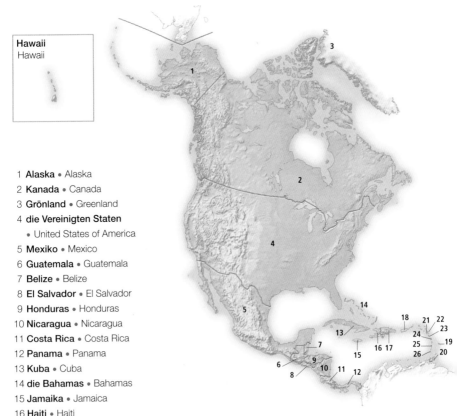

Hawaii
Hawaii

1 **Alaska** • Alaska
2 **Kanada** • Canada
3 **Grönland** • Greenland
4 **die Vereinigten Staten**
   • United States of America
5 **Mexiko** • Mexico
6 **Guatemala** • Guatemala
7 **Belize** • Belize
8 **El Salvador** • El Salvador
9 **Honduras** • Honduras
10 **Nicaragua** • Nicaragua
11 **Costa Rica** • Costa Rica
12 **Panama** • Panama
13 **Kuba** • Cuba
14 **die Bahamas** • Bahamas
15 **Jamaika** • Jamaica
16 **Haiti** • Haiti
17 **die Dominikanische Republik**
   • Dominican Republic
18 **Puerto Rico** • Puerto Rico
19 **Barbados** • Barbados
20 **Trinidad und Tobago** • Trinidad and Tobago
21 **Saint Kitts und Nevis** • St. Kitts and Nevis

22 **Antigua und Barbuda** • Antigua and Barbuda
23 **Dominica** • Dominica
24 **Saint Lucia** • St Lucia
25 **Saint Vinzent und die Grenadinen**
   • St Vincent and The Grenadines
26 **Granada** • Grenada

Südamerika • South America

1 **Venezuela** • Venezuela

2 **Kolumbien** • Colombia

3 **Ecuador** • Ecuador

4 **Peru** • Peru

5 **die Galapagosinseln**
   • Galapagos Islands

6 **Guyana** • Guyana

7 **Suriname** • Suriname

8 **Französisch-Guayana**
   • French Guiana

9 **Brasilien** • Brazil

10 **Bolivien** • Bolivia

11 **Chile** • Chile

12 **Argentinien** • Argentina

13 **Paraguay** • Paraguay

14 **Uruguay** • Uruguay

15 **die Falklandinseln**
   • Falkland Islands

Vokabular • vocabulary

der Staat	die Kolonie	die Zone
state	colony	zone
das **Land**	die **Provinz**	die **Region**
country	province	region
die **Nation**	das **Territorium**	der **Bezirk**
nation	territory	district
der **Kontinent**	das **Fürstentum**	die **Hauptstadt**
continent	principality	capital

Europa • Europe

1 **Irland** • Ireland
2 **das Vereinigte Königreich**
• United Kingdom
3 **Portugal** • Portugal
4 **Spanien** • Spain
5 **die Balearen**
• Balearic Islands
6 **Andorra** • Andorra
7 **Frankreich** • France
8 **Belgien** • Belgium
9 **die Niederlande**
• Netherlands
10 **Luxemburg** • Luxembourg
11 **Deutschland** • Germany
12 **Dänemark** • Denmark
13 **Norwegen** • Norway
14 **Schweden** • Sweden
15 **Finnland** • Finland
16 **Estland** • Estonia
17 **Lettland** • Latvia
18 **Litauen** • Lithuania
19 **Kaliningrad** • Kaliningrad
20 **Polen** • Poland
21 **die Tschechische Republik**
• Czech Republic
22 **Österreich** • Austria
23 **Liechtenstein**
• Liechtenstein
24 **die Schweiz**
• Switzerland
25 **Italien** • Italy
26 **Monaco**
• Monaco
27 **Korsika** • Corsica
28 **Sardinien** • Sardinia
29 **San Marino** • San Marino

30 **die Vatikanstadt**
• Vatican City
31 **Sizilien** • Sicily
32 **Malta** • Malta
33 **Slowenien** • Slovenia
34 **Kroatien** • Croatia
35 **Ungarn** • Hungary
36 **die Slowakei** • Slovakia
37 **die Ukraine** • Ukraine
38 **Weißrussland** • Belarus
39 **Moldawien** • Moldova

40 **Rumänien** • Romania
41 **Serbien** • Serbia
42 **Bosnien und Herzegowina**
• Bosnia and Herzogovina
43 **Albanien** • Albania
44 **Mazedonien** • Macedonia
45 **Bulgarien** • Bulgaria
46 **Griechenland** • Greece
47 **Kosovo** • Kosovo
48 **Montenegro** • Montenegro
49 **Island** • Iceland

deutsch • english

Afrika • Africa

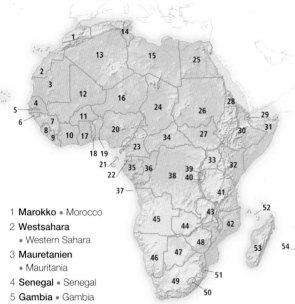

1 **Marokko** • Morocco

2 **Westsahara**
 • Western Sahara

3 **Mauretanien**
 • Mauritania

4 **Senegal** • Senegal

5 **Gambia** • Gambia

6 **Guinea-Bissau**
 • Guinea-Bissau

7 **Guinea** • Guinea

8 **Sierra Leone** • Sierra Leone

9 **Liberia** • Liberia

10 **Elfenbeinküste** • Ivory Coast

11 **Burkina Faso** • Burkina Faso

12 **Mali** • Mali

13 **Algerien** • Algeria

14 **Tunesien** • Tunisia

15 **Libyen** • Libya

16 **Niger** • Niger

17 **Ghana** • Ghana

18 **Togo** • Togo

19 **Benin** • Benin

20 **Nigeria** • Nigeria

21 **São Tomé und Príncipe**
 • São Tomé and Principe

22 **Äquatorialguinea**
 • Equatorial Guinea

23 **Kamerun** • Cameroon

24 **Tschad** • Chad

25 **Ägypten** • Egypt

26 **der Sudan** • Sudan

27 **Südsudan** • South Sudan

28 **Eritrea** • Eritrea

29 **Dschibuti** • Djibouti

30 **Äthiopien** • Ethiopia

31 **Somalia** • Somalia

32 **Kenia** • Kenya

33 **Uganda** • Uganda

34 **die Zentralafrikanische
 Republik** • Central African
 Republic

35 **Gabun** • Gabon

36 **Kongo** • Congo

37 **Kabinda** • Cabinda

38 **die Demokratische Republik
 Kongo** • Democratic Republic
 of the Congo

39 **Ruanda** • Rwanda

40 **Burundi** • Burundi

41 **Tansania** • Tanzania

42 **Mosambik** • Mozambique

43 **Malawi** • Malawi

44 **Sambia** • Zambia

45 **Angola** • Angola

46 **Namibia** • Namibia

47 **Botsuana** • Botswana

48 **Simbabwe** • Zimbabwe

49 **Südafrika** • South Africa

50 **Lesotho** • Lesotho

51 **Swasiland** • Swaziland

52 **die Komoren** • Comoros

53 **Madagaskar** • Madagascar

54 **Mauritius** • Mauritius

Asien • Asia

1 **die Türkei** • Turkey
2 **Zypern** • Cyprus
3 **die Russische Föderation**
  • Russian Federation
4 **Georgien** • Georgia
5 **Armenien** • Armenia
6 **Aserbaidschan** • Azerbaijan
7 **der Iran** • Iran
8 **der Irak** • Iraq
9 **Syrien** • Syria
10 **der Libanon** • Lebanon
11 **Israel** • Israel
12 **Jordanien** • Jordan
13 **Saudi-Arabien**
  • Saudi Arabia
14 **Kuwait** • Kuwait
15 **Bahrain** • Bahrain
16 **Katar** • Qatar
17 **Vereinigte Arabische Emirate**
  • United Arab Emirates
18 **Oman** • Oman
19 **der Jemen** • Yemen
20 **Kasachstan** • Kazakhstan
21 **Usbekistan** • Uzbekistan
22 **Turkmenistan** • Turkmenistan
23 **Afghanistan** • Afghanistan
24 **Tadschikistan** • Tajikistan
25 **Kirgisistan** • Kyrgyzstan
26 **Pakistan** • Pakistan
27 **Indien** • India
28 **die Malediven** • Maldives
29 **Sri Lanka** • Sri Lanka
30 **China** • China
31 **die Mongolei** • Mongolia
32 **Nordkorea** • North Korea
33 **Südkorea** • South Korea
34 **Japan** • Japan

35 **Nepal** • Nepal
36 **Bhutan** • Bhutan
37 **Bangladesch** • Bangladesh
38 **Birmania (Myanmar)**
  • Burma (Myanmar)
39 **Thailand** • Thailand
40 **Laos** • Laos
41 **Vietnam** • Vietnam

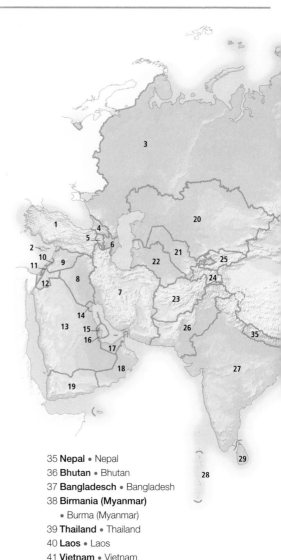

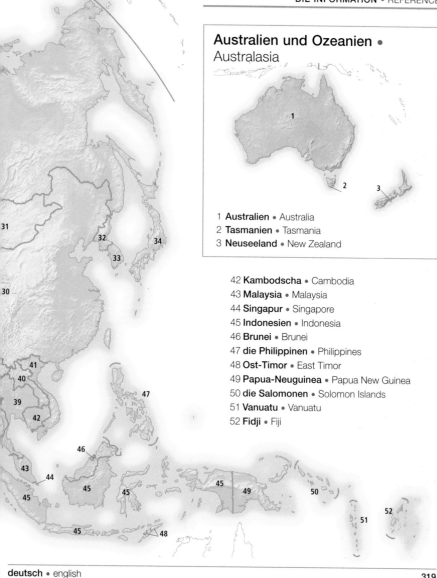

Australien und Ozeanien •
Australasia

1 **Australien** • Australia
2 **Tasmanien** • Tasmania
3 **Neuseeland** • New Zealand

42 **Kambodscha** • Cambodia
43 **Malaysia** • Malaysia
44 **Singapur** • Singapore
45 **Indonesien** • Indonesia
46 **Brunei** • Brunei
47 **die Philippinen** • Philippines
48 **Ost-Timor** • East Timor
49 **Papua-Neuguinea** • Papua New Guinea
50 **die Salomonen** • Solomon Islands
51 **Vanuatu** • Vanuatu
52 **Fidji** • Fiji

Partikeln und Antonyme • particles and antonyms

zu, nach to	**von, aus** from	**für** for	**zu** towards
über over	**unter** under	**entlang** along	**über** across
vor in front of	**hinter** behind	**mit** with	**ohne** without
auf onto	**in** into	**vor** before	**nach** after
in in	**aus** out	**bis** by	**bis** until
über above	**unter** below	**früh** early	**spät** late
innerhalb inside	**außerhalb** outside	**jetzt** now	**später** later
hinauf up	**hinunter** down	**immer** always	**nie** never
an, bei at	**jenseits** beyond	**oft** often	**selten** rarely
durch through	**um** around	**gestern** yesterday	**morgen** tomorrow
auf on top of	**neben** beside	**erste** first	**letzte** last
zwischen between	**gegenüber** opposite	**jede** every	**etwas** some
nahe near	**weit** far	**gegen** about	**genau** exactly
hier here	**dort** there	**ein wenig** a little	**viel** a lot

groß large	**klein** small	**heiß** hot	**kalt** cold
breit wide	**schmal** narrow	**offen** open	**geschlossen** closed
groß tall	**kurz** short	**voll** full	**leer** empty
hoch high	**niedrig** low	**neu** new	**alt** old
dick thick	**dünn** thin	**hell** light	**dunkel** dark
leicht light	**schwer** heavy	**leicht** easy	**schwer** difficult
hart hard	**weich** soft	**frei** free	**besetzt** occupied
nass wet	**trocken** dry	**stark** strong	**schwach** weak
gut good	**schlecht** bad	**dick** fat	**dünn** thin
schnell fast	**langsam** slow	**jung** young	**alt** old
richtig correct	**falsch** wrong	**besser** better	**schlechter** worse
sauber clean	**schmutzig** dirty	**schwarz** black	**weiß** white
schön beautiful	**hässlich** ugly	**interessant** interesting	**langweilig** boring
teuer expensive	**billig** cheap	**krank** sick	**wohl** well
leise quiet	**laut** noisy	**der Anfang** beginning	**das Ende** end

praktische Redewendungen • useful phrases

wesentliche Redewendungen
• essential phrases

Ja
Yes

Nein
No

Vielleicht
Maybe

Bitte
Please

Danke
Thank you

Bitte sehr
You're welcome

Entschuldigung
Excuse me

Es tut mir Leid
I'm sorry

Nicht
Don't

Okay
OK

In Ordnung
That's fine

Das ist richtig
That's correct

Das ist falsch
That's wrong

Begrüßungen
• greetings

Guten Tag
Hello

Auf Wiedersehen
Goodbye

Guten Morgen
Good morning

Guten Tag
Good afternoon

Guten Abend
Good evening

Gute Nacht
Good night

Wie geht es Ihnen?
How are you?

Ich heiße…
My name is…

Wie heißen Sie?
What is your name?

Wie heißt er/sie?
What is his/her name?

Darf ich… vorstellen
May I introduce…

Das ist…
This is…

Angenehm
Pleased to meet you

Bis später
See you later

Schilder • signs

Touristen-Information
Tourist information

Eingang
Entrance

Ausgang
Exit

Notausgang
Emergency exit

Drücken
Push

Lebensgefahr
Danger

Rauchen verboten
No smoking

Außer Betrieb
Out of order

Öffnungszeiten
Opening times

Eintritt frei
Free admission

Sonderangebot
Special offer

Reduziert
Reduced

Ausverkauf
Sale

Bitte anklopfen
Knock before entering

Betreten des Rasens verboten
Keep off the grass

Hilfe • help

Können Sie mir helfen?
Can you help me?

Ich verstehe nicht
I don't understand

Ich weiß nicht
I don't know

Sprechen Sie Englisch, Französisch…?
Do you speak English, French…?

Ich spreche Englisch, Spanisch…
I speak English, Spanish…

Sprechen Sie bitte langsamer
Please speak more slowly

Schreiben Sie es bitte für mich auf
Please write it down for me

Ich habe… verloren
I have lost…

Richtungsangaben
- directions

Ich habe mich verlaufen
I am lost

Wo ist der/die/das…?
Where is the…?

Wo ist der/die/das nächste…?
Where is the nearest…?

Wo sind die Toiletten?
Where are the toilets?

Wie komme ich nach…?
How do I get to…?

Nach rechts
To the right

Nach links
To the left

Geradeaus
Straight ahead

Wie weit ist…?
How far is…?

die Verkehrsschilder
- road signs

Langsam fahren
Slow down

Achtung
Caution

Keine Zufahrt
No entry

Umleitung
Diversion

Rechts fahren
Keep to the right

Autobahn
Motorway

Parkverbot
No parking

Sackgasse
No through road

Einbahnstraße
One-way street

Vorfahrt gewähren
Give way

Anlieger frei
Residents only

Baustelle
Roadworks

gefährliche Kurve
Dangerous bend

Unterkunft
- accommodation

Haben Sie Zimmer frei?
Do you have any vacancies?

Ich habe ein Zimmer reserviert
I have a reservation

Wo ist der Speisesaal?

Wann gibt es Frühstück?
What time is breakfast?

Ich bin um … Uhr wieder da
I'll be back at … o'clock

Ich reise morgen ab
I'm leaving tomorrow

Essen und Trinken
- eating and drinking

Zum Wohl!
Cheers!

Es ist köstlich/ scheußlich
It's delicious/awful

Ich trinke/rauche nicht
I don't drink/smoke

Ich esse kein Fleisch
I don't eat meat

Nichts mehr, danke
No more for me, thank you

Könnte ich noch etwas mehr haben?
May I have some more?

Wir möchten bitte zahlen
May we have the bill?

Ich hätte gerne eine Quittung
Can I have a receipt?

Nichtraucherbereich
No-smoking area

die Gusundheit
- health

Ich fühle mich nicht wohl
I don't feel well

Mir ist schlecht
I feel sick

Können Sie einen Arzt holen?
Can you get me a doctor?

Wird er/sie sich wieder erholen?
Will he/she be all right?

Es tut hier weh
It hurts here

Ich habe Fieber
I have a temperature

Ich bin im … Monat schwanger
I'm … months pregnant

Ich brauche ein Rezept für …
I need a prescription for …

Ich nehme normalerweise …
I normally take …

Ich bin allergisch gegen …
I'm allergic to …

deutsches register • German index

deutsch

A

à la carte 152
Aal m 294
Abdeckband n 83
Abdecktuch n 83
Abend m 305
Abenddämmerung f 305
Abendessen n 64
Abendkleid n 34
Abendmenü n 152
Abenteuerfilm m 255
Abfahrtslauf m 247
Abfalleimer m 61
Abfallentsorgung f 61
Abfallsortiereinheit f 61
Abfertigungsschalter m 213
Abflug m 213
Abflughalle f 213
Abfluss m 61, 72
Abflussrohr n 61
Abführmittel n 109
abheben 99
Abhebungsformular m 96
Abkühlgitter n 69
Ablage für Ausgänge f 172
Ablage für Eingänge f 172
Ablasshahn m 61
Ableger m 91
Abmessungen f 165
Absatz m 37
Abschlag m 232
abschleppen 195
Abschleppwagen m 203
Abschnitt m 96
Abschürfung f 46
Abschuss m 281
Abschussrampe f 281
Abseilen n 248
Abseits n 223
abseits der Piste 247
Absender m 98
Absperrhahn m 61
Abspielen n 269
Abteil n 209
Abteilungen f 49
Abtropfbrett n 67
Abzeichen n 189
abziehen 82
Abzug m 271
Accessoires m 36
Achat m 289
Achillessehne f 16
Achse f 205
Achselhöhle f 13
acht 308
Achteck n 164
achter 309
achthundert 308

achtzehn 308
achtzehnter 309
achtzig 308
achtzigster 309
Ackerbaubetrieb m 183
Ackerland n 182
Acrylfarbe f 274
Adamsapfel m 19
addieren 165
Adler m 292
Adresse f 98
Adzukibohnen f 131
Affe m 291
Afghanistan 318
Afrika 317
After-Sun-Lotion f 108
Ägypten 317
Ahorn m 296
Ahornsirup m 134
Aikido n 236
Airbag m 201
akademische Grad m 169
Akazie f 110
Aktenordner m 173
Aktenschrank m 172
Aktentasche f 37
Aktien f 97
Aktienpreis m 97
Aktionen f 227, 229, 233
Aktivitäten f 162, 245, 263
Aktivitäten im Freien f 262
Akupressur f 55
Akupunktur f 55
Alarmanlage f 58
Alaska 314
Albanien 316
Algerien 317
alkoholfreie Getränk n 154
alkoholfreien Getränke n 144
alkoholischen Getränke n 145
Allee f 299
Allergie f 44
Alligator m 293
Allzweckraum m 76
Alpenpflanze f 87
alpine Kombination f 247
als Fänger spielen 229
alt 321
Alternativtherapien f 54
Aluminium n 289
Amazonien 312
ambulante Patient m 48
Ameise f 295
Amethyst m 288
Amniozentese f 52
Ampère n 60
Amphibien f 294

an Bord gehen 217
an, bei 320
analog 179
Ananas f 128
Ananassaft m 149
Anästhesist m 48
Anbau m 58
anbeißen 245
anbraten 67
anbringen 82
Anden 312
Andenken n 260
andere Geschäfte n 114
andere Kunstfertigkeiten f 275
andere Schiffe n 215
andere Sportarten f 248
Andorra 316
Anfang m 321
Angebot n 174
Angebote n 106
Angeklagte n 180, 181
Angelgeräte n 245
Angelhaken m 244
Angelrute f 244
Angelschein m 245
Angelsport m 244
angemacht 159
angereicherte Mehl n 139
Angler m 244
Angola 317
angreifen 220, 223
Angriff m 220, 237
Angriffszone f 224
Anhang m 177
Anhänger m 36, 266
Anker m 214, 240
Ankerwinde f 214
Anklage f 94, 180
Ankunft f 213
anlegen 217
Anorak m 31, 33
Anprobe f 104
Anreden f 23
Anrufbeantworter m 99
Anspielkreis m 224
anstreichen 83
Antifalten- 41
Antigua und Barbuda 314
Antiquitätenladen m 114
Antiseptikum n 47
Antwort f 163
antworten 163
Anwaltsbüro n 180
Anwendung f 176
Anzeigetafel f 104, 225
Aperitif m 153
Apfel m 126
Apfelsaft m 149
Apfelstecher m 68
Apfelwein m 145

Apfelweinessig m 135
Apotheke f 108
Apotheker m 108
Apothekerin f 189
App f 99
Apparat m 99
applaudieren 255
Aprikose f 126
April m 306
Aquamarin m 288
Aquarellfarbe f 274
Äquator m 283
Äquatorialguinea 317
Arabische Meer n 313
Arbeit f 172
Arbeitgeberin f 24
Arbeitnehmer m 24
Arbeitsessen n 175
Arbeitsfläche f 66
Arbeitszimmer n 63
Architekt m 190
architektonische Garten m 84
Architektur f 300
Architrav m 301
Argentinien 315
Arithmetik f 165
Arm m 13
Armaturen f 201
Armaturenbrett n 201
Armband n 36
Ärmel m 34
ärmellos 34
Armenien 318
Armlehne f 210
Armstütze f 200
Aromatherapie f 55
aromatisch 130
aromatische Öl n 134
Art-déco- 301
Arterie f 19
Artischocke f 124
Arzt m 45, 189
Aschbecher m 150
Asche f 283
Aserbaidschan 318
Asien 318
Asphalt m 187
Ass n 230, 273
Assistentin f 24
assistierte Entbindung f 53
Ast m 296
Asteroid m 280
Asthma n 44
Astigmatismus m 51
Astronaut m 281
Astronomie f 281
Atemloch n 290
ätherischen Öle m 55
Äthiopien 317
Atlantische Ozean m 312

Atmosphäre f 282, 286
Atmung f 47
Atmungssystem n 19
Atrium n 104
Aubergine f 125
auf 320
auf der Stelle joggen 251
aufgehen 139
aufgenommen 48
aufgeregt 25
Aufhängung f 203, 205
aufkreuzen 241
Auflaufform f 69
Auflaufförmchen n 69
auflockern 91
Auflösungszeichen n 256
Aufnahme f 269
Aufsatz m 163, 233
Aufschlag m 231
aufschlagen 231
Aufschlaglinie f 230
aufstehen 71
auftauen 67
auftrennen 277
aufwachen 71
aufwärmen 154
Auge n 14, 51
Augenbraue f 14, 51
Augenbrauenstift m 40
Augenoptiker m 51
August m 306
aus 225, 226, 228, 320
aus Freilandhaltung 118
ausblasen 141
ausbrechen 283
Ausfahrt f 194
Ausfall m 251
Ausgang m 210
Ausgehen n 75
Auskunft f 99, 168
Auskunft f 99
ausländische Währung f 97
Auslandsflug m 212
Auslass m 61
auslaufen 217
Ausleger m 95
Auslegerkorb m 95
Ausleihe f 168
Ausleihe m 168
ausleihen 168
Auslöser m 270
Auspuff m 203
Auspuffrohr n 204
Auspufftopf m 203
ausrollen 67
Ausrüstung f 165, 233, 238
Aussage f 180
Außenbordmotor m 215
Außenfeld n 229
Außentür f 59

Äussere n 198
äussere Erscheinung f 30
äussere Kern m 282
außerhalb 320
ausspülen 38
Ausstellung f 261
Ausstellungsstück n 261
ausstrecken 251
Auster f 121
Australien 319
Auswechslung f 223
auswerfen 245
Auszeit f 220
Auto n 198, 200
Autobahn f 194
Automatiktür f 196
Autostereoanlage f 201
Autotür f 198
Autounfall m 203
Autoverleih m 213
Autowaschanlage f 198
Avocado f 128
Ayurveda m 55

B

Baby n 23, 30
Babybecher m 75
Babyflasche f 75
Babyhandschuhe m 30
Babyprodukte n 107
Babyschuhe m 30
Babysprechanlage f 75
Babytasche f 75
Babytrageschlinge f 75
Babywanne f 74
Bach m 285
Backe f 14
backen 67, 138
Backenzahn m 50
Bäcker m 139
Bäckerei f 114, 138
Backgammon n 272
Backofen m 66
Backpflaume f 129
Backpinsel m 69
Backwaren f 107
Badeanzug m 238, 265
Badehose f 238
Badekappe f 238
Bademantel m 32, 73
Badematte f 72
Bademeister m 239
baden 72
Badetuch n 73
Badewanne f 72
Badezimmer n 72
Badminton n 231
Bagger m 187
baggern 227
Baguette n 138
Bahamas 314
Bahn f 234, 238
Bahnhof m 208
Bahnhofshalle f 209
Bahnnetz n 209
Bahnsteig m 208

Bahrain 218
Baiser n 140
Balearen 316
Balken m 186
Balkon m 59, 254
Ball m 75
Ballen m 15, 184
Ballett n 255
Ballettröckchen n 191
Balljunge m 231
Ballwechsel m 230
Bambus m 86, 122
Banane f 128
Band n 27, 39, 47, 141
Bandage f 47
Bangladesch 318
Bank f 96, 250, 262
Bankgebühr f 96
Banküberweisung f 96
Bar f 150, 152
Bär m 291
Bar Mizwa f 26
Barbados 314
Barhocker m 150
Barkeeper m 150, 191
barock 301
Barren m 235
Basalt m 288
Baseball m 228
Basilikum n 133
Basketball m 226
Basketballspieler m 226
Bassgitarre 258
Bassklarinette f 257
Bassschlüssel m 256
Batterie f 78, 167, 202,
Batterien f 260
Bau m 186
Bauarbeiter m 186
Bauch m 12
Bauchmuskeln m 16
Bauchspeicheldrüse f 18
bauen 186
Bauer m 182, 189, 272
Bauerngarten m 84
Bauernhaus n 182
Bauernhof m 182, 184
Bauhandwerker m 188
Bauholz n 187
Baum m 86, 240, 296
Baumwolle f 184, 277
Baustelle f 186
Baustile m 301
Beat m 259
Beben n 283
Becher m 65
Becherglas n 167
Becken n 17, 61, 257
Bedienung 152
Beere f 296
Befestigungen f 89
Befruchtung f 20
Begräbnis n 26
Behälter m 311
Behandlungslampe f 50
Behandlungsschürze f 50

Behindertenparkplatz m 195
Beil n 95
Beilage f 153
Beilagenteller m 65
Bein n 12, 64
Beinstütz m 251
Beize f 79
Bekannte m 24
belegt 321
belegte Brot n 155
Beleuchtung f 178
Belgien 316
Belichtung f 271
Belichtungsmesser m 270
Belize 314
Benin 317
Benzin n 199
Benzinpreis m 199
Benzintank m 203
Beraterin f 55
Berg m 284
Berg-und-Talbahn f 262
Bericht m 174
Berufe m 188, 190
Berufung f 181
Beruhigungsmittel n 109
berühmte Ruine f 261
Besatzungsluke m 281
beschneiden 91
Beschwerde f 94
Besen m 77
besetzt 99, 321
Besetzung f 254
Besichtigungstour m 260
besorgt 25
Besteck n 64
bestellen 153
Bestuhlung f 254
bestürzt 25
Besuchszeiten f 48
Betonblock m 187
Betonmischmaschine f 186
Betrag m 96
Betrieb für Milchproduktion m 183
Bett n 70
Bettcouch f 63
Bettdecke f 71
Bettlaken n 71
Bettwäsche f 71
Bettzeug n 74
beugen 251
Beutel m 291, 311
bewässern 183
Beweismittel n 181
bewölkt 286
bewusstlos 47
bezahlen 153
Beziehungen f 24
Bezirk m 315
Bhutan 318
Biathlon n 247
Bibliothek f 168, 299
Bibliothekar m 190

Bibliothekarin f 168
Bidet n 72
Biene f 295
Bier n 145, 151
Bifokal- 51
Bikini m 264
Bilderrahmen m 62
Bildhauer m 191
Bildhauerei f 275
Bildschirm m 97, 172, 176, 269
Bildsucher m 271
Bimsstein m 73, 288
Binse f 86
Bio-Abfall m 61
biodynamisch 91, 122
Biologie f 162
biologisch kontrolliert 118
Birke f 296
Birma 318
Birne f 60, 127
bis 320
Biskuittörtchen n 140
Biss m 46
bitter 124
bittere Schokolade f 113
Bizeps m 16
Bizepsübung f 251
Blase f 46
Blatt n 78, 122, 296
Blätter n 110
Blätterteig m 140
blau 274
Blauschimmelkäse m 136
Blazer m 33
Blechblasinstrumente n 256
bleifrei 199
Bleigürtel m 239
Bleistift m 163, 275
Blendenregler m 270
Blinddarm m 18
Blinker m 198, 204
Blitz m 270, 287
Block m 237
blocken 227
blond 39
Blues m 259
blühende Pflanze f 297
Blumen f 110
Blumenampel f 84
Blumenarrangements n 111
Blumenbeet n 85, 90
Blumengeschäft n 110
Blumengirlande f 111
Blumenkohl m 124
Blumentopf m 89
Blumenvase f 111
Blutdruck m 44
Blutdruckmesser m 45
Blüte f 297
Blütenblatt n 297
Blutung f 46
Blutuntersuchung f 48

Blutwurst f 157
Bob m 247
Bockshornklee m 132
Boden m 85
Bodenakrobatik f 235
Bodendecker f 87
Bodenturnen n 235
Bogen m 85, 164, 249, 300
Bogenschießen n 249
Bohnen f 131, 144
bohren 79
Bohrer m 50, 78, 80
Bohrer mit Batteriebetrieb m 78
Bohrfutter m 78
Bohrwinde f 78
Boiler m 61
Boje f 217
Bolivien 315
Bombenflugzeug n 211
Bonbons m 113
Bongos m 257
Booster m 281
Bordkante f 298
Bordkarte f 213
Börse f 97
Börsenmakler m 97
Bosnien und Herzegowina 316
Botsuana 317
Boutique f 115
Bowling n 249
Bowlingkugel f 249
Box f 268
Boxen n 236
Boxershorts 33
Boxgymnastik f 251
Boxhandschuhe m 237
Boxring m 237
Brand m 95
Brandteig m 140
Brandung f 241
Brandungsangeln m 245
Brandwunde f 46
Brasilien 315
Braten m 158
braten 67
Bratenblech n 69
bratfertige Huhn n 119
Bratfisch mit Pommes frites m 155
Bratpfanne f 69
Bratsche f 256
Brauenbürstchen n 40
braun 274
braunen Linsen f 131
Brause f 89
breit 321
Breite f 165
Breitengrad m 283
Bremsbacke f 207
Bremse f 200, 204bremsen 207
Bremsflüssigkeitsbehälter m 202
Bremshebel m 207
Bremslicht n 204

Bremspedal n 205
Brenner m 67
Brettspiele n 272
Bridge n 273
Brie m 142
Brief m 98
Brieffreund m 24
Briefkasten m 58, 99
Briefmarke f 98
Briefmarken f 112
Briefmarkensammeln n 273
Brieftasche f 37
Briefträger m 98, 190
Briefumschlag m 173
Brille f 51
Brillengestell n 51
Brioche f 157
Brokkoli m 123
Brombeere f 127
Bronze f 235
Brosche f 36
Broschüre f 175
Broschüren n 96
Brot n 138, 157
Brot backen 138
Brötchen n 139, 143, 155
Brotfrucht f 124
Brotmesser n 68
Brotschneider m 139
browsen 177
Browser m 177
Bruch m 165
Brücke f 300
Bruder m 22
Brühe f 158
Brunei 319
brünett 39
Brunnenkresse f 123
Brust f 12, 119
Brustbein n 17
Brustflosse f 294
Brustkorb m 17
Brustmuskel m 16
Brustpumpe f 53
Brustschwimmen n 239
Brustübung f 251
Brustwarze f 12
Brustwirbel m 17
Brutkasten m 53
Bube m 273
Bubikopf m 39
Buch n 168
Buche f 296
Bücherregal n 63, 168
Buchhaltung f 175
Buchladen m 115
buchstabieren 162
Buffet n 152
Bug m 210, 215, 240
Bügelbrett n 76
Bügeleisen n 76
bügeln 76
Bugfahrwerk n 210
Buggy m 232
Bühne f 254, 258
Bühnenbild n 254

Bukett n 35, 111
Bulgarien 316
Bullauge n 214
Bull's eye n 273
Bund m 258
Bungalow m 58
Bungeejumping n 248
Bunker m 232
Bunsenbrenner m 166
bunte Mischung f 113
Buntstift m 163
Burg f 300
Bürgersteig m 298
Burggraben m 300
Burkina Faso 317
Büro n 24, 172, 174
Büroausstattung f 172
Bürobedarf m 173
Bürogebäude n 298
Büroklammer f 173
bürsten 38, 50
Burundi 317
Bus m 196
Busbahnhof m 197
Busfahrer m 190
Bushaltestelle f 197, 299
Businessclass f 211
Büstenhalter m 35
Bustier n 35
Bustypen m 196
Butter f 137, 156
Butterfly m 239
Buttermilch f 137
Butternusskürbis m 125
Bytes n 176

C

Caddie m 233
Café n 148, 262
Cafetière f 65
Camcorder m 260, 269
Camembert m 142
Campari m 145
Camping n 266
Campingplatz m 266
Campingplatzverwaltung f 266
Campus m 168
Capoeira n 237
Cappuccino m 148
Cashewnuss f 129
Cashewnüsse f 151
CD-Platte f 269
CD-Spieler m 268
Cello n 256
Champagner m 145
Chassis n 203
Check-up m 50
Cheddar m 142
Cheerleader m 220
Chef m 24
Chemie f 162
Chickenburger m 155
Chicorée m 122
Chile 315
Chili m 132
China 318
Chinakohl m 123

chippen 233
Chips m 113
Chiropraktik f 54
Chirurg m 48
Chirurgie f 48
Chor n 301
Chorizo f 143
Chutney n 134
Cockpit n 210
Cocktail m 151
Cocktailrührer m 150
Cocktailshaker m 150
Cola f 144
Collage f 275
Cornicheft n 112
Computer m 172, 176
Container m 216
Containerhafen m 216
Containerschiff n 215
Costa Rica 314
Couchtisch m 62
Countrymusic f 259
Cousin m 22
Creme f 109
Crêpes f 155
Crew f 241
Croissant n 156
Curling n 247
Curry n 158
Currypulver n 132

D

Dach n 58, 203
Dachboden m 58
Dachgarten m 84
Dachgepäckträger m 198
Dachrinne f 58
Dachsparren m 186
Dachvorsprung m 58
Dachziegel m 58, 187
Dame f 272, 273
Damenbinde f 108
Damenkleidung f 34
Damenoberbekleidung f 105
Damensattel m 242
Damenschneiderin f 191
Damenwäsche f 105
Damespiel n 272
Dammschnitt m 52
dämpfen 67
Dampflokomotive f 208
Dänemark 316
Darlehen n 96
Darts n 273
Dartscheibe f 273
das Bett machen 71
das Fruchtwasser geht ab 52
das Radio einstellen 269
Datei f 177
Dattel f 129
Datum n 306
Daumen m 15
Deck n 214
Deckanstrich m 83

Decke f 62, 71, 74
Deckel m 61, 66, 69
decken 227
Degen m 236
Dekoration f 141
Delphin m 290
Deltamuskel m 16
Demokratische Republik Kongo 317
den Anker werfen 217
den Ball abgeben 220, 223
den Fernseher abschalten 269
den Fernseher einschalten 269
den Kanal wechseln 269
den Tisch decken 64
den Vorsitz führen 174
den Wecker stellen 71
Deo n 73
Deos m 108
Dermatologie f 49
Designer m 191
Desinfektionsmittel n 51
Desinfektionstuch n 47
Desktop m 177
Dessertwagen m 152
Deutschland 316
Dezember m 306
Diagonale f 164
Diamant m 288
Diaphragma n 21
dichte Nebel m 287
Dichtung f 61
Dichtungsring m 80
dick 321
Dickdarm m 18
dicke Bohne f 122
die Geburt einleiten 53
Diele f 59
Dienstag m 306
Diesel m 199
Diesellokomotive f 208
digital 179, 269
Digitale Box f 269
Digitalkamera f 270
Digitalprojecktor m 163
Digitalradio n 268
Dill m 133
Dioptrie f 51
Diplom n 169
Dirigent m 256
Diskjockey m 179
Diskuswerfen n 234
diskutieren 163
Dissertation f 169
Distel f 297
Disziplinen f 247
dividieren 165
Diwali n 27
Dock n 214, 216
Dokumentarfilm m 178
Dominica 314
Dominikanische Republik 314
Domino n 273
Donner m 286

Donnerstag m 306
Doppel n 230
Doppel(haus) 58
Doppelbett n 71
Doppeldecker m 196, 211
doppelt 151
Doppelzimmer n 100
Dorf n 299
Dörrobst n 156
Dose f 145, 311
Dosengetränk n 154
Dosenöffner m 68
Dosierung f 109
Dozent m 169
Drachen m 248
Drachenfliegen n 248
Draht m 79
Drahtnetz n 167
Drahtschneider m 80
drechseln 79
Drehscheibe f 275
Drehstuhl m 172
Drehzahlmesser m 201
drei 308
Dreieck n 164
Dreifuß m 166
dreihundert 308
Dreipunktlinie f 226
dreißig 308
dreißigster 309
dreistöckige Haus n 58
dreitürig 200
dreiundzwanzigster 309
dreizehn 308
dreizehnter 309
Dress m 222
Dressurreiten n 243
dribbeln 223
dritter 309
driven 233
Drucken n 275
drucken 172
Drucker m 172, 176
Druckfarbe f 275
Druckknopf m 30
Druckluftflasche f 239
Drüse f 19
Dschibuti 317
Duffelcoat m 31
Duftsträußchen n 111
düngen 91
Dünger m 91
dunkel 41, 321
Dunkelkammer f 271
dünn 321
Dünndarm m 18
Dunstabzug m 66
durch 320
Durchfall m 44, 109
Durchmesser m 164
Durchschwung m 233
Dusche f 72
Duschen f 266
duschen 72
Duschgel n 73
Duschkopf m 72
Duschtür f 72

deutsch

Duschvorhang m 72
Düse f 89
Duty-free-Shop m 213
DVD-Platte f 269
DVD-Spieler m 268
Dynamo m 207

E

Eau de Toilette n 41
Ebene f 285
EC-Karte f 96
Eckball m 223
Eckfahne f 223
Eckzahn m 50
Eclair n 140
Economyclass f 211
Ecuador 315
Edamer m 142
Edelstein m 36
Ehefrau f 22
Ehemann m 22
Ei n 20
Eiche f 296
Eichelkürbis m 125
Eichhörnchen m 290
Eidechse f 293
Eier n 137
Eierbecher m 65, 137
Eierschale f 137
Eierstock m 20
Eigelb n 137, 157
Eileiter m 20
Eimer m 77, 82, 265
ein Baby bekommen 26
ein Feuer machen 266
ein Rad wechseln 203
ein Tor schießen 223
ein Zelt aufschlagen 266
Einbahn- 194
Einbahnstraße f 298
Einbauschrank m 71
Einbruchdiebstahl m 94
einchecken 212
eine halbe Stunde 304
eine Stelle bekommen 26
eine Viertelstunde 304
einen Dunk spielen m 227
einen Flug buchen 212
einen Rekord brechen 234
einfach 151
einfädeln 277
einfrieren 67
Eingang m 59
Eingangssperre f 209
eingelegt 159
eingemachte Obst n 134
einholen 245
einjährig 86
Einkauf m 104
Einkaufskorb m 106
Einkaufstasche f 106
Einkaufswagen m 106
Einkaufszentrum m 104
Einlagen f 53
einlochen 233

einloggen 177
einlösen 97
Einmachglas n 135
eins 308
Einsatzpapier n 83
Einschienenbahn f 208
einschlafen 71
Einschreiben n 98
Einstand m 230
einstellen 179
Einstellknopf m 167
Einstellung f 203, 271
eintausend 309
Eintopf m 158
eintopfen 91
Eintrittsgeld n 260
einundzwanzig 308
einundzwanzigster 309
Einwegkamera f 270
Einwegrasierer m 73
einweichen 130
Einwickelpapier n 111
Einwurf m 223, 226
einzahlen 96
Einzahlungsscheine m 96
Einzel n 230
Einzel(haus) 58
Einzelbett n 71
Einzelzimmer n 100
Einzugsauftrag m 96
Eis n 120, 137, 149, 287
Eis und Zitrone 151
Eisbär m 291
Eisen n 109, 233, 289
Eisenwarenhandlung f 114
Eisfach n 67
Eisfläche f 224
Eishockey n 224
Eishockeyspieler m 224
Eiskaffee m 148
Eisklettern n 247
Eiskübel m 150
Eiskunstlauf m 247
Eislaufen n 247
Eisprung m 20, 52
Eisschnelllauf m 247
Eistee m 149
Eiswürfel m 151
Eiszange f 150
Eiszapfen m 287
Eiweiß n 137
Ekzem n 44
El Salvador 314
Elefant m 291
Elektriker m 188
elektrische
  Blutdruckmessgerät n 45
elektrische Gitarre f 258
elektrische Schlag m 46
Elektrizität f 60
Elektroartikel m 105, 107
Elektroauto m 199
Elektrobohrer m 78
Elektrokessel m 66
Elektrolokomotive f 208
Elektronenblitz m 270

Elektrorasierer m 73
elf 308
Elfenbeinküste 317
Elfmeter m 222
elfter 309
Ellbogen m 13
Elle f 17
Eltern 23
E-Mail f 98, 177
E-Mail-Adresse f 177
E-Mail-Konto n 177
Embryo m 52
emigrieren 26
Empfang m 100
empfangen 20
Empfängnis f 52
Empfängnisverhütung f 21, 52
Empfangsdame f 100, 190
Empfangshalle f 100
Empfehlungszettel m 173
empfindlich 41
Emulsionsfarbe f 83
Ende n 321
Endivie f 123
Endlinie f 226
endokrine System n 19
Endokrinologie f 49
Endzone f 220
Energiesparbirne f 60
englische Frühstück n 157
englische Kuchen m 140
englische Senf m 135
Englischhorn n 257
Enkel m 22
Enkelin f 22
Enkelkinder n 23
Entbindung f 52
Entbindungsstation f 48, 49
Ente f 119, 185
Entenei n 137
Entenküken n 185
Entfernung f 310
entgrätet 121
Enthaarung f 41
enthäutet 121
Entisolierzange f 81
entlang 320
entlassen 48
entschuppt 121
Entspannung f 55
Entwässerung f 91
entwickeln 271
Entzündungshemmer m 109
Epilepsie f 44
Erbsen f 131
Erdbeben n 283
Erdbeere f 127
Erdbeermilchshake m 149
Erde f 85, 280, 282
Erdgeschoss n 104
Erdkruste f 282

Erdkunde f 162
Erdnuss f 129
Erdnussbutter f 135
Erdnüsse f 151
Erdnussöl n 135
Erdung f 60
Erdzonen f 283
Ereignisse des Lebens n 26
Erfrischungstuch n 75
Ergänzung f 55
Ergebnis n 49
erhalten 177
Eritrea 317
Erkältung f 44
Erkennungsetikett n 53
Ermittlung f 94
ernten 91, 183
Ersatzrad n 203
Ersatzspieler m 223
erschrocken 25
erste Etage f 104
erste Hilfe f 47
Erste-Hilfe-Kasten m 47
erste Rang m 254
erster 309
ersticken 47
ertrinken 239
eruptiv 288
Erwachsene m 23
Erweiterung f 52
Esel m 185
Espresso m 148
Essen n 64, 75, 149
essen 64
Essig m 135, 142
Esskastanie f 129
Essteller m 65
Esszimmer n 64
Estland 316
Estragon m 133
externe Festplatte f 176
Extraktion f 50
Eyeliner m 40

F

Fabrik f 299
Fach n 100
Facharzt m 49
Fachbereich m 169
Fächerordner m 173
Fachhochschulen f 169
Fadenleiter m 276
Fagott n 257
Fahne f 221
fahrbare Liege f 48
Fähre f 215, 216
fahren 195
Fahrer m 196
Fahrerkabine f 95
Fahrersitz m 196
Fahrkarte f 209
Fahrkartenschalter m 209

Elektrorasierer m 73
Erdkunde f 162
Fahrplan m 197, 209, 261
Fahrpreis m 197, 209
Fahrrad n 206
Fahrradhelm m 206
Fahrradkette f 206
Fahrradlampe f 207
Fahrradschloss n 207
Fahrradständer m 207
Fahrradweg m 206
Fahrschein m 197
Fahrstuhl m 59, 100, 104
Fährterminal m 216
Fairway n 232
Falke m 292
Falklandinseln 315
Fallen n 237
Fallschirm m 248
Fallschirmspringen n 248
Faltbett n 266
Falte f 15
Familie f 22
fangen 220, 225, 227, 229, 245
Fänger m 229
Fans m 258
Farbe f 83, 273
Farben f 274
Farbton m 41
Farbtopf m 83
Farn m 86
Fasan m 119, 293
Faser f 127
Fassungsvermögen n 311
faul 127
Faust f 15, 237
Fax n 98, 172
Faxgerät n 172
Februar m 306
Fechten n 249
Feder f 163, 293
Federball m 231
Federhalter m 172
Federmäppchen n 163
Federwaage f 166
fegen 77
Fehler m 230
Fehlgeburt f 52
Feier f 140
Feige f 129
Feijoa f 128
Feile f 81
feine Nebel m 287
Feinkost f 107, 142
Feld n 182, 234, 272
Feldauslinie f 221
Feldfrucht f 183
Felge f 206
Felgenbremse f 206
Felsen m 284
Fenchel m 122, 133
Fenchelsamen m 133
Feng Shui n 55
Fenster n 58, 177, 186, 197, 210
Fensterladen m 58

deutsch

Ferkel n 185
Fernbedienung f 269
Fernglas n 281
fernsehen 269
Fernseher m 268
Fernsehserie f 178, 179
Fernsehstudio n 178
Fernsehtelefon n 99
Ferse f 13, 15
Fertiggerichte n 107
Fertigkeiten f 79
Fesseln f 237
fest 124
Feste n 27
feste Honig m 134
festlichen Kuchen m 141
festmachen 217
Festnahme f 94
Feststation f 99
Fett n 119
fettarme Sahne f 137
fettfrei 137
fettig 39, 41
Fettpflanze f 87
Fetus m 52
feucht 286
Feuchtigkeitscreme f 41
Feueranzünder m 266
feuerfest 69
Feuerlöscher m 95
Feuermelder m 95
Feuerstein m 288
Feuertreppe f 95
Feuerwache f 95
Feuerwehr f 95
Feuerwehrleute 95
Feuerwehrmann m 189
Feuerzeug n 112
Fidschi 319
Fieber n 44
Figur f 260
Filet n 119, 121
filetiert 121
Filialleiter m 96
Film m 260, 271
Filmfach n 270
Filmspule f 271
Filter m 270
Filterkaffee m 148
Filterpapier n 167
Finanzberaterin f 97
Fingerabdruck m 94
Fingerhut m 276, 297
Fingernagel m 15
Finnland 316
Finsternis f 280
Firma f 175
Fisch m 107, 120
Fische m 294
Fischer m 189
Fischerboot n 217
Fischereihafen m 217
Fischfangarten f 245
Fischgeschäft n 114,
  120
Fischhändlerin f 188
Fischkorb m 245
Fischzucht f 183

Fitness f 250
Fitnesscenter n 250
Fitnessgerät n 250
Fitnessraum m 101
Flachbildfernseher m
  269
Fläche f 165, 310
flache Ende n 239
Flachholzbohrer m 80
Flachrennen n 243
Flachs m 184
Flachzange f 80
Fladenbrot n 139
Flagge f 232
Flamingo m 292
Flasche f 61, 135, 311
Flaschenöffner m 68,
  150
Flaschenwasser n 144
Flauschdecke f 74
Fledermaus f 290
Fleisch n 119, 124
Fleisch und das Geflügel n
  106
Fleischerhaken m 118
Fleischklopfer m 68
Fleischklöße m 158
Fleischsorten f 119
Flicken m 207
Fliege f 36, 244, 295
fliegen 211
Fliegenangeln n 245
Fließhecklimousine f 199
Flipchart n 174
Florentiner m 141
Florett n 249
Floristin f 188
Flosse f 290
Flöte f 139
Flugbegleiterin f 190,
  210
Flügel m 60, 119, 293
Fluggastbrücke f 212
Flughafen m 212
Fluginformationsanzeige f
  213
Flugnummer f 213
Flugticket n 213
Flugverbindung f 212
Flugzeug n 210
Flugzeugträger m 215
Fluss m 284
flüssige Honig m 134
Flüssigkeit f 77
Flüssigkeitsmaß n 311
Flussmündung f 285
Fock f 240
Fohlen n 185
Föhn m 38
föhnen 38
Folk m 259
Follikel m 20
Football m 220
Footballspieler m 220
Forelle f 120
formell 34
Formen f 164
Formschnitt m 87

Forschung f 169
Fortpflanzung f 20
Fortpflanzungsorgane n
  20
Fortpflanzungssystem n
  19
Foto n 271
Fotoalbum n 271
Fotoapparattypen m 270
Fotofinish n 234
Fotogeschäft n 115
Fotograf m 191
Fotografie f 270
fotografieren 271
fotokopieren 272
Fotorahmen m 271
Foul n 222, 226
Foullinie f 229
Foyer n 255
Fracht f 216
Frachtraum m 215
Frachtschiff n 215
Frage f 163
fragen 163
Fraktur f 46
Frankreich 316
französische Senf m 135
französischen Bohnen f
  131
Französisch-Guyana 315
Frau f 12, 23
Fräulein n 23
Freesie f 110
frei 321
freigesprochen 181
Freistoß m 222
Freitag m 306
Freiwurflinie f 226
Freizeit f 254, 258, 264
Freizeitkleidung f 33
Fremdenführerin f 260
Frequenz f 179
Freund m 24
Freundin f 24
Fries m 301
frisch 121, 127, 130
frische Fleisch n 142
Frischkäse m 136
Friseur m 188
Friseurin f 38
Frisierartikel m 38
Frisiersalon m 115
Frisiertisch m 71
Frisierumhang m 38
Frisuren f 39
frittiert 159
Frosch m 294
Frost n 287
Frostschutzmittel n 199,
  203
Früchtejoghurt m 157
Fruchtfleisch n 127, 129
Fruchtgummi m 113
Fruchtmark n 127
Fruchtwasser n 52
früh 305
Frühkohl m 123
Frühling m 307

Frühlingszwiebel f 125
Frühstück n 64, 156
Frühstücksbuffet n 156
Frühstücksspeck m 157
Frühstückstablett n 101
Frühstückstisch m 156
Fuchs m 290
Fuchsschwanz m 80
Fugenkitt m 83
Fühler m 295
Führerstand m 208
Führung f 260
füllen 76
Füller m 163
Füllung f 140, 155
fünf 308
Fünfeck n 164
fünfhundert 308
fünfter 309
fünfundfünfzigtausend-
  fünfhundert 309
fünfzehn 308
fünfzehnter 309
fünfzig 308
fünfzigster 309
fünfzigtausend 309
Funkantenne f 214
für 320
Furche f 183
Fürstentum n 315
Fuß m 12, 15, 310
Fußabtreter m 59
Fußball m 222
Fußball m 222
Fußballdress m 31
Fußballfeld n 222
Fußballschuh m 223
Fußballspieler m 222
Fußboden m 62, 71
Fußende n 71
Fußgängerübergweg m
  195
Fußgängerzone f 299
Fußpedal n 257
Fußrücken m 15
Fußschlaufe f 241
Fußsohle f 15
Fußweg m 262
Futter n 32
Futteral n 51
füttern 183

G

Gabel f 65, 88, 153, 207
Gabelstapler m 186, 216
Gabun 317
gähnen 25
Galapagosinseln 315
Galaxie f 280
Gallone f 311
Galopp m 243
galvanisiert 79
Gambia 317
Gang m 106, 168, 210,
  254
Gänge m 153, 206
Gans f 119, 293
Gänseei n 137

ganz 129, 132
Garage f 58
Gardine f 63
Garn n 276
Garnele f 121
Garten m 84
Gartenanlagen f 262
Gartenarbeit f 90
Gartencenter m 115
Gartengeräte m 88
Gartenhandschuhe m 89
Gartenkorb m 88
Gartenkürbis m 124
Gartenornamente m 84
Gartenpflanzen f 86
Garten-Sauerampfer m
  123
Gartenschlauch m 89
Gartenspritze f 89
Gartenstöcke m 89
Gartentypen m 84
Gärtner m 188
Gasbrenner m 61, 267
Gashebel m 204
Gaspedal n 200
Gasse f 298
Gast m 100
Gästebuch n 100
Gastgeber m 64
Gastgeberin f 64
Gatenummer f 213
Gaumen m 19
Gaze f 47
Gebäck n 140, 149
gebacken 159
Gebärmutter f 20, 52
Gebärmutterhals m 20,
  52
Gebäude n 299
Gebäudereiniger m 188
geben 273
Gebirgskette f 282
gebogen 165
geboren werden 26
gebratene Hähnchen n
  155
Gebrauchsanweisung f
  109
Gebrauchtwarenhändler
  m 115
Geburt f 52, 53
Geburtsgewicht n 53
Geburtshelfer m 52
Geburtstag m 27
Geburtstagsfeier f 27
Geburtstagskerzen f 141
Geburtstagskuchen m
  141
Geburtsurkunde f 26
Geburtszange f 53
gedämpft 159
Gedeck n 65
Gedränge n 221
Gefahr f 195
Gefängnis n 181
Gefängniswärter m 181
Gefängniszelle f 181
gefärbt 39

Geflügel n 119
Gefrierfach n 67
Gefrier-Kühlschrank m 67
Gefrierware f 107
gefrorene Joghurt m 137
Gefühle n 25
gefüllt 159
gefüllte Fladenbrot n 155
gefüllte Olive f 143
gegenüber 320
Gegner f 236
gegrillt 159
Gehalt n 175
gehen lassen 139
Gehirn n 19
Gehirnerschütterung f 46
Gehrungslade f 81
Geige f 256
Geißblatt n 297
gekochte Ei n 137, 157
gekochte Fleisch n 118, 143
gekrümmt 165
Gel n 109
geladen 60
Geländemotorrad n 205
Geländer n 59
Geländewagen m 199
gelangweilt 25
gelb 274
gelbe Karte f 223
Geld n 97
Geldautomat m 97
Geldwirtschaft f 97
Geleebonbon m 113
Gelenk n 17
gemahlen 132
gemahlene Kaffee m 144
Gemälde n 62, 261, 274
gemischte Salat m 158
Gemüse n 107, 122, 124
Gemüsefach n 67
Gemüsegarten m 85, 182
Gemüsehändler m 188
Gemüseladen m 114
Generaldirektor m 175
Generation f 23
Generator m 60
geöffnet 260
Geometrie f 165
Georgien 318
Gepäck n 100, 198, 213
Gepäckablage f 209
Gepäckabteilung f 104
Gepäckanhänger m 212
Gepäckausgabe f 213
Gepäckband n 212
Gepäckfach n 196, 210
Gepäckröntgenmaschine f 212
Gepäckträger m 204
Gepäckwaage f 212
gepökelt 118, 143
gerade 165
geradeaus 260
geraspelt 132

geräuchert 118, 121, 143, 159
Gerbera f 110
Gerichtsdiener m 180
Gerichtssaal m 180
Gerichtsstenograf m 181
Gerichtstermin m 180
geriebene Käse m 136
geröstet 129
Gerste f 130, 184
Gerüst n 186
gesalzen 121, 129, 137
Gesäßmuskel m 16
Geschäft n 175
Geschäftsabkommen n 175
Geschäftsbogen m 173
Geschäftsfrau f 175
Geschäftsmann m 175
Geschäftspartnerin f 24
Geschäftsreise f 175
geschält 129
geschälten Garnelen f 120
Geschenk n 27
Geschenkartikelladen m 114
Geschichte f 162
Geschirr n 64
Geschirr und das Besteck n 65
Geschlechtskrankheit f 20
Geschlechtsteile 12
Geschlechtsverkehr m 20
geschlossen 260, 321
Geschwindigkeitsbegrenzung f 195
Geschworenen m 180
Geschworenenbank f 180
Gesicht n 14
Gesichtsbehandlung f 41
Gesichtscreme f 73
Gesichtsmaske f 41
Gesichtspuder m 40
Gesichtsschutzmaske f 225
Gesichtswasser f 41
Gesims n 300
gespaltenen Haarspitzen f 39
gestalten 91
Gestänge n 267
Gestein n 288
Gestell n 166, 174
gestern 306
Gesundheit f 44
Gesundheitsfürsorge n 168
geteilt durch 165
getoastete Sandwich m 149
Getränke n 107, 144, 156
Getreide n 130
Getreideflocken f 107, 130, 156

Getriebe n 202, 204
getrocknet 129, 143, 159
getrockneten Erbsen f 131
Gewächshaus n 85
Geweih n 291
Gewicht n 166, 244
Gewichte n 250
Gewichthantel f 251
Gewinnanteile m 97
gewinnen 273
Gewinner m 273
Gewitter n 287
Gewölbe n 15, 300
Gewürze n 132
Gewürzessig m 135
Gewürznelke f 133
Geysir m 285
Ghana 317
Giebel m 300
Giebeldreieck n 301
gießen 67, 90
Gießen n 89
Gießkanne f 89
Gin m 145
Gin Tonic m 151
Gips m 83
Giraffe f 291
Girokonto n 96
Gitarrist m 258
Gitterstäbe m 74
Gladiole f 110
Glanz- 83
Glas n 51, 134, 152, 311
Glas- 69
Gläser n 150
Glasflasche f 166
glasieren 139
Glaskeramikkochfeld n 66
Glasstäbchen n 167
Glaswaren f 64
glatt 39
glätten 39
Glattrochen m 294
gleich 165
Gleichstand n 230
Gleichstrom m 60
Gleichung f 165
Gleis n 208
Gleisnummer f 208
Gleitschirmfliegen n 248
Gletscher m 284
Glied n 36
Glimmer m 289
glücklich 25
Glühfaden m 60
Gneis m 288
Gold n 235, 289
Goldfisch m 294
Golf n 232
Golfball m 233
Golferin f 232
Golfhandicap n 233
Golfplatz m 232
Golfschläger m 233

Golftasche f 233
Golfturnier n 233
Gong m 257
Gorilla m 291
gotisch 301
Gottesanbeterin f 295
GPS-System m 201
graben 90
graduieren 26
Graduierte f 169
Graduierungsfeier f 169
Gramm n 310
Granat m 288
Granatapfel m 128
Granit m 288
Grapefruit f 126
Graphit m 289
Gras n 86, 262
Grasfangsack m 88
Grasland n 285
Gräte f 121
grau 39, 274
Graubrot n 139, 149
graue Star m 51
Gravieren n 275
Greifzange f 167
Grenada 314
Griechenland 316
Grieß m 130
Griff m 36, 88, 230, 237
Griffe m 37
Grill m 267
Grillblech n 69
Grille f 295
grillen 67
Grippe f 44
grobe Senf m 135
Grönland 314
groß 321
große Zeh m 15
Großeltern 23
Großmutter f 22
Großraumlimousine f 199
Großsegel n 240
Großvater m 22
Grübchen m 15
grün 129, 274
Grün n 232
Grundfläche f 164
Grundhobel m 78
Grundierfarbe f 83
Grundierung f 40, 83
Grundlinie f 230
Grundriss m 261
grüne Bohne f 122
grüne Erbse f 122
grüne Olive f 143
grüne Salat m 158
grüne Tee m 149
grünen Erbsen f 131
Grünkohl m 123
Gruppentherapie f 55
Guatemala 314
Guave f 128
Guinea 317
Guinea-Bissau 317
Gummiband n 173

Gummihose f 30
Gummiknüppel m 94
Gummistiefel m 31, 89
Gurke f 125
Gürtel m 32, 36, 236
Gürtelschnalle f 36
gut 321
gut geschnitten 35
Güterzug m 208
Guyana 315
Gymnastikband n 235
Gynäkologe m 52
Gynäkologie f 49

H

Haar n 14, 38
Haarband n 39
Haarbürste f 38
Haarfärbemittel n 40
Haarfarben f 39
Haargel n 38
Haarglätter m 39
Haarklammer f 38
Haarknoten m 39
Haarreif m 38
Haarspray n 38
Haarspülung f 38
Hackbrett n 68
Hacke f 88
Hackfleisch n 119
Hackmesser n 68
Hafen m 214, 216, 217
Hafenmeister m 217
Hafer m 130
Haftbefehl m 180
Haftentlassung auf Bewährung f 181
Hagel m 286
Hahn m 61, 185
Hähnchen n 119
Hähnchenstückchen n 155
Hahnenfuß m 297
Haifisch m 294
Haiti 314
Häkelhaken m 277
Häkeln n 277
Haken m 187, 276
halbdunkle Bier m 145
halbe Liter m 311
halbfeste Käse m 136
Halbfettmilch f 136
Halbinsel f 282
Halbpension f 101
Halbzeit f 223
Halfter n 243
Halloween n 27
Hals m 12, 258
Halskette f 36
Halskrawatte f 36
Halspastille f 109
Halstuch n 36
Halswirbel m 17
Haltegriff m 196
Halteknopf m 197
halten 223
Halten verboten 195
Haltung f 232

deutsch

deutsch

Hämatit m 289
Hamburger m 154
Hamburger mit Pommes frites m 154
Hammer m 80
hämmern 79
Hamster m 290
Hand f 13, 15
Handbohrer m 81
Handbremse f 203
Handfeger m 77
Handfläche f 15
Handgabel f 89
Handgelenk n 13, 15
Handgepäck n 211, 213
Handknöchel m 15
Handrad n 276
Handsäge f 89
Handschellen f 94
Handschuh m 224, 228, 233, 236, 246
Handschuhe m 36
Handtasche f 37
Handtuch n 73
Handtücher n 73
Handtuchhalter m 72
Handy n 99
Hang m 284
Hängematte f 266
Hängeordner m 173
Hantel f 251
Hardware f 176
Harfe f 256
harken 90
Harnblase f 20
Harnleiter m 21
Harnröhre f 20
Harnsystem n 19
hart 129, 321
Hartfaserplatte f 79
Hartholz n 79
Hartkäse m 136
Haselnuss f 129
Haselnussöl n 134
Hauptfahrwerk n 210
Hauptgericht n 153
Hauptmahlzeit f 158
Hauptstadt f 315
Haus n 58
Hausanschlüsse m 60
Hausapotheke f 72
Hausaufgaben f 163
Haushaltswaage f 69
Haushaltswaren f 107
Hausschuhe m 31
Haustür f 58
Haustürlampe f 58
Haut f 14, 119
Hautausschlag m 44
Hautpflege f 108
Hawaii 314
Heavymetal n 259
Hebamme f 53
Hebel m 61, 150
Heck n 198, 210, 240
Hecke f 85, 90, 182
Heckenschere f 89
Hefe f 138

Hefebrötchen n 139
Heft n 163
heften 277
Hefter m 173
hegen 91
Heidekraut n 297
Heidelbeere f 127
Heilbuttfilets n 120
Heilkräuter m 55
Heimwerkstatt f 78
heiraten 26
heiß 286, 321
heiße Schokolade f 144
heißen Getränke n 144
Heißluftballon m 211
Heißwasserhahn m 72
Heizdecke f 71
Heizelement n 61
Heizkörper m 60
Heizlüfter m 60
Heizofen m 60
Heizungsregler m 201
hell 41, 321
Helm m 204, 220, 228
Hemd n 33, 251
Henkel m 106
Herbizid n 183
Herbst m 31, 307
Herde f 183
Hering m 266
Herr m 23
Herrenbekleidung f 105
Herrenfriseur m 39
Herrenhalbschuh m 37
Herrenkleidung f 32
herunterladen 177
Herz n 18, 119, 122, 273
Herz- und Gefäßsystem n 19
Herzinfarkt m 44
Herzmuschel f 121
Heu n 184
Heuschnupfen m 44
Heuschrecke f 295
heute 306
Hieb m 237
hier essen 154
Hi-Fi-Anlage f 268
Hilfskoch m 152
Himalaja m 313
Himbeere f 127
Himbeerkonfitüre f 134
hinauf 320
Hindernis n 243
hinter 320
Hinterbacke f 13
hinterherlaufen 229
Hinterrad n 197
hinunter 320
Hirsch m 291
Hirse f 130
historische Gebäude n 261
HNO-Abteilung f 49
Hobel m 81
hobeln 79
hoch 271, 321
hochauflösend 269

hochbinden 91
Hochfrisur f 39
Hochgeschwindigkeitszug m 208
Hochglanz- 271
Hochschule f 168
Hochseefischerei f 245
Hochsprung m 235
Höchstlademarke f 214
Hochzeit f 26, 35
Hochzeitsfeier f 26
Hochzeitskleid n 35
Hochzeitsreise f 26
Hochzeitstag m 26
Hochzeitstorte f 141
hochziehen 251
Höcker m 291
Hockey n 224
Hockeyball m 224
Hockeyschläger m 224
Hoden m 21
Hodensack m 21
Hof m 58, 84, 182
Höhe f 165, 211
Höhenleitwerk n 210
Höhle f 284
Hole-in-One n 233
Holz n 79, 233, 275
Holzarbeit f 275
Holzblasinstrumente n 257
Holzbohrer m 80
Holzkohle f 266
Holzleim m 78
Holzlöffel m 68
Holzspäne m 78
homogenisiert 137
Homöopathie f 55
Honduras 314
Honigwabe f 135
Hörer m 99
Hormon n 20
Horn n 257, 291
Hornhaut f 51
Horrorfilm m 255
Hörsaal m 169
Hose f 32, 34
Hot Dog n 155
Hotel n 100, 264
Hoteldiener m 100
Hubschrauber m 211
Huf m 242, 291
Hufeisen n 242
Hüfte f 12
Hügel m 284
Huhn n 185
Hühnerbein n 119
Hühnerei n 137
Hühnerfarm f 183
Hühnerstall m 185
Hülse f 130
Hülsenfrüchte f 130
Hummer m 121, 295
Hund m 290
hundert 308
hundertster 309
hunderttausend 308
hundertzehn 308

Hundeschlittenfahren n 247
hungrig 64
Hupe f 201, 204
Hürdenlauf m 235
Hurrikan m 287
Husten m 44
Hustenmedikament n 108
Hut m 36
Hüttenkäse m 136
Hydrant m 95
Hypnotherapie f 55
hypoallergen 41
Hypotenuse f 164
Hypothek f 96

I

Igel m 290
Imbissstand m 154
Imbissstube f 154
immergrün 86
Immobilienmakler m 115
Immobilienmaklerin f 189
impotent 20
in 320
in den Ruhestand treten 26
indigoblau 274
in Ei gebratene Brot n 157
in Lake 143
in Ohnmacht fallen 25, 44
in Öl 143
in Saft 159
in Sicherheit 228
in Soße 159
Inbox f 177
Indien 318
Indische Ozean m 312
Indonesien 319
Industriegebiet n 299
Infektion f 44
Information f 261
Ingwer m 125, 133
Inhalationsapparat m 44
Inhalierstift f 109
Inlandsflug m 212
Inlinerfahren n 263
Inlineskaten n 249
Innenausstattung f 200
Innenfeld n 228
innere Kern m 282
Innereien f 118
innerhalb 320
Inning n 228
ins Bett gehen 71
Insektenschutzmittel n 108
Insektenspray m 267
Insel f 282
Inspektor m 94
Installation f 61
installieren 177
Instrumente n 258
Insulin n 109
Intensivstation f 48

Intercity m 209
Internet n 177
Interviewer m 179
Ionosphäre f 286
iPad n 176
iPod n 268
Irak 318
Iran 318
Iris f 51, 110
Irland 316
Island 316
Isolierband n 81
Isolierung f 61
Israel 318
Italien 316

J

Jacht f 215
Jacke f 32, 34
Jade f 288
Jagdflugzeug n 211
Jagdrennen n 243
Jahr n 306
Jahreszeiten f 306
Jahrhundert n 307
jährlich 307
Jahrmarkt m 262
Jahrtausend n 307
Jahrzehnt n 307
Jakobsmuschel f 121
Jalousie f 63
Jamaika 314
Jamswurzel f 125
Januar m 306
Japan 318
jäten 91
Jazz m 259
Jeans f 31, 33
Jemen 318
jenseits 320
Jett m 288
jetzt
Jogging n 251, 263
Joghurt m 137
Joker m 273
Jordanien 318
Journalist m 190
Judo n 236
Jugendliche f 23
Jugendstil m 301
Jugoslawien 316
Juli m 306
Junge m 23, 290
Juni m 306
Jupiter m 280
Juwelier 188
Juwelierarbeit f 275
Juweliergeschäft n 114

K

Kabel n 79, 207
Kabelfernsehen n 269
Kabeljau m 120
Kabinda 317
Kabine f 210, 214
Kabinenlift m 246
Kabriolett n 199
kacheln 82

deutsch

Käfer m 295
Kaffee m 144, 148, 153, 156, 184
Kaffee mit Milch m 148
Kaffeelöffel m 153
Kaffeemaschine f 148, 150
Kaffeemilchshake m 149
Kaffeetasse f 65
kahl 39
Kai m 216
Kaiserschnitt m 52
Kakadu m 293
Kakaopulver m 148
Kakerlak m 295
Kaktus m 87
Kaktusfeige f 128
Kalb n 185
Kalbfleisch n 118
Kalender m 306
Kalk m 85
Kalkstein m 288
kalt 286, 321
kaltgepresste Öl n 135
Kaltwasserhahn m 72
Kalzit m 289
Kalzium n 109
Kambodscha 318
Kamel m 291
Kamera f 178, 260
Kamera-Handy n 270
Kamerakran m 178
Kameramann m 178
Kameratasche f 271
Kamerun 317
Kamillentee m 149
Kamin m 63
Kamm m 38
kämmen 38
Kammer f 283
Kampf m 237
Kampfsport m 236
Kampfsportarten f 237
Kanada 314
Kanal m 178, 269, 299
Kanalschacht m 299
Kanarienvogel m 292
Kandare f 242
kandierten Früchte f 129
Känguru n 291
Kaninchen n 118, 290
Kännchen n 65
Kante f 246
Kanter m 243
Kanu n 214
Kanusport m 241
Kapern f 143
Kapitalanlage f 97
Kapitän m 214
Kapsel f 109
Kapstachelbeere f 128
Kapuze f 31
Kapuzenmuskel m 16
Karamell m 113
Karamellpudding m 142
Karate m 236
Kardamom m 132
Kardanwelle f 202

Kardiologie f 49
Karibische Meer m 312
Karies f 50
Karneval m 27
Karo n 273
Karosserie f 202
Karotte f 124
Karte f 27
Kartenreiter m 173
Kartenschlitz m 97
Kartenspiel n 273
Kartoffel f 124
Kartoffelchips m 151
Kartoffelstampfer m 68
Kasachstan 318
Käse m 136, 156
Kasino n 261
Kaspische Meer n 313
Kasse f 106, 150, 255
Kasserolle f 69
Kassette f 269
Kassettenrekorder m 269
Kassierer m 96, 106
Katamaran m 215
Katar 318
Kathedrale f 300
Katheter m 53
Kätzchen n 290
Katze f 290
Katzenauge n 204
Kaufhaus n 105
Kaugummi m 113
Kaulquappe f 294
Kaution f 181
Kajak n 241
Kebab m 155
Kegel m 164, 249
Kehldeckel m 19
Kehle f 19
Kehlkopf m 19
Kehre f 238
Keilriemen m 203
Keilschuh m 37
keine Einfahrt 195
Keks m 113, 141
Kelch m 297
Kelle f 187
Kellergeschoss n 58
Kellner m 148, 152
Kellnerin f 191
Kendo n 236
Kenia 317
Kennmarke f 94
kentern 241
Kern m 122, 127, 128, 129, 130
Kerngehäuse n 127
kernlos 127
Kescher m 244
Kessel m 61
Kesselpauke f 257
Ketchup m 135
Kette f 36
Kettenzahnrad n 207
Keule f 119, 167, 228
Keyboard n 258

Kichererbsen f 131
Kickboxen n 236
kicken 221, 223
Kiefer f 296
Kieferknochen m 17
Kiel m 214
Kieme f 294
Kies m 88
Kilogramm n 310
Kilometer m 310
Kilometerzähler m 201
Kind n 23, 31
Kinder n 23
Kinderabteilung f 104
Kinderbett n 74
Kinderkleidung f 30
Kinderportion f 153
Kindersicherung f 75
Kindersitz m 198, 207
Kinderstation f 48
Kinderstuhl m 75
Kinderwagen m 75
Kinderzimmer n 74
Kinn n 14
Kinnlade f 14
Kino n 255, 299
Kinosaal m 255
Kipper m 187
Kirche f 298, 300
Kirsche f 126
Kirschtomate f 124
Kissenbezug m 71
Kiwi f 128
Klammer f 166
Klammern f 173
Klampe f 240
Klappe f 179
Klapptisch m 210
Klarinette f 257
Klasse f 163
Klassenzimmer n 162
klassische Musik f 255, 259
klassizistisch 301
Klatschmohn m 297
Klaue f 291
Klavier n 256
Klebstoff m 275
Klee m 297
Kleid n 31, 34
Kleiderbügel m 70
Kleiderschrank m 70
Kleidung f 205
Kleie f 130
klein 321
Kleinbus m 197
kleine Finger m 15
kleine Trommel f 257
kleine Zeh m 15
Kleinkind n 30
Kleisterbürste f 82
Klementine f 126
Klemmbrett n 173
Klempner m 188
Klettergerüst n 263
Klettern n 248
Kletterpflanze f 87

Klient m 180
Klimaanlage f 200
Klinge f 89
Klingel f 197
Klinik f 48
Klippe n 285
Klitoris f 20
Klöppel m 277
Klubhaus n 232
Klubsandwich m 155
Knabbereien f 151
Knäckebrot n 139, 156
knackig 127
Knebelknopf m 31
kneten 138
Knie n 12
Kniebeuge f 251
knielang 34
Kniescheibe f 17
Knieschützer m 205, 227
Kniesehnenstrang m 16
Knoblauch m 125, 132
Knoblauchpresse f 68
Knöchel m 13, 15
knöchellang 34
Knochen m 17, 119
Knochenasche f 88
Knockout m 237
Knopf m 32
Knopfloch n 32
Knorpel m 17
Knospe f 111, 297
Koalabär m 291
Koch m 190
köcheln lassen 67
kochen 67
Kochen n 67
Köcher m 249
Kochfeld n 67
Kochmütze f 190
Kochtopf m 69
Köder m 244
Köderhaken m 244
ködern 245
Kofferkuli m 100, 208, 213
Kofferraum m 198
Kohl m 123
Kohle f 288
Kohlestift m 275
Kohlrabi m 123
Kohlrübe f 125
Koikarpfen m 294
Kokon m 295
Kokosnuss f 129
Kolben m 166
Kolibri m 292
Kollege m 24
Kolonie 315
Kolumbien 315
Kombinationszange f 80
Kombiwagen m 199
Kombüse f 214
Komet m 280
Kommandobrücke f 214
Kommandoturm m 215
Kommode f 70

Kommunikation f 98
Komödie f 255
Komoren 317
Kompass m 240, 312
Komposterde f 88
Komposthaufen m 85
Kondensmilch f 136
Konditor m 113
Konditorcreme f 140
Konditorei f 114
Kondom n 21
Konfitüre f 134, 156
Konglomerat n 288
Kongo 317
König m 272, 273
Königsberg 316
Konserven f 107
Konsultation f 45
Kontaktlinsen f 51
Kontaktlinsenbehälter m 51
Kontinent m 282, 315
Kontonummer f 96
Kontoüberziehung f 96
Kontrabass m 256
Kontrafagott n 257
Kontrollturm m 212
Konzert m 255, 258
Kopf m 12, 19, 112, 230
köpfen 91, 222
Kopfende n 70
Kopfhaut f 39
Kopfhörer m 268
Kopfkissen n 70
Kopfschmerzen m 44
Kopfschutz m 74, 236
Kopfstütze f 200
Kopfverletzung f 46
kopieren 172
Kopilot m 211
Koppel f 242
Korallenriff n 285
Korb m 207, 226
Korbbrett n 226
Körbchen n 74
Korbring m 226
Koriander m 133
Korinthe f 129
Korken m 134
Korkenzieher m 150
Körner n 131
Körnerbrot n 139
Körper m 12, 164
Körperlotion f 73
Körperpuder m 73
Körpersysteme n 19
Körperverletzung f 94
Korrekturstift m 40
Korsett n 35
Korsika 316
Kotelett n 119
Krabbe f 121
Kraftstoffanzeige f 201
Kraftstofftank m 204
Krafttraining n 251
Kragen m 32
Krähe f 292
Kralle f 293

deutsch

Krampf m 239
Krämpfe m 44
Kran m 187, 216
Kranich m 292
Krankenhaus n 48
Krankenhausstation f 48
Krankenschwester f 45, 48, 52, 189
Krankenwagen m 94
Krankheit f 44
Kranz m 111
Krater m 283
kratzen 77
Kraulen m 239
kraus 39
Kraut n 86
Kräuter n 133, 134
Kräuter und Gewürze n 132
Kräutergarten m 84
Kräuterheilkunde f 55
Kräuterheilmittel n 108
Kräutermischung f 132
Kräutertee m 149
Krawatte f 32
Krawattennadel f 36
Krebs m 121, 295
Kreditkarte f 96
Kreide f 162, 288
Kreis m 165
Kreissäge f 78
Kreisverkehr m 195
Kreuz n 13, 256, 273
Kreuzblume f 300
Kreuzkümmel m 132
Kreuzschlitzschraubenzieher m 80
Kreuzung f 194, 298
Kricket n 225
Kricketball m 225
Kricketspieler m 225
Krickettor n 225
Kriechpflanze f 87
Kriegsschiff n 215
Kriminalbeamte m 94
Kristalltherapie f 55
Kroatien 316
Krokodil n 293
Krokodilklemme f 167
Krone f 50
Kröte f 294
Krug m 151
Kruste f 139
Kuba 314
Küche f 66, 152
Kuchen m 141
Kuchen backen m 69
Kuchenblech n 69
Küchenchef m 152
Kuchenform f 69
Küchengeräte n 66, 68, 105
Küchenmaschine f 66
Küchenmesser n 68
Küchenregal n 66
Küchenschrank m 66
Kugel f 149, 164

Kugelstoßen n 234
Kuh f 185
Kühler m 202
Kühlmittelbehälter m 202
Kühlschrank m 67
Kuhmilch f 136
Küken n 185
Kulisse f 254
Kultivator m 182
Kümmel m 131
Kumquat f 126
Kunde m 96, 104, 106, 152
Kundendienst m 104
Kundendienstabteilung f 175
Kundin f 38, 175
Kung-Fu n 236
Kunst f 162
Kunstgalerie f 261
Kunstgeschichte f 169
Kunsthandlung f 115
Kunsthandwerk n 274, 276
Kunsthochschule f 169
Künstlerin f 274
kunststoffbeschichtet 69
Kupfer n 289
Kuppel f 300
Kupplung f 200, 204
Kürbiskern m 131
Kurierdienst m 99
Kurkuma f 132
kurz 32, 321
kurz gebraten 159
Kurzhaarschnitt m 39
Kurzsichtigkeit f 51
Kurzwaren f 105
Kurzwelle f 179
Kuscheltier n 75
Kuskus m 130
Küste f 285
Küstenwache f 217
Kuwait 318

L

Labor n 166
Laborwaage f 166
lächeln 25
lachen 25
Lachs m 120
Lack m 79, 83
Lacrosse n 249
Lacrosseschläger m 249
Laden m 298
Lagerfeuer n 266
Laib m 139
Laken n 74
Lakritze f 113
Laktose f 137
Lamm n 118, 185
Lampe f 62
Lampen f 105
Land n 282, 315
landen 211
Landschaft f 284
Landungsbrücke f 214
Landungssteg m 217

landwirtschaftlichen Betriebe m 183
lang 32
Länge f 165, 310
Längengrad m 283
Langkorn- 130
Langlauf m 247
Langlaufmaschine f 250
langsam 321
Längsschnitt m 282
Langwelle f 179
Laos 318
Laptop m 175, 176
Lärche f 296
Lastwagen m 194
Lastwagenfahrer m 190
Laterne f 217
Latte f 235
Lätzchen n 30
Latzhose f 30
Laubbaum m 86
Laubrechen m 88
Lauch m 125
Lauf m 228
Laufband n 106, 250
Läufer m 272
Laufstall m 75
Lautsprecher m 176, 209, 258
Lautstärke f 179, 269
Lava f 283
Lawine f 247
Leadsänger m 258
Lebensmittel n 106
Lebensmittelabteilung f 105
Lebensmittelgeschäft n 114
Leber f 18, 118
Lederanzug m 205
Lederschuhe m 32
leer 321
Leerung f 98
legen 38
leger 34
Leggings n 31
Leguan m 293
Lehm m 85
Lehne f 64
Lehrerin f 162, 191
leicht 321
Leichtathlet m 234
Leichtathletik f 234
Leichtflugzeug n 211
Leimpistole f 78
Leinen n 277
Leinwand f 255, 274
Leiste f 12
leitende Angestellte m 174
Leiter f 95, 186
Leitkegel m 187
Leitplanke f 195
Leitung f 60
Leitungswasser n 144
Leitz-Ordner m 173
Lende f 121
Lendensteak n 119

Lendenwirbel m 17
Lenkrad n 201
Lenkstange f 207
lernen 163
Lernen n 162
Leselampe f 210
lesen 162
Leserausweis m 168
Lesesaal m 168
Lesotho 317
letzte Woche 307
Leuchtrakete f 240
Leuchtstreifen m 205
Leuchtturm m 217
Leukoplast n 47
Levkoje f 110
Libanon 318
Libelle f 295
Liberia 317
Libyen 317
Licht n 94
Lichtmaschine f 203
Lichtschalter m 201
Lid n 51
Lidschatten m 40
Liebesfilm m 255
Liechtenstein 316
Lied n 259
Lieferung ins Haus f 154
Liegestuhl m 265
Liegestütz m 251
Liga f 223
Likör m 145
Lilie f 110
Limonade f 144
Limone f 126
Limousine f 199
Linde f 296
Lineal n 163, 165
Linien f 165
Liniennummer f 196
Linienrichter m 220, 223, 230
Liniensystem n 256
linke Feld n 228
links 260
Linkssteuerung f 201
Linse f 51, 270
Lipgloss n 40
Lippe f 14
Lippenkonturenstift m 40
Lippenpinsel m 40
Lippenstift m 40
Litauen 316
Liter m 311
Literatur f 162, 169
Literaturliste f 168
Litschi f 128
live 178
Lob m 230
Loch n 232
Locher m 173
Lockenstab m 38
Löffel m 65
Löffelbiskuits n 141
Loganbeere f 127

Loge f 254
Logo n 31
Lohnliste f 175
Lokomotive f 208
Lorbeerblatt n 133
Löschfahrzeug n 95
loslassen 245
löslich 109
Lösungsmittel 83
löten 79
Lotion f 109
Lötkolben m 81
Lottoscheine m 112
Lötzinn m 79, 80
Löwe m 291
Löwenzahn m 123, 297
Luffaschwamm m 73
Luftdüse f 210
Luftfilter m 202, 204
Luftkissenboot n 215
Luftmanschette f 45
Luftmatratze f 267
Luftpostbrief m 98
Luftpumpe f 207
Luftröhre f 18
Lunge f 18
Lungenautomat m 239
Lupinen f 297
Lutscher m 113
Luxemburg 316
Luzerne f 184
lymphatische System n 19

M

Macadamianuss f 129
Madagaskar 317
Mädchen n 23
Magen m 18
Magenschmerzen m 44
magere Fleisch n 118
Magermilch f 136
Magister m 169
Magma f 283
Magnesium n 109
Magnet m 167
Mähdrescher m 182
mähen 90
Mähne f 242, 291
Mai m 306
Mais m 122, 124, 130, 184
Maisbrot n 139
Maiskeimöl n 135
Majonäse f 135
Majoran m 133
Make-up n 40
Makramee n 277
Makrele f 120
mal 165
Malachit m 288
Malawi 317
Malaysia 318
Malediven 318
Malerei f 274
Malerin f 191
Mali 317

deutsch

Malspieler m 228
Malta 316
Malzessig m 135
Malzgetränk n 144
Manager m 174
Manchego m 142
Mandarine f 126
Mandel f 129
Mandeln f 151
Mandelöl n 134
Mango f 128
Mangold m 123
Maniküre f 41
Maniok m 124
Mann m 12, 23
männlich 21
Mannschaft f 220
Mansarde f 58
Mansardenfenster n 58
Manschette f 32
Manschettenknopf m 36
Mantel m 32, 282
Maracas f 257
Marathon m 234
Margarine f 137
Margerite f 110, 297
Marienkäfer m 295
Marina f 217
mariniert 143, 159
Marketingabteilung f 175
Markise f 148
Markt m 115
Marmor m 288
Marokko 317
Mars m 280
Marshmallow n 113
Martini m 151
März m 306
Marzipan n 141
Maschinen f 187
Maschinenbau m 169
Maschinengewehr n
189
Maschinenraum m 214
Masern f 44
Maske f 189, 236, 249
Maß n 150, 151
Massage f 54
Maße n 165
Mast m 240
Mastdarm m 21
Match n 230
Material n 187
Materialien n 79
Mathematik f 162, 164
Matratze f 70, 74
matt 83, 271
Matte f 54, 235
Mauer f 58, 186, 222
Mauerturm m 300
Mauerwerkbohrer m 80
Mauretanien 317
Mauritius 317
Maus f 176, 290
Mautstelle f 194
Mazedonien 316
MDF-Platte f 79
Mechanik f 202

Mechaniker m 188, 203
Medaillen f 235
Medien f 178
Medikament n 109
Meditation f 54
Medizin f 169
Meer n 264, 282
Meeresfrüchte f 121
Meerrettich m 125
Mehl n 138
Mehl mit Backpulver n
139
Mehl ohne Backpulver n
139
mehrjährig 86
Mehrkornbrot n 139
Meile f 310
Meißel m 81, 275
Meisterschaft f 230
melken 183
Melodie f 259
Melone f 127
Memorystick m 176
Mensa f 168
Menschen m 12, 16, 39
Menstruation f 20
Menübalken m 177
Merkur m 280
Mesosphäre f 286
Messbecher m 69, 150,
311
messen 310
Messer n 65, 66
Messerschärfer m 68,
118
Messlöffel m 109
Metall n 79
Metallbohrer m 80
Metalle n 289
Metallsäge f 81
metamorph 288
Meteor m 280
Meter m 310
Metermaß m 80
Metzger m 118, 188
Metzgerei f 114
Mexiko 314
Mieder n 35
Miesmuschel f 121
Miete f 58
mieten 58
Mieter m 58
Migräne f 44
Mikrophon n 179, 258
Mikrophongalgen m 179
Mikroskop n 167
Mikrowelle f 66
Milch f 136, 156
Milchprodukte n 107,
136
Milchpulver n 137
Milchreis m 130, 140
Milchschokolade f 113
Milchshake m 137
Milchtüte f 136
Milliarde 309
Milligramm n 310
Milliliter m 311

Millimeter m 310
Million 309
Milz f 18
Mineralien n 289
Mineralwasser n 144
Minibar f 101
minirock m 34
minus 165
Minute f
Minutenzeiger m
Minze f 133
mischen 273
Mischpult n 179
mit 320
mit Automatik 200
mit Formbügeln 35
mit Handschaltung 200
mit Kohlensäure 144
mit Kopfdünger düngen
90
mit offenem Oberdeck
260
mit Rasen bedecken 90
mit Schokolade
überzogen 140
mit
Schokoladenstückchen
141
mit Zahnseide reinigen
50
Mittag 305
Mittagessen n 64
Mittagsmenü n 152
Mittelfeld n 228
Mittelfinger m 15
Mittelfußknochen m 17
Mittelhandknochen m 17
mittelharte Käse f 136
Mittelkreis m 222, 224,
226
Mittellinie f 226
Mittelmeer n 313
Mittelpunkt m 164
Mittelstreifen m 194
Mittelstürmer m 222
Mittelwelle f 179
Mitternacht f 305
mittlere Spur f 194
Mittwoch m 306
Mixer m 66
Mixerschüssel f 66
Möbel n 105
Möbelgeschäft m 115
Mobile n 74
Mode f 277
Modedesigner m 277
Modell n 169, 190
Modellbau m 275
Modellierholz m 275
Moderator m 178
Mohn m 138
Moldawien 316
Monaco 316
Monat m 306
monatlich 307
Monatshygiene
f 108
Mond m 280

Mondbohnen f 131
Mondfähre f 281
Mondsichel f 280
Mondstein m 288
Mongolei 318
Monitor m 53
Monopoly n 272
Monsun m 287
Montag m 306
Montenegro 316
Monument n 261
Mopp m 77
Morgen m 305
morgen 306
Morgendämmerung f
305
Morgenmantel m 35
Morgenrock m 31
Mörser m 68, 167
Mörtel m 187
Mosambik 317
Moschee f 300
Moskitonetz n 267
Motocross n 249
Motor m 88, 202,
204
Motorhaube f 198
Motorrad n 204
Motorradrennen n 249
Motorradständer m
205
Motte f 295
Mountainbike n 206
Mousse f 141
Möwe f 292
Mozzarella m 142
Muffin m 140
mulchen 91
Mülleimer m 67, 266
Müllschaufel f 77
Müllschlucker m 61
multiplizieren 165
Multivitaminmittel m 109
Mumps m 44
Mund m 14
Mundschutz m 237
Mundwasser n 72
Mungbohnen f 131
Münze f 97
Münzfernsprecher m
99
Münzrückgabe f 99
Muschel f 265
Museum n 261
Musical n 255
Musik f 162
Musiker m 191
Musikhochschule f 169
Musikinstrumente n
256
Musikstile f 259
Muskatblüte f 132
Muskatnuss f 132
Muskeln m 16
Mutter f 22, 80
Muttermal n 14
Mütze f 36
Myanmar 318

N

Naan m 139
Nabe f 206
Nabel m 12
Nabelschnur f 52
nach 320
Nachbar m 24
Nachmittag m 305
Nachrichten f 100, 178
Nachrichtensprecherin f
179
nachschneiden 39
Nachspeisen f 140
nächste Woche 307
Nacht f 305
Nachthemd n 31, 35
Nachtisch m 70, 153
Nachttischlampe f 70
Nachtwäsche f 31
Nacken m 13
Nadel f 109, 276
Nadelbaum m 86
Nadelkissen n 276
Nagel m 80
Nagelfeile f 41
Nagelhaut f 15
Nagelknipser m 41
Nagelkopf m 81
Nagellack m 41
Nagellackentferner m 41
Nagelschere f 41
nahe 320
nähen 277
Näherin f 277
Nähkorb m 276
Nähmaschine f 276
Nahrungsmittel n 118,
130
Nahrungsmittel in
Flaschen n 134
Naht f 34, 52
Namibia 317
Nascherei f 113
Nase f 14
Nasenbluten n 44
Nasenklemme f 238
Nasenloch n 14
Nasenriemen m 242
Nashorn n 291
nass 286, 321
Nation f 315
Nationalpark m 261
Naturfaser f 31
Naturheilkunde f 55
Naturreis m 130
Naturwissenschaft f 162
Navi m 195
navigieren 240
Nebelfleck m 280
neben 320
Nebengebäude n 182
Nebenwirkungen f 109
Neffe m 23
Negativ n 271
negative Elektrode f 167
Nektarine f 126
Nelke f 110
Nenner m 165

Nennwert m 97
Nepal 318
Neptun m 280
Nerv m 19, 50
Nervensystem n 19
nervös 25
Nessel f 297
Netz n 217, 226, 227, 231
netzen 245
Netzhaut f 51
Netzwerk n 176
neu 321
Neubelag m 187
neue Kartoffel f 124
Neugeborene n 53
Neujahr n 27
Neumond m 280
neun 308
neunhundert 308
neunter 309
neunzehn 308
neunzehnhundert 307
neunzehnhunderteins 307
neunzehnhundertzehn 307
neunzehnter 309
neunzig 308
neunzigster 309
Neurologie f 49
Neuseeland 319
neutral 60
neutrale Zone f 224
Nicaragua 314
nicht falten 98
Nichte f 23
Nickel m 289
Niederlande 316
niedrig 321
Niere f 18, 119
Niesen n 44
Niger 317
Nigeria 317
Nilpferd n 291
Nockenriemen m 203
Nord- und Mittelamerika 314
Norden m 312
Nordkorea 318
nördliche Halbkugel f 283
nördliche Polarkreis m 283
Nordpol m 283
Nordpolarmeer n 312
Nordsee f 312
normal 39
Norwegen 316
Notation f 256
Notaufnahme f 48
Notausgang m 210
Note f 163, 256
Noten f 255, 256
Notfall m 46
Nothebel m 209
Notizblock m 173
Notizbuch n 172

Notizen f 191
Notizen machen 163
Notrufsäule f 195
November m 306
Nudelholz n 69
Nudeln f 158
Nugat m 113
null 230, 308
Nummernschild n 198
Nüsse f 151
Nüsse und das Dörrobst f, n 129
Nylon n 277

O

oben 98
Oberarmknochen m 17
obere Kuchenteil m 141
Oberschenkel m 12
Oberschenkelknochen m 17
Oberschenkelmuskeln m 16
Objektivlinse f 167
Objektträger m 167
Oboe f 257
Obsidian m 288
Obst n 107, 126, 128, 157
Obstanbau m 183
Obstkorb m 126
Obstkuchenform f 69
Obstsaft m 156
Obsttortelette n 140
Obus m 196
offen 321
offene Gedränge n 221
ohne 320
ohne Bedienung 152
ohne Kohlensäure 144
Ohr n 14
Öhr n 244
Ohrring m 36
Okra f 122
Oktober m 306
Okular n 167
Okularmuschel f 269
Öl n 142, 199
Öle n 134
Ölfarben f 274
Oliven f 151
Olivenöl n 134
Ölmessstab m 202
Ölsumpf m 204
Öltanker m 215
Oman 318
Omelett n 158
Onkel m 22
Onkologie f 49
online 177
Onyx m 289
Opal m 288
Oper f 255
Operation f 48
Operationssaal m 48
Ophthalmologie f 49
Optiker m 189
orange 274

Orange f 126
Orangeade f 144
Orangenmarmelade f 134, 156
Orangensaft m 148
Orchester n 254, 256
Orchestergraben m 254
Orchidee f 111
Ordner m 172, 177
Oregano m 133
Origami n 275
Orthopädie f 49
Öse f 37, 276
Osten m 312
Osteopathie f 54
Osterglocke f 111
Ostern n 27
Österreich 316
Ostsee f 313
Ost-Timor 319
Otter m 290
Ouvertüre f 256
Oval n 164
Overall m 82
Ozean m 282
Ozeandampfer m 215
Ozonschicht f 286

P

Paar n 24
Päckchen n 311
Päckchen Zigaretten n 112
Packung f 311
Paddel n 241
Pädiatrie f 49
Paket n 99
Pakistan 318
Palette f 186, 274
Palme f 86, 296
Palmherzen n 122
Panama 314
Pandabär m 291
Paniermehl n 139
Panzer m 293
Papagei m 293
Papaya f 128
Papierbehälter m 172
Papierklammer f 173
Papierkorb m 172, 177
Papiermaché n 275
Papierserviette f 154
Papiertaschentuch n 108
Papiertaschentuch-schachtel f 70
Pappe f 275
Pappel f 296
Paprika f 124
Paprika m 132
Papua-Neuguinea 319
Par n 233
Paraguay 315
parallel 165
Parallelogramm n 164
Paranuss f 129
Parfum n 41
Parfümerie f 105
Park m 261, 262

parken 195
Parkett n 254
Parkplatz m 298
Parkuhr f 195
Parmesan m 142
Partner m 23
Partnerin f 23
Parfümerie f 105
Pass m 213, 226
Passagier m 216
Passagierhafen m 216
Passah m 27
Passcode m 99
Passionsfrucht f 128
Passkontrolle f 212, 213
Pastellstifte m 274
Pastete f 142, 156, 158
Pasteten f 143
Pastetenform f 69
pasteurisiert 137
Pastinake f 125
Patchwork n 277
Pathologie f 49
Patientenstuhl m 50
Patient-tabelle f 48
Patientin f 45
Patio m 85
Pause f 254, 269
Pausenzeichen n 256
Pay-Kanal m 269
Pazifische Ozean m 312
Pecannuss f 129
Pedal n 206
Pediküre f 41
Peeling n 41
Pelikan m 292
Pendler m 208
Penguin m 292
Penis m 21
Peperoni f 124, 143
Pepperoni f 142
per Luftpost 98
Pergola f 84
Periduralanästhesie f 52
Periodikum n 168
Perlenkette f 36
Persimone f 128
Personal m 175
Personalabteilung f 175
Personenwaage f 45
persönliche Bestleistung f 234
Peru 315
Perücke f 39
Pessar n 21
Petersilie f 133
Petrischale f 166
Pfannenwender m 68
Pfannkuchen m 157
Pfau m 293
Pfeffer m 64, 152
Pfefferkorn n 132
Pfefferminz f 113
Pfefferminztee m 149
Pfeife f 112
Pfeil m 249
Pferch m 185

Pferd n 185, 235, 242
Pferderennen n 243
Pferdeschwanz m 39
Pferdestall m 243
Pfingstrose f 111
Pfirsich m 126, 128
pflanzen 183
Pflanzen f 296
Pflanzenarten f 86
Pflanzenöl n 135
Pflanzenschildchen n 89
Pflanzschaufel f 89
Pflaster n 47
Pflaume f 126
pflücken 91
pflügen 183
pfropfen 91
Pfund n 310
Phantombild n 181
Philippinen 319
Philosophie f 169
Physik f 162, 169
Physiotherapie f 49
Picknick n 263
Picknickbank f 266
Picknickkorb m 263
Pier m 217
Pik n 273
pikante Wurst f 142
Pikkoloflöte f 257
Pilates f 251
Pille f 21, 109
Pilot m 190, 211
Pilz m 125
Piment m 132
Piniennuss f 129
PIN-Kode m 96
Pinne f 240
Pinnwand f 173
Pinsel m 274
Pint n 311
Pintobohnen f 131
Pinzette f 40, 47, 167
Pipette f 167
Pistazie f 129
Pistole f 94
Pitabrot n 139
Pizza f 154
Pizzabelag m 155
Pizzeria f 154
Plädoyer n 180
Plakat n 255
Plakatfarbe f 274
Planet m 280, 282
Planken f 85
Planschbecken n 263
Plastiktüte f 122
plastische Chirurgie f 49
Plateau n 284
Platin n 289
Platte f 283
Platten n 85
Plattengeschäft n 115
Plattenspieler m 268
Platz m 299
Platzanweiser m 255
Platzverweis m 223
Plazenta f 52

deutsch

plus 165
Pluto m 280
pochieren 67
pochiert 159
Podium n 256
Poker n 273
Pol m 60, 282
Polarlicht n 286
Polaroidkamera f 270
Polen 316
polieren 77
Politologie f 169
Politur f 77
Polizei f 94
Polizeiauto n 94
Polizeiwache f 94
Polizeizelle f 94
Polizist m 94, 189
Poller m 214, 298
Polo n 243
Polster n 220, 224, 225
Polyester n 277
Pommes frites 154
Poolbillard n 249
Pop m 259
Popcorn n 255
Pore f 15
Porridge m 157
Port m 176
Portefeuille n 97
Portemonnaie n 37
Portion f 64
Portionierer m 68
Portugal 316
Portwein m 145
Porzellan n 105
Posaune f 257
Pose f 244
positive Elektrode n 167
Post f 98
Postanweisung f 98
Postbeamte m 98
Postgebühr f 98
postgraduierte 169
Postkarte f 112
Postleitzahl f 98
Postsack m 98
Poststempel m 98
Posttasche f 190
Praline f 113
Präsentation f 174
Preis m 152
Preiselbeere f 127
Preisliste f 154
Prellung f 46
Premiere f 254
Presse f 178
Pressluftbohrer m 187
Privatbadezimmer n 100
private Fitnesstrainerin f 250
Privatjet m 211
Privatunterhaltung f 268
Privatzimmer n 48
Probleme n 271
Profilsäge f 81

Programm n 176, 254, 269
Programmgestaltung f 178
Promenade f 265
Promotion f 169
Propeller m 211
Prosciutto f 143
Prospekt m 254
Prostata f 21
Protokoll n 174
Protokollführer m 180
Provinz f 315
Provision f 97
Prozentsatz m 165
Prozessor m 176
Prüfung f 163
Psychiatrie f 49
Psychotherapie f 55
Publikum n 254
Puck m 224
Puder m 109
Puderdose f 40
Puderpinsel m 40
Puderquaste f 40
Puderrouge f 40
Puerto Rico 314
Pullover m 33
Puls m 47
Pult n 162, 269
Pulver n 77
Pumps m 37
Punkmusik f 259
pünktlich
Pupille f 51
Puppe f 75
Puppenhaus n 75
püriert 159
Pute f 119
Putter m 233
putzen 77
Puzzle n 273
Pyramide f 164

Q
Quadrat n 164
Quadratfuß m 310
Quadratmeter m 310
Qualle f 295
Quappe f 120
Quart n 311
Quarz m 289
Quecksilber n 289
quer 271
Querflöte f 257
Querlatte f 222
Querruder n 210
Quiche f 142
Quitte f 128
Quittung f 152

R
Rachen m 19
Rack n 268
Racquetball n 231
Rad n 198, 207
Rad fahren 207

Radar n 214, 281
Radfahren n 263
Radicchio n 123
Radiergummi m 163
Radieschen n 124
Radio n 179, 268
Radiologie f 49
Radiowecker m 70
Radius m 164
Radkappe f 202
Radmuttern f 203
Radschlüssel m 203
Rafting n 241
Rahmen m 206, 230
Rahmkäse m 136
Rakete f 211
Rallyefahren n 249
RAM n 176
Ramadan m 26
Rap m 259
Raps m 184
Rapsöl m 135
Rasen m 85, 90
Rasenmäher m 88, 90
Rasenrandschere f 88
Rasensprenger m 89
Rasieren n 73
Rasierklinge f 73
Rasierschaum m 73
Rasierwasser n 73
Rassel f 74
Rathaus n 299
Ratte f 290
Rauch m 95
Rauchen n 112
Räucherfisch m 143
Räucherheringe m 157
Rauchmelder m 95
Raumanzug m 281
Raumfähre f 281
Raumforschung f 281
Raumstation f 281
Raupe f 295
Raureif m 287
Reagenzglas n 166
Rebound m 227
Rechen m 88
Rechnung f 152
Recht n 180
rechte Feld n 229
rechte Spur f 194
Rechteck n 164
rechte Spur f 194
rechts 260
Rechtsabteilung f 175
Rechtsanwalt m 180, 190
Rechtsberatung f 180
Rechtsfall m 180
Rechtssteuerung f 201
Rechtswissenschaft f 169
Reck n 235
Recyclingbehälter m 61
Redakteurin f 191
Reflexzonenmassage f 54
Reformhaus n 115
Regen m 287

Regenbogen m 287
Regenbogenforelle f 120
Regenhaut f 245, 267
Regenmantel m 31, 32
Regenschirm m 36
Regenwald m 285
Reggae m 259
Region f 315
Regisseur m 254
Reibahle f 80
Reibe f 68
reiben 67
reif 129
Reifen m 198, 205, 206
Reifendruck m 203
Reifenpanne f 203, 207
Reifenprofil n 207
Reifenschlüssel m 207
Reihe f 210, 254
Reihen(haus) 58
Reiki n 55
Reiniger m 41
Reinigung f 115
Reinigungsartikel m 77
Reinigungsmittel n 51, 77
Reinigungstuch n 108
Reis m 130, 158, 184
Reisebüro n 114
Reisebürokauffrau f 190
Reisebus m 196
Reiseführer m 260
Reisekrankheitstabletten f 109
Reisescheck m 97
Reisetasche f 37
Reiseziel n 213
Reismelde f 130
Reißnagel m 173
Reißverschluss m 277
Reiten n 263
Reiter m 242
Reitgerte f 242
Reithelm m 242
Reithose f 242
Reitsport m 242
Reitstiefel m 242
Reitweg m 263
Rekord m 234
Rennbahn f 234, 243
Rennboot n 214
Rennbügel m 207
Rennen n 234
rennen 228
Rennfahrer m 249
Rennmaschine f 205
Rennpferd n 243
Rennrad n 206
Rennrodeln n 247
Rennsport m 249
Reparaturkasten m 207
Reporterin f 179
Reproduktion f 20
Reptilien n 293
Restaurant n 101, 152
Rettungsboot n 214, 240

Rettungsring m 240
Rettungssanitäter m 94
Rettungsschwimmer m 265
Rettungsturm m 265
Return n 231
Revers n 32
Rezept n 45
R-Gespräch n 99
Rhabarber m 127
Rhombus m 164
rhythmische Gymnastik f 235
Richter m 180
Richtungsangaben f 260
Riemen m 207
Riesenslalom m 247
Rinde f 136, 142, 296
Rindfleisch n 118
Ring m 36
Ringbefestigungen f 89
Ringe m 235
Ringen n 236
Ringfinger m 15
Rinnstein m 299
Rippe f 17, 126
Rippen f 155
Rippenstück n 119
Robbe f 290
Robe f 169
Rochen m 120, 294
Rochenflügel m 120
Rock m 30, 34
Rockbund m 35
Rockkonzert n 258
Rocky Moutains 312
Rodeo n 243
Roggenbrot n 138
Roggenmehl n 138
roh 124, 129
Rohr n 202
Rohrabschneider m 81
Rohrzange f 81
Rokoko- 301
Rolle f 244, 245, 311
Rolle Toilettenpapier f 72
Rollenheft n 254
Roller m 83, 205
Rollo n 63
Rollstuhl m 48
Rollstuhlzugang m 197
Rolltreppe f 104
Röntgenaufnahme f 48, 50
Röntgenbild n 50
Röntgenbildbetrachter m 45
rosa 274
Röschen n 122
Rose f 110
rosé 145
Rosenkohl m 122
Rosenschere f 89
Rosine f 129
Rosinenbrot n 139
Rosmarin m 133
Rost m 67
rostfreie Stahl m 79

deutsch

rot 39, 145, 274
rotbraun 39
Rote Bete f 125
rote Fleisch f 118
rote Karte f 223
Rote Meer n 313
rote Meeräsche f 120
roten Bohnen f 131
roten Linsen f 131
Rotfärbung der Augen f 271
Rotorblatt n 211
Rotzunge f 120
Rough n 232
Route f 260
Ruanda 317
Rübe f 124
Rubin m 288
Rücken m 13
Rückenbürste f 73
Rückenflosse f 294
rückenfrei 35
Rückenlehne f 210
Rückenmuskel m 16
Rückenschwimmen f 239
Rückgabedatum n 168
Rückhand f 231
Rücklauf m 269
Rücklicht n 207
Rucksack m 31, 37, 267
Rücksitz m 200
Rückspiegel m 198
Rückstrahler m 207
rückwärts fahren 195
Ruder n 241
Ruderboot n 214
Ruderer m 241
Rudermaschine f 250
rudern 241
Rufknopf m 48
Rugby n 221
Rugbyball m 221
Rugbyspieler m 221
Rugbytrikot n 221
Rührei n 157
rühren 67
Rührschüssel f 69
Rukula n 123
Rum m 145
Rum mit Cola n 151
Rumänien 316
Rumpf m 210, 214, 240
Rumpfheben n 251
Rumpsteak n 119
Runde f 237
runde Ausschnitt m 33
Rundfunkstation f 179
Rundkorn- 130
Rüssel m 291
Russische Föderation 318
Rutsche f 263
rutschen 229

S

säen 90, 183

Safaripark m 262
Safran m 132
Saft m 109, 127
Säfte und Milchshakes m 149
saftig 127
sägen 79
Sahara f 313
Sahne f 137, 140, 157
Sahnetorte f 141
Saint Kitts und Nevis 314
Saint Lucia 314
Saint Vinzent und die Grenadinen 314
Saison- 129
Saite f 230, 258
Saiteninstrumente n 256
Salamander m 294
Salami f 142
Salat m 123, 149
Salatsoße f 158
Salbe f 47, 109
Salbei m 133
Salomonen 319
Salto m 235
Salz n 64, 152
salzig 155
Sambia 317
Samen m 88, 122, 130
Samenausführungsgang m 21
Samenbläschen n 21
Samenleiter m 21
Sämling m 91
Samstag m 306
San Marino 316
Sand m 85, 264
Sandale f 37
Sandalen f 31
Sandburg f 265
Sandkasten m 263
Sandsack m 237
Sandstein m 288
Sandwich m 155
Sandwichtheke f 143
Sängerin f 191
Sao Tomé und Príncipe 317
Saphir 288
Sardine f 120
Sardinien 316
Satellit m 281
Satellitenschüssel f 269
Satsuma f 126
satt 64
Sattel m 206, 242
Sattelgurt m 242
Sattelstütze f 206
Saturn m 280
Satz m 230
Sattel m 206, 242
Sauber 127
Sauerteigbrot n 139
Sauger m 75
Säugetiere n 290
Saugglocke f 53

Säuglingspflege f 74
Saugschlauch m 77
Säule f 300
Saum m 34
Sauna f 250
saure Sahne f 137
Saxophon n 257
Scan m 48
Scanner m 106, 176
Schablone f 83
Schach n 272
Schachbrett n 272
Schachtel Pralinen f 113
Schädel m 17
Schaf n 185
Schaffarm f 183
Schaffner m 209
Schafsmilch f 137
Schal m 31
Schale f 126, 127, 128, 129
schälen 67
Schäler m 68
Schalldämpfer m 204
Schalotte f 125
schalten 207
Schalter m 60, 96, 98, 100
Schalthebel m 201, 207
Schamlippen f 20
scharf 124
Schaschlik m 158
Schattenpflanze f 87
Schauer m 286
Schaufel f 187
Schaukel f 263
Schaum m 148
Schaumbad n 73
Schaumlöffel m 68
Schauspieler m 179, 254
Schauspielerin f 191, 254
Scheck m 96
Scheckheft n 96
Scheibe f 119, 139
Scheibenbrot n 138
Scheibenputzmittel-behälter m 202
Scheibenschießen n 249
Scheibenwaschanlage f 199
Scheibenwischer m 198
Scheide f 20
Scheidenmuschel f 121
Scheidung f 26
Schein m 97
Scheinwerfer m 198, 205, 259
Schellfisch m 120
Schenkel m 119
Schere f 38, 47, 276
Scheune f 182
Schiebedach n 202
Schiedsrichter m 222, 225, 226, 229, 230
Schiedsrichterball m 226
Schiefer m 288

Schienbein n 12, 17
Schiene f 47, 208
schießen 223, 227
Schiff n 214
Schiffsschraube f 214
Schilddrüse f 18
Schildkröte f 293
Schinken m 119, 143, 156
Schirm m 233
Schirmständer m 59
Schlafabteil n 209
Schlafanzug m 30, 33
Schläfe f 14
Schlafen n 74
Schlaflosigkeit f 71
Schlafmatte f 267
Schlafmittel n 109
Schlafsack m 267
Schlafzimmer n 70
Schlag m 233
Schlaganfall m 44
Schläge m 231
schlagen 67, 224, 225, 229
Schläger m 224
Schlägerspiele n 231
Schlagfehler m 228
Schlagholz n 225
Schlaginstrumente n 257
Schlagmal n 228
Schlagmann m 225, 228
Schlagsahne f 137
Schlagzeug n 258
Schlagzeuger m 258
Schlange f 293
Schlauch m 95, 207
Schlauchboot n 215
Schlauchwagen m 89
schlecht 321
Schlegel m 275
Schleier m 35
Schleierkraut n 110
Schleifmaschine f 78
Schleppdampfer m 215
Schleppe f 35
schleudern 76
Schleudertrauma n 46
Schlick m 85
Schließfächer n 239
Schlinge f 46
Schlittenfahren n 247
Schlittschuh laufen 224
Schloss n 59
Schlot m 283
Schlucht f 284
Schlüssel m 59, 80, 207
Schlüsselbein n 17
Schlüsselblume f 297
schmal 321
Schmerzmittel n 109
Schmerztabletten f 47
Schmetterball m 231
Schmetterling m 295
schmirgeln 82
Schmirgelpapier n 81, 83
Schmortopf m 69

Schmuck m 36
Schmuckkasten m 36
Schmucksteine m 288
schmutzige Wäsche f 76
Schnabel m 293
schnarchen 71
Schnauze f 293
Schnecke f 295
Schnee m 287
Schneeanzug m 30
Schneebesen m 68
Schneemobil n 247
Schneeregen m 286
schneiden 38, 67, 79, 277
Schneider m 80, 88, 191
Schneiderei f 115
Schneiderkreide f 276
Schneiderpuppe f 276
Schneidezahn m 50
schnell 321
schnell zubereitet 130
Schnellbootsport n 241
Schnellbratgericht n 158
Schnellimbiss m 154
Schnellstraße f 195
Schnitt m 46
Schnitte f 121
Schnittlauch m 133
Schnittmuster m 276
schnitzen 79
Schnorchel m 239
Schnur f 244
schnurlose Telefon n 99
Schnurrhaare m 290
Schnürschuh m 37
Schnürsenkel m 37
Schock m 47
schockiert 25
Schokolade f 156
Schokoladenaufstrich m 135
Schokoladenmilchshake m 149
Schokoladentorte f 140
Schönheit f 40
Schönheitsbehandlungen f 41
Schönheitspflege f 105
Schöpflöffel m 68
Schornstein m 58, 214
Schot f 241
Schote f 122
Schraube f 80
Schraubenschlüssel m 80
Schraubenzieher m 80
Schraubenziehereinsätze m 80
Schraubstock m 78
schreiben 162
Schreibtisch m 172
Schreibwaren f 105
schreien 25
Schreiner m 188
Schriftart f 177
Schritt m 243
schrubben 77

deutsch

Schubkarren m 88
Schublade f 66, 70, 172
schüchtern 25
Schuh m 233
Schuh mit hohem
  Absatz m 37
Schuhabteilung f 104
Schuhe m 34, 37
Schuhgeschäft n 114
Schulbuch n 163
Schulbus m 196
schuldig 181
Schule f 162, 299
Schüler m 162
Schuljunge m 162
Schulleiter m 163
Schulmädchen n 162
Schultasche f 162
Schulter f 13
Schulterblatt n 17
Schulterpolster m 35
Schulterriemen m 37
Schuppe f 121, 294
Schuppen f 39, 293
Schuppen m 84
Schürze f 30, 69
Schuss m 151
Schüssel f 65
Schutz m 88
Schutzanstrich m 83
Schutzblech n 205
Schutzbrille f 81, 167
Schutzhelm m 95, 186,
  224
Schutzkappe f 270
Schutzmaske f 228
schwach 321
Schwager m 23
Schwägerin f 23
Schwalbe f 292
Schwamm m 73, 74, 83
Schwan m 293
schwanger 52
Schwangerschaft f 52
Schwangerschaftstest m
  52
Schwanz m 121, 242,
  290, 294
Schwänzchen n 39
Schwarte f 119
schwarz 39, 272, 274
schwarze Gürtel m 237
schwarze Johannisbeere f
  127
schwarze Kaffee m 148
schwarze Loch n 280
Schwarze Meer n 313
schwarze Olive f 143
schwarze Tee m 149
Schwebebalken m 235
Schweden 316
Schwefel m 289
Schweif m 280
Schweifsäge f 81
Schwein n 185
Schweinefarm f 183
Schweinefleisch n 118
Schweinestall m 185

Schweißband n 230
Schweiz f 316
schwer 321
Schwerkraft f 280
Schwert n 241
Schwertfisch m 120,
  294
Schwester f 22
Schwiegermutter f 23
Schwiegersohn m 22
Schwiegertochter f 22
Schwiegervater m 23
Schwimmbad n 101
Schwimmbecken n 238,
  250
Schwimmbrille f 238
schwimmen 238
Schwimmer m 61, 238
Schwimmfloß n 238
Schwimmflosse f 239
Schwimmflügel m 238
Schwimmreifen m 265
Schwimmsport m 238
Schwimmstile m 239
Schwimmweste f 240
schwingen 232
Science-Fiction-Film m
  255
Scotch mit Wasser m 151
Scrabble n 272
Scrollbalken m 177
sechs 308
Sechseck n 164
sechshundert 308
sechster 309
sechzehn 308
sechzehnter 309
sechzig 308
sechzigster 309
sedimentär 288
See m 285
Seebarsch m 120
Seebrassen m 120
Seefischerei f 245
Seelöwe m 290
Seemann m 189
Seepferd m 294
Seepolyp m 121, 295
Seestern m 295
Seezunge f 120
Segel n 241
Segelboot n 215
Segelfliegen n 248
Segelflugzeug n 211,
  248
Segeljacht f 240
Segelsport m 240
Sehenswürdigkeiten f
  261
Sehkraft f 51
Sehne f 17
Sehnenband n 17
Sehnerv m 51
Sehtest m 51
Seide f 277
Seife f 73
Seifenoper f 178
Seifenschale f 73

Seil n 248
Seilspringen n 251
sein Testament machen
  26
Seite f 164
Seitendeck n 240
Seitenleitwerk n 210
Seitenlinie f 220, 221,
  226, 230
Seitenpferd n 235
Seitenruder n 210
Seitenspiegel m 198
Seitenstraße f 299
Seitenstreifen m 194
Seitfußstoß m 237
Sekretariat n 168
Sekunde f 304
Sekundenzeiger m
Selbstbräunungscreme f
  41
selbstsicher 25
Selbstverteidigung f 237
Sellerie m 124
senden 177, 178
Sendung f 179
Senegal 317
Senf m 155
Senfkorn n 131
Senkblei n 82
senkrecht 165
Sepie f 121
September m 306
Serbien 316
Server m 176
Serviceprovider m 177
servieren 64
Servierlöffel m 68
Serviette f 65
Serviettenring m 65
Sesamkorn n 131
Sesamöl n 134
Sessel m 63
Sessellift m 246
Set n 64, 179
Setzkasten m 89
Setzkescher m 244
seufzen 25
Shampoo n 38
Sherry m 145
Shiatsu n 54
Shorts 30, 33
Sibirien 313
sich aufwärmen 251
sich befreunden 26
sich übergeben 44
sich verlieben 26
Sicherheit f 75, 240
Sicherheitsbohrer m 80
Sicherheitsgurt m 198,
  211
Sicherheitsnadel f 47
Sicherheitssperre f 246
Sicherheitsventil n 61
Sicherheitsvorkehrungen f
  212
sichern 177
Sicherung f 60
Sicherungskasten m 60,

203
Sieb n 68, 89
sieben 91, 138, 308
siebenhundert 308
siebter 309
siebzehn 308
siebzehnter 309
siebzig 308
siebzigster 309
Siegerpodium m 235
Sierra Leone 317
Signal n 209
Silber n 235, 289
Silo m 183
Simbabwe 317
Singapur 319
Sinus m 19
Sirene f 94
Sitz m 204, 209, 210,
  242
Sitzfläche f 64
Sitzung f 174
Sitzungsraum m 174
Sizilien 316
Skalpell n 81, 167
Skateboard n 249
Skateboardfahren n 249,
  263
Skelett n 17
Ski m 246
Skibrille f 247
Skijacke f 246
Skiläuferin f 246
Skipiste f 246
Skisport m 246
Skisprung m 247
Skistiefel m 246
Skistock m 246
Skizze f 275
Skizzenblock m 275
Skorpion m 295
Slalom f 247
Slice m 230
Slip m 33, 35
Slipeinlage f 108
Slipper m 37
Slowakei 316
Slowenien 316
Smaragd m 288
Smartphone n 176
SMS f 99
Snackbar f 148
Snooker n 249
Snowboarding n 247
Socken f 33
Sodabrot n 139
Sodawasser n 144
Sofa n 62
Sofakissen n 62
Sofortbildkamera f 270
Software f 176
Sohle f 37
Sohn m 22
Sojabohnen f 131
Sojasprosse f 122
Soldat m 189
Somalia 317

Sommer m 31, 307
Sommersprosse f 15
Sonate f 256
Sonde f 50
Sonne f 280
Sonnenaufgang m 305
sonnenbaden 264
Sonnenbank f 41
Sonnenblock m 108,
  265
Sonnenblume f 184, 297
Sonnenblumenkern m
  131
Sonnenblumenöl n 134
Sonnenbrand m 46
Sonnenbräune f 41
Sonnenbrille f 51, 265
Sonnenhut m 30, 265
Sonnenmilch f 265
Sonnenschein m 286
Sonnenschirm m 264
Sonnenschutzcreme f
  108
Sonnensystem n 280
Sonnenuhr f 262
Sonnenuntergang m 305
sonnig 286
Sonntag m 306
Sorbett n 141
Soße f 134, 143, 155
Soufflé n 158
Souffléform f 69
Soziussitz m 204
Spachtel m 68, 82
Spachtelmasse f 83
spachteln 82
Spalier n 84
Spanholz n 79
Spanien 316
Spann m 15
Spannung f 60
Spareinlagen f 96
Spargel m 124
Sparkonto n 97
Sparren m 237
spät 305
Spatel m 167
Spaten m 88, 265
später 304
Spatz m 292
Specht m 292
Speck m 118
Speckscheibe f 119
Speerfischen n 245
Speerwerfen n 234
Speibecken n 50
Speiche f 17, 207
Speicher m 176
Speisekarte f 148, 153,
  154
Speiseröhre f 19
Speisewagen m 209
Spermium m 20
Sperrholz n 79
Spezialitäten f 152
Spiegel m 40, 71, 167
Spiegelei n 157
Spiel n 230, 273

deutsch

Spielanzug m 30
Spielbahn f 225, 233
Spiele n 272
spielen 229, 273
Spielen n 75
Spieler m 273
Spielerbank f 229
Spielergebnis n 273
Spielernummer f 226
Spielfeld n 220, 221, 226, 228
Spielfeldgrenze f 225
Spielfilm m 269
Spielhaus n 75
Spielmarke f 272
Spielplatz m 263
Spielshow f 178
Spielstand m 220
Spielwaren f 105
Spielzeug n 75
Spielzeugkorb m 75
Spieß m 68
Spikes m 233
Spin m 230
Spinat m 123
Spinne f 295
Spinnerkasten m 244
Spion m 59
Spirale f 21
Spitze f 35, 37, 122, 165, 246
Spitzenklöppelei f 277
Spitzer m 163
Spitzhacke f 187
Splitter m 46
Sport m 162, 220, 236
Sportangeln n 245
Sportartikel m 105
Sportjackett n 33
Sportkabriolett n 198
Sportler m 191
Sportplatz m 168
Sportschuh m 37
Sportschuhe m 31
Sportwagen m 75
Sprachen f 162
Sprachmitteilung f 99
Spray m 109
Sprechanlage f 59
Sprecherin f 174
Sprechzimmer n 45
Springbrunnen m 85
springen 227
springen lassen 227
Springer m 238, 272
Springreiten n 243
Sprinter m 234
Spritzbeutel m 69
Spritze 48, 109, 167, 311
Spritzschutz m 66
Sprühdose f 311
sprühen 91
Sprung m 235, 237, 239, 243
Sprungbrett n 235, 238
Sprungfeder f 71
Spülbecken n 66

Spule f 276
Spüle f 61
spülen 76, 77
Spuler m 276
Spülkasten m 61
Spülmaschine f 66
Squash n 231
Sri Lanka 318
Staat m 315
Staatsanwaltschaft f 180
Stab m 225, 235
Stabhochsprung m 234
Stachel m 295
Stachelbeere f 127
Stadien n 23
Stadion n 223
Stadt f 298, 299
Stadtplan m 261
Stadtrundfahrtbus m 260
Staffelei f 274
Staffellauf m 235
Stahlwolle f 81
Stake f 245
Stall m 185
Stallbursche m 243
Stamm m 296
Stammaktie f 97
Ständer m 88, 268
Stange f 90, 207, 250
Stangen f 133
Stangenbohne f 122
Stangensellerie m 122
stark 321
Start- und Landebahn f 212
Startblock m 234, 238
starten 211
Startlinie f 234
Startsprung m 239
Stativ n 166, 270, 281
Staub wischen 77
Staubgefäß n 297
Staubsauger m 77, 188
Staubtuch n 77
Staudamm m 300
Staudenrabatte f 85
stechen 90
Stechmücke f 295
Stechpalme f 296
Steckdose f 60
Stecker m 60
Stecknadel f 276
Steckschlüssel m 80
Steg m 258
Steigbügel m 242
Stein m 272, 275
Steingarten m 84
Steinobst n 126
Steiß- 52
Steißbein n 17
Stempel m 173
Stempelkissen n 173
Stengel m 111, 297
Steppdecke f 71
sterben 26
stereo 269
steril 20, 47
Stern m 280

Sternarnis m 133
Sternbild n 281
Sternfrucht f 128
Sternhyazinthen f 297
Stethoskop n 45
Steuer f 96
Steuerhebel m 269
Steuerrakete f 281
Steuerung f 204
Stich m 46, 277
Stichplatte f 276
Stichsäge f 78
Stichwähler m 276
Stickerei f 277
Stickrahmen m 277
Stiefel m 37, 220
Stiefmutter f 23
Stiefsohn m 23
Stieftochter f 23
Stiefvater m 23
Stiel m 112, 187, 297
Stier m 185
Stillbüstenhalter m 53
stillen 53
Stillen n 53
Stimmbänder m 19
Stipendium n 169
Stirn f 14
Stirnmuskel m 16
Stirnriemen m 242
Stirnrunzeln n 25
Stock m 58, 91
Stoff m 276, 277
Stoffdrücker m 276
Stoffwindel f 30
stolz 25
Stop m 269
stopfen 277
Stoppball m 230
Stoppuhr f 234
Stöpsel m 72, 166
Storch m 292
Stoß m 237, 239
Stößel m 68
Stoßstange f 198
Stoßzahn m 291
Stoßzeit f 209
Stout m 145
Strafmaß n 181
Strafraum m 223
Strafregister n 181
Straftäter m 181
Strähnen f 39
Strampelanzug m 30
Strand m 264
Strandhäuschen n 264
Strandsandale f 37
Strandtasche f 264
Strandtuch n 265
Strang m 277
Straße f 298
Straßen f 194
Straßenanzug m 32
Straßenarbeiten f 187
Straßenbahn f 196, 208
Straßenbaustelle f 195
Straßencafé n 148
Straßenecke f 298

Straßenlaterne f 298
Straßenmarkierungen f 194
Straßenrad n 206
Straßenschild n 298
Stratosphäre f 286
Strauß m 111, 292
Streaming n 269
Strebepfeiler m 301
Strecken n 251
Streichbürste f 83
Stress m 55
Strichkode m 106
Stricken n 277
Strickjacke f 32
Stricknadel f 277
Strohhalm m 144, 154
Strom m 60
Stromanschluss m 266
Stromausfall m 60
stromführende Schiene f 209
Stromkabel n 176
Stromnetz n 60
Stromschnellen f 284
Stromzähler m 60
Strumpf m 35
Strumpfband n 35
Strumpfhalter m 35
Strumpfhose f 251
Strunk m 122
Stück m 63
Stück n 140, 311
Student m 169
Studentenheim n 168
Studioeinrichtung f 178
Stufenbarren m 235
Stuhl m 64
Stunde f 163
Stundenzeiger m
Sturm m 286
Sturz m 186
Stütze f 187
stutzen 90
Stützräder m 207
subtrahieren 165
suchen 177
Südafrika 317
Sudan 317
Süden m 312
Südfrüchte f 128
Südkorea 318
südliche Halbkugel f 283
Südpolarmeer n 313
Südsudan 317
Sultanine f 129
Sumo n 237
Sumpf m 285
Supermarkt m 106
Suppe f 153, 158
Suppenlöffel m 65
Suppenteller m 65
Surfbrett n 241
Surfer m 241
Suriname 315
süß 124, 127, 155
süße Aufstrich m 134
Süßkartoffel f 125

Süßwaren f 107, 113
Süßwarengeschäft n 113
Süßwasserangeln n 245
Swasiland 317
Sweatshirt n 33
Symbol n 177
Symphonie f 256
Synagoge f 300
Synchronschwimmen n 239
synthetisch 31
Syrien 318
System n 176

T

Tabak m 112, 184
Tablett n 152, 154
Tachometer m 201, 204
Tadschikistan 318
Taekwondo n 236
Tafel f 162
Tafel Schokolade f 113
Tag m 306
Tagesdecke f 70
Tagesordnung f 174
Tai Chi n 236
Taille f 12
Takelung f 215, 240
Taktstock m 256
Taktstrich m 256
Tal n 284
Tamarillo f 128
Tamburin n 257
Tampon m 108
Tandem m 206
Tangelo f 126
Tankstelle f 199
Tankstellenplatz m 199
Tansania 317
Tante f 22
Tanzakademie f 169
Tänzerin f 191
Tanzmusik f 259
Tapedeck n 268
Tapete f 82, 177
Tapetenkleister m 82
Tapezierbürste f 82
Tapezieren n 82
tapezieren 82
Tapezierer m 82
Tapeziermesser n 82
Tapezierschere f 82
Tapeziertisch m 82
Tapisserie f 277
Tarowurzel f 124
Tasche f 32
Taschen f 37
Taschenlampe f 267
Taschenrechner m 165
Taschentuch n 36
Tasmanien 319
Tastatur f 172, 176
Taste f 176
Tastenfeld n 97, 99
Tätigkeiten f 77, 183
Tätowierung f 41
Taube f 292
tauchen 238

Tauchen n 239
Taucheranzug m 239
Tauchermaske f 239
Taufe f 26
Tausendfüßler m 295
Taxifahrer m 190
Taxistand m 213
Team n 229
Techniken f 237
Teddy m 75
Tee m 144, 149, 184
Tee mit Milch m 149
Tee mit Zitrone m 149
Teebeutel m 144
Teeblätter n 144
Teekanne f 65
Teelöffel m 65
Teetasse f 65
Teich m 85
Teig m 138, 140
Teilchen n 140
Teiler m 173
teilnehmen 174
Teint m 41
Telefon n 99
Telefonzelle f 99
Telegramm n 98
Teleprompter m 179
Teleskop n 281
Teller m 65
Tempel m 300
Temperatur f 286
Temperaturanzeige f 201
Tennis n 230
Tennisball m 230
Tennisplatz m 230
Tennisschläger m 230
Tennisschuhe m 231
Tennisspieler m 231
Teppich m 63, 71
Tequila m 145
Termin m 45, 175
Terminal m 212
Terminkalender m 173, 175
Terminplaner m 175
Termite f 295
Terparybohnen f 131
Terpentin n 83
Terrassencafé n 148
Territorium n 315
Tesafilm m 173
Tesafilmhalter m 173
Text m 259
Thailand 318
Thanksgiving Day m 27
Theater n 254, 299
Theaterkostüm n 255
Theaterstück n 254
Theke f 142, 150
Therapeutin f 55
Thermometer m 45, 167
Thermosflasche f 267
Thermosphäre f 286
Thermostat m 61
Thermounterwäsche f 35
Thermowäsche f 267
Thriller m 255

Thymian m 133
Tiefe f 165
tiefe Ende n 239
tiefgefroren 121, 124
Tiegel m 166
Tierärztin f 189
Tiere n 292, 294
Tierfutter n 107
Tierhandlung f 115
Tiger m 291
Tintenfisch m 121, 295
Tisch m 64, 148, 167
Tischdecke f 64
Tischtennis n 231
Tischtennisschläger m 231
Titel m 168
Toast m 157
Toaster m 66
Tochter f 22
Toffee n 113
Togo 317
Toilette f 72
Toiletten f 104, 266
Toilettenartikel m 41, 107
Toilettenbürste f 72
Toilettensitz m 61, 72
Tomate f 125, 157
Tomatenketchup m 154
Tomatensaft m 144, 149
Ton m 275
Tonabnehmer m 258
Tonhöhe f 256
Tonicwater n 144
Tonleiter f 256
Tonmeister m 179
Tonne f 310
Tonspur f 255
Tonstudio n 179
Topas m 288
Töpfchen n 74
Töpferei f 275
Topfhandschuh m 69
Topfpflanze f 87, 110
Topinambur m 125
Tor n 85, 182, 221, 223, 224, 247
Torlinie f 220, 223, 224
Tornado m 287
Tornetz n 222
Torpfosten m 220, 222
Torraum m 221, 223
Törtchenform f 69
Torwächter m 225
Torwart m 222, 224
Touchdown m 220
Tourenfahrrad n 206
Tourer m 205
Tourist m 260
Touristenattraktion f 260
Touristenbus m 197
Touristeninformation f 261
Trab n 243
Trabbrennen n 243
Tragbahre f 94
Tragebettchen n 75
Träger m 35, 186

trägerlos 34
Tragfläche f 210
Tragflügelboot n 215
trainieren 251
Trainingsanzug m 31, 32
Trainingsrad m 250
Trainingsschuhe m 251
Traktor m 182
Tranchiergabel f 68
Träne f 51
Transfer m 223
Transformator m 60
Transmission f 202
Trapez n 164
Traubenkernöl m 134
Traubensaft m 144
traurig 25
Trekking n 243
Treppe f 59
Treppenabsatz m 59
Treppengeländer m 59
Treppengitter m 75
treten 207
Trethebel m 61
Tretmaschine f 250
Triangel m 257
Trichter m 166
Triebwerk n 210
Trifle n 141
Trimester n 52
Trinidad und Tobago 314
Trittleiter f 82
Trizeps m 16
trocken 39, 41, 130, 145, 286, 321
Trockenblumen f 111
Trockendock n 217
trocknen 76
Trockner m 76
Trog m 183
Trommel f 258
Trompete f 257
Tropen f 283
Tropfen m 109
Tropfer m 109, 167
Tropfinfusion f 53
Troposphäre f 286
Trüffel m 113, 125
Truthahn m 185, 293
Tschad 317
Tschechische Republik 316
T-Shirt m 30, 33, 54
Tuba f 257
Tube f 311
Tülle f 80
Tulpe f 111
Tunesien 317
Tunfisch m 120
Tür f 196, 209
Turbolader m 203
Türgriff m 200
Türkei f 316
Türkette f 59
Türkis m 289
Türklingel f 59
Türklopfer m 59
Turkmenistan 318

Türknauf m 59
Turm m 272, 300
Turmalin m 288
Turmspitze f 300
Turmsprung m 239
Turnen m 235
Turnerin f 235
Turnierplatz m 243
Türriegel m 59
Türverriegelung f 200
Tüte f 311
Typen m 205

U

U-Bahn m 209
U-Bahnplan m 209
Übelkeit f 44
über 320
überbelichtet 271
Überdach n 266
Überführung f 194
Übergepäck m 212
überholen 195
Überholspur f 194
Überlauf m 61
übermorgen 307
Übernachtung mit Frühstück f 101
Überpar n 233
überrascht 25
Überschwemmung f 287
Überweisung f 49
U-Boot n 215
Übungen f 251
Übungsschwung m 233
Ufer n 284
Uganda 317
Uhr f 36
Ukraine f 316
Ulme f 296
Ultraleichtflugzeug n 211
Ultraschall m 52
Ultraschallaufnahme f 52
Ultraviolettstrahlen m 286
um 320
Umfang m 164
Umhängetasche f 37
Umlaufbahn f 280
Umleitung f 195
umpflanzen 91
Umschlag m 98
umsteigen 209
Umwelt f 280
Umzug m 27
Unentschieden n 223
Unfall m 46
Ungarn 316
ungesalzen 137
ungültige Schlag m 228
Uniform f 94, 189
Universität f 299
Universum n 280
Unkraut n 86
Unkrautvernichter m 91
unpasteurisiert 137
unscharf 271
unschuldig 181
unsichere Fangen des

Balls n 220
unter 320
Unterarm m 12
unterbelichtet 271
unterbrochen 99
untere Kuchenteil m 141
Unterführung f 194
Untergrund m 91
Unterhemd n 33, 35
Unterpar n 233
Unterrock m 35
Unterschrift f 96, 98
Untersetzer m 150
Untersuchung f 45, 49
Unterwäsche f 32, 35
Unze f 310
Uranus m 280
Urlaub m 212
Urlaubsprospekt m 212
Urologie f 49
Urteil n 181
Uruguay 315
Usbekistan 318

V

Vanille f 132
Vanillepudding m 140
Vanuatu 319
Vase f 63
Vater m 22
Vatikanstadt f 316
V-Ausschnitt m 33
vegetarische Hamburger m 155
Vene f 19
Venezuela 315
Ventil n 207
Ventilator m 60, 202
Venus f 280
Venusmuschel f 121
Verankerung f 217
Veranstaltungen f 243
verarbeiteten Getreidearten f 130
verärgert 25
Verband m 47
verbinden 177
verbleit 199
Verbrechen n 94
Verdächtige m 94, 181
Verdauungssystem n 19
Verdeck n 75
Verdünnungsmittel n 83
Vereinigte Arabische Emirate 318
Vereinigte Königreich n 316
Vereinigten Staaten von Amerika 314
Verfallsdatum n 109
Verfügung f 180
Vergiftung f 46
Vergnügungspark m 262
vergrößern f 172
Vergrößerung f 271
Verkäufer m 104
Verkäuferin f 188
Verkaufsabteilung f 175

deutsch

Verkehr *m* 194
Verkehrsampel *f* 194
Verkehrsflugzeug *n* 210, 212
Verkehrsinsel *f* 194
Verkehrspolizist *m* 195
Verkehrsschilder *n* 195
Verkehrsstau *m* 195
verkleinern *f* 172
Verkühlung *f* 44
verlängern 168
verlängerte Limousine *f* 199
Verlängerung *f* 223
Verlängerungsschnur *f* 78
verlegen 25
Verletzung *f* 46
verlieren 273
Verlierer *m* 273
Verlobte *m* 24
Verlobte *f* 24
Verlobten *m*, *f* 24
vermehren 91
Vermieter *m* 58
Vermittlung *f* 99
Verordnung *f* 109
verputzen 82
verrühren 67, 138
Verschluss *m* 36
Versicherung *f* 203
Versiegelungsmittel *m* 83
Versorgungsfahrzeug *n* 212
Verspätung *f* 209
Verstärker *m* 268
Verstauchung *f* 46
verstellbare
   Schraubenschlüssel *m* 80
Versuch *m* 166, 221
Verteidiger *m* 223
Verteidigung *f* 181, 220
Verteidigungszone *f* 224
Verteiler *m* 203
Verwandten *m* 23
verwirrt 25
Vibraphon *m* 257
Videospiel *n* 269
Vieh *n* 183, 185
vier 308
vierhundert 308
vierter 309
viertürig 200
vierzehn 308
vierzehn Tage 307
vierzehnter 309
vierzig 308
vierzig Minuten 304
vierzigster 309
Vietnam 318
Violinschlüssel *m* 256
Virus *m* 44
Visier *n* 205
Visum *n* 213
Vitamintabletten *f* 108
Vögel *m* 292
Vögelbeobachten *n* 263

Vogelscheuche *f* 184
Volant *m* 71
voll 266, 321
Voll tanken, bitte 199
Volley *m* 231
Volleyball *m* 227
Vollkorn- 131
Vollkornbrot *n* 139
Vollkornmehl *n* 138
Vollmilch *f* 136
Vollmond *m* 280
Vollpension *f* 101
Volumen *n* 165, 311
vom Abschlag spielen 233
von Bord gehen 217
von, aus 320
vor 320
vorbestellen 168
Vordach *n* 58
vordere Backenzahn *m* 50
Vorderrad *n* 196
Vorderzwiesel *m* 242
Vorfeld *n* 212
vorgeburtlich 52
vorgestern 307
Vorhand *f* 231
Vorhang *m* 63, 254
Vorhaut *f* 21
vorher aufgezeichnet 178
Vorkriegsmodell *n* 199
Vorladung *f* 180
Vorlauf *m* 269
Vorort *m* 299
Vorschlaghammer *m* 187
Vorspeise *f* 153
Vorteil *m* 230
vorzeitig 52
Vulkan *m* 283

W

Waage *f* 53, 98, 118, 310
Waagschale *f* 310
Wachtel *f* 119
Wachtelei *n* 137
Wächter *m* 189
Wade *f* 13
Wadenbein *n* 17
Wadenmuskel *m* 16
Waffeln *f* 157
Wagen *m* 208
Wagenheber *m* 203
Wagentypen *m* 199
wählen 99
Wal *m* 290
Wald *m* 285
Walnuss *f* 129
Walnussöl *n* 134
Walross *n* 290
Walze *f* 187
Wandern *n* 263
Wanderschuh *m* 37
Wanderschuhe *m* 267
Wandlampe *f* 62

Wanne *f* 83
Warenlager *n* 216
Warenregal *n* 106
warm 286
Wärmflasche *f* 70
Warnlichter *n* 201
Wartehäuschen *n* 197
Warteraum *m* 45
Waschautomat mit
   Trockner *m* 76
Waschbär *m* 290
Waschbecken *n* 38, 72
Wäsche *f* 76, 105
Wäschedienst *m* 101
Wäscheklammer *f* 76
Wäschekorb *m* 76
Wäscheleine *f* 76
waschen 38
Wäscheschleuder *f* 76
Waschmaschine *f* 76
Waschmittel *n* 77
Waschsalon *m* 115
Wasser *n* 144, 238
Wasser treten 239
Wasserball *m* 239, 265
Wasserbehandlung *f* 55
Wasserfall *m* 285
Wasserflasche *f* 206, 267
Wasserflugzeug *n* 211
Wassergarten *m* 84
Wasserglas *n* 65
Wasserhahn *m* 66
Wasserhindernis *n* 232
Wasserkastanie *f* 124
Wassermelone *f* 127
Wassermotorradsport *m* 241
Wasserpflanze *f* 86
Wasserraum *m* 61
Wasserreis *m* 130
Wasserschildkröte *f* 293
Wasserski *n* 241
Wasserskifahrer *m* 241
Wassersport *m* 241
Wasserstrahl *m* 95
Wasserwaage *f* 80, 187
Watstiefel *m* 244
Wattebällchen *n* 41
Wattieren *n* 277
WC *n* 61
Weben *n* 277
Web-Site *f* 177
Webstuhl *m* 277
Wechselkurs *m* 97
Wechselstrom *m* 60
Wechselstube *f* 97
Wecker *m* 70
Wedge *n* 233
Weg *m* 58, 85
Wegschnecke *f* 295
Wegwerf- 109
Wegwerfwindel *m* 30
Wehe *f* 52
weiblich 20
weich 129, 321
weiche Brötchen *n* 139
Weichholz *n* 79

Weichkäse *m* 136
Weichspüler *m* 76
Weide *f* 182, 296
Weihnachten *n* 27
Wein *m* 145, 151
Weinberg *m* 183
Weinbrand *m* 145
weinen 25
Weinessig *m* 135
Weinglas *n* 65
Weinhandlung *f* 115
Weinkarte *f* 152
Weinstock *m* 183
weiß 39, 145, 272, 274
Weißbrot *n* 139
weiße Fleisch *n* 118
weiße Haut *f* 126
weiße Johannisbeere *f* 127
weiße Reis *m* 130
weiße Schokolade *f* 113
weißen Bohnen *f* 131
Weißfisch *m* 120
Weißrussland 316
weit 320
Weitsichtigkeit *f* 51
Weitsprung *m* 235
Weizen *m* 130, 184
Weizenmehl *n* 138
Weizenschrot *m* 130
Welle *f* 241, 264
Wellenlänge *f* 179
Wellenreiten *n* 241
Welpe *m* 290
Weltkarte *f* 312
Weltraum *m* 280
Wendekreis des
   Krebses *m* 283
Wendekreis des
   Steinbocks *m* 283
Werbung *f* 269
werdende Mutter *f* 52
werfen 221, 225, 227, 229
Werfer *m* 225, 229
Werferplatte *f* 228
Werft *f* 217
Werkbank *f* 78
Werkstatt *f* 199, 203
Werktag *m* 306
Werkzeuge *n* 187
Werkzeuggestell *n* 78
Werkzeuggürtel *m* 186
Werkzeugkasten *m* 80
Werkzeugleiste *f* 177
Wertpapiere *n* 97
Wespe *f* 295
Weste *f* 33
Westen *m* 312
Western *m* 255
Westsahara 317
Wette *f* 273
Wetter *n* 286
Wetzstein *m* 81
Whisky *m* 145
Wickelmatte *f* 74
Wickelraum *m* 104

Widerhaken *m* 244
Wiederbelebung *f* 47
wiegen 310
Wiese *f* 285
Wild *n* 118, 119
Wildwasser *n* 240
Wimper *f* 14, 51
Wimperntusche *f* 40
Wind *m* 241, 286
Windel *f* 75
windig 286
Windpocken *f* 44
Windschutz *m* 265
Windschutzscheibe *f* 198, 205
Windsurfer *m* 241
Windsurfing *n* 241
Winkel *m* 164
Winkelmesser *m* 165
Winter *m* 31, 307
Wintersport *m* 247
Wippe *f* 263
Wirbel *m* 259
Wirbellosen *n* 295
Wirbelsäule *f* 17
Wirtschaftsprüfer *m* 97, 190
Wirtschaftswissenschaft *f* 169
wischen 77
Wissenschaft *f* 166
Wissenschaftlerin *f* 190
WLAN 269
Woche *f* 306
Wochenende *n* 306
wöchentlich 307
Wodka *m* 145
Wodka mit Orangensaft *m* 151
Wohnblocke *m* 59, 298
Wohngegend *f* 299
Wohnmobil *n* 266
Wohnung *f* 59
Wohnwagen *m* 266
Wohnzimmer *n* 62
Wok *m* 69
Wolf *m* 290
Wolke *f* 287
Wolkenkratzer *m* 299, 300
Wolle *f* 277
Wörterbuch *n* 163
Wunde *f* 46
Wundsalbe *f* 74
Wurf *m* 237
Würfel *m* 164, 272
Wurflinie *f* 225
Wurm *m* 295
Wurst *f* 155
Würstchen *n* 118, 157
Wurzel *f* 124, 296
Wüste *f* 285

Y

Yard *n* 310
Yoga *n* 54